People to People Fundraising

Social Networking and Web 2.0 for Charities

TED HART
JAMES M. GREENFIELD
SHEERAZ D. HAJI

John Wiley & Sons, Inc.

This book is printed on acid-free paper.♾

Copyright © 2007 by Ted Hart, James M. Greenfield and Sheeraz D. Haji. All rights reserved.

Published by John Wiley & Sons, Inc., Hoboken, New Jersey.

Wiley Bicentennial Logo: Richard J. Pacifico.

Published simultaneously in Canada.

No part of this publication may be reproduced, stored in a retrieval system, or transmitted in any form or by any means, electronic, mechanical, photocopying, recording, scanning, or otherwise, except as permitted under Section 107 or 108 of the 1976 United States Copyright Act, without either the prior written permission of the Publisher, or authorization through payment of the appropriate per-copy fee to the Copyright Clearance Center, Inc., 222 Rosewood Drive, Danvers, MA 01923, (978) 750-8400, fax (978) 750-4470, or on the Web at www.copyright.com. Requests to the Publisher for permission should be addressed to the Permissions Department, John Wiley & Sons, Inc., 111 River Street, Hoboken, NJ 07030, (201) 748-6011, fax (201) 748-6008, or online at http://www.wiley.com/go/permission.

Limit of Liability/Disclaimer of Warranty: While the publisher and author have used their best efforts in preparing this book, they make no representations or warranties with respect to the accuracy or completeness of the contents of this book and specifically disclaim any implied warranties of merchantability or fitness for a particular purpose. No warranty may be created or extended by sales representatives or written sales materials. The advice and strategies contained herein may not be suitable for your situation. You should consult with a professional where appropriate. Neither the publisher nor authors shall be liable for any loss of profit or any other commercial damages, including but not limited to special, incidental, consequential, or other damages.

For general information on our other products and services or for technical support, please contact our Customer Care Department within the United States at (800) 762-2974, outside the United States at (317) 572-3993 or fax (317) 572-4002.

Wiley also publishes its books in a variety of electronic formats. Some content that appears in print may not be available in electronic books.

For more information about Wiley products, visit our Web site at http://www.wiley.com.

Library of Congress Cataloging-in-Publication Data:

ISBN-13: 978-0-470-12077-4

Printed in the United States of America.

10   9   8   7   6   5   4   3   2   1

Contents

FOREWORD

James E. Austin
Harvard Business School

REFLECTIONS ON THE ePHILANTHROPY REVOLUTION

The ePhilanthropy Revolution continues its evolution. It is a revolution because it is transforming philanthropic resource mobilization structurally, significantly, and irreversibly. This transformation is an evolutionary process because it involves technology adoption and behavioral adaptation, both of which require time to test, assess, and adjust. This change process is well underway and accelerating.

The first stage of the ePhilanthropy Revolution was its *birth* during the Internet boom. Web-based social enterprises (WEBSEs) emerged as a follow-on entrepreneurial wave to the emergence of commercial Internet companies: online giving directories, click-to-donate sites, charity shopping malls, online charity auctions, workplace giving systems, online donor-advised funds, alumni portals, nonprofit information hubs, and volunteer clearinghouses. These transactional WEBSEs were accompanied by the emergence of support WEBSEs that created a variety of software programs and services to enable nonprofits to incorporate Internet-based resource mobilization into their fundraising and stakeholder relationship activities.

The second stage in the revolution was the *shakeout*, which hit the WEBSEs just like their commercial counterparts. The bubble burst for everyone. Between 2001 and 2006 the WEBSE population shrunk by about one-third. Only volunteer clearinghouses increased. But while this blow slowed the adoption process, the revolution continued. The early trends and timetable projections needed to be adjusted to a longer time horizon, but the direction remained clear.

A third stage that in fact began simultaneously with the first stage and lived through the second was *early adoption*. This stage is populated by the new WEBSEs that were created and survived and by some bold nonprofits that saw significant potential in the new technology and so began trying it out. These early adopters tended to be the larger nonprofits that had already a certain amount of information technology experience and expertise for their regular operations.

A fourth stage, in which we find ourselves today, is *accelerating adoption*. The benefits of ePhilanthropy have been proven by the early adopters, and the support technology has advanced significantly, thereby reducing risks and making even more robust the payoff from adoption. Whereas in 2001 only about half of the larger nonprofits had incorporated online giving capabilities, by 2007 nearly all have it. While online giving still is a small portion of total giving—less than 2 percent, it has reached sizable absolute levels, probably over $6 billion in 2006. The growth rate is impressive, given that in 2000 only about $250 million was raised. Somewhere between 7 and 12 percent of the U.S. population now donates online. A useful indicator of the growing reliance on the Internet is online donations after disasters, where the Internet's distinctive capacity to enable an immediate response is particularly attractive to donors. After 9/11, 11 percent of the donations were online; after the Asian tsunami, 25 percent; and after Hurricane Katrina, 50 percent. For several nonprofits, the share of their giving coming online has become quite significant: for example, 35 percent for Mercy Corps.

The fifth stage will be *widespread usage*. This will likely emerge over the next decade when over a quarter of the donors will do so online at least for part of their giving. Currently, online giving rates track eCommerce usage rates. As the population continues to become more comfortable using the Internet for monetary transactions, online giving will also rise. Almost two-thirds of the adult U.S. population is online regularly, so the technological barrier has been overcome. Plus, most of these online users are also donors albeit not yet online. Some industry studies indicate that a majority of those who give, whether online or off, visit a nonprofit's Web site first. So there is a large percentage of the population that is close to migrating to online giving. And when they give, they tend to give more than offline donors.

The sixth stage is *standard practice*. This will likely occur by midcentury as our society is completely connected electronically and the convergence of the different modes of communication has reached full integration. Almost all nonprofits will have integrated online fundraising and other resource mobilization as a core part of their operations. The vast majority of donors will consider quite normal online giving in whatever new form technology has created by then. Although the timetable may be elastic, the destination is clear.

The power of the Internet is connectivity. This enables nonprofits efficiently, economically, and effectively to develop powerful relationships with a multitude of stakeholders: funders, volunteers, advocates, peers, employees, beneficiaries. Relationships are the social glue of communities, so community building is at the core of the mission of internet based communication.

But realizing this potential is not simple. Accelerating the evolution of the revolution requires strategic thinking, clear analytical frameworks, and effective operating techniques. The chapters that follow are abundant sources of these critical ingredients. They have the virtue of emerging from actual operating experiences that the contributing authors have lived or observed. Readers will be able to harvest an abundance of smart practices. Your journey in the ePhilanthropy Revolution will be enriched and accelerated.

ABOUT THE AUTHOR

Dr. James E. Austin holds the Eliot I. Snider and Family Professor of Business Administration, Emeritus at the Harvard Business School. Previously he held the John G. McLean Professorship and the Richard Chapman Professorship. He has been a member of the Harvard University faculty since 1972. He was the Co-Founder and Chair of the HBS Social Enterprise Initiative.

He is Doctor of Business Administration and Master of Business Administration from Harvard University with Distinction; Bachelor of Business Administration from The University of Michigan with High Distinction, elected to Beta Gamma Sigma.

Dr. Austin has been the author or editor of 16 books, dozens of articles, and over a hundred case studies on business and nonprofit organizations. His most recent book is Social Partnering in Latin America published in 2004 (Harvard University Press), a collaborative research publication of the Social Enterprise Knowledge Network (SEKN).

Introduction

Ted Hart
tedhart.com

P*eople to People Fundraising: Social Networking and Web 2.0 for Charities* is a book filled with cutting-edge strategies, data, and techniques offered by the world's foremost experts in ePhilanthropy.

Web 1.0 was typically nothing more than an online version of offline materials and content: Articles would be printed online, just as they were offline. Some charities would prepare content that word for word would reflect what you would find in their direct mail campaigns.

In short, Web 1.0 was the Web that *talked at* people. Web 2.0 is a Web where users generate content themselves, create communities, and connect around the world with people they may never meet but can connect with for causes they collectively support.

The true power of ePhilanthropy-based methods lies in their ability to do more than simply function as a novel way to raise money. It lies in the communication and relationship-building promise of Web 2.0. In fact, these are the real drivers of fundraising success, both offline and online. The Internet is an ideal platform from which to reach, inform, and engage potential donors, many of whom may be beyond the reach of normal fundraising channels. Communication and relationship building are key components in the successful application of Web 2.0 techniques.

Giving donors the chance to participate and to contribute to the success of a charity beyond the gift online is proving to be successful for nonprofits. Although using these new techniques has proven a serious area of growth, it challenges the traditional top-down, ask-give relationship that charities have traditionally had with their supporters.

Through the harnessing of passionate advocates and donors, charities can develop online communities of support far beyond their direct mail lists or even e-mail lists. Online social networking techniques have become the strongest and most important differences between what is traditionally practical offline and what is now possible for charities.

Along with these changes in the way charities interact with donors come more demands from donors for transparency and disclosure. ePhilanthropy is a transformative force that is propelling charities around the world toward a new way of doing business characterized by donor participation, open and full disclosure, and social networking.

Charities should approach the Internet as a communication and stewardship tool first and a fundraising tool second. Any seasoned fundraiser will tell you that when you can build and enhance a relationship with a prospective donor, you have a much higher chance of successfully soliciting a gift.

In March 2001, Harvard's professor James Austin wrote:

> *Make no mistake; the ePhilanthropy revolution is here to stay, and it will transform charitable giving in as profound a way as technology is changing the commercial world. Charities that have dismissed ePhilanthropy as a fad, or run from it in confusion, will sooner or later, need to become reconciled to it. If they don't, they risk losing touch with donors and imperiling the vitality of their work.*[1]

As Dr. Austin notes in the Forward of this book: "The benefits of ePhilanthropy have been proven by the early adopters and the support technology has advanced significantly, thereby reducing risks and making even more robust the payoff from adoption." In an earlier article, he reminds us that charities who fail to follow this path "risk losing touch with donors and imperiling the vitality of their work."[2]

We can now say that Web 2.0 and the social networking techniques of ePhilanthropy are no fad, but rather are tools and techniques that have already and will continue to change the way charities communicate with their supporters in the online world.

Every charity will learn, either now or later, that these techniques are important to their ability to remain charitable, to their ability to reach out and give the opportunity to supporters to connect to important causes. Giving up absolute control is one of the tenets of Web 2.0, inviting supporters and communities of people to comment and become part of the cause instead of just supporting the cause with a check. For nonprofits that like to keep a tight rein over all communications, Web 2.0 can create an uncomfortable scenario, but increasingly charities will grow to understand the power and necessity of these tools.

An example of a charity that took this to the extreme is the Wikimedia Foundation, Inc., a nonprofit charitable organization dedicated to encouraging the growth, development, and distribution of free, multilingual content and to providing the full content of these wiki-based projects to the public free of charge.

"Wikis"[3] are another "output" of Web 2.0. The amazing thing about them is that the entries are entirely maintained by the site's users. There is no overarching content owner on the site. Anyone can log in and contribute and also correct content placed on there. The Wikipedia community is provided with an edit history function, allowing users to view who has made which updates.

One of the huge success stories of the Internet has been Google's YouTube.com. Some charities, including Greenpeace, are counting on the large traffic on that site and ease of use to promote their content. For example, at the time of printing, Greenpeace had posted a video playing off the popular IBM/Mac television commercials (search for "Hi. I'm a Mac—Greenpeace Apple parody"). However, the Greenpeace version promoted a "greener" iPod. Between September 2006 and February 2007, over 41,000 people had viewed this video, which cost Greenpeace nothing to post.

Those who support nonprofits tend to be passionate about their cause. Many can easily be called on to become *advocates* for the cause, forwarding and recommending content to family, friends, and colleagues. This important reality forms the basis of understanding the great opportunity that can be had by harnessing their passion.

A Web site is the 24/7 advocacy and education hub for charities, but it is the legions of supporters and the networks they represent that make the promise a reality.

In this book you will find many creative ideas, techniques, and suggestions that can help harness social networking and Web 2.0 for your charity. The time to begin is now.

ABOUT THE AUTHOR

Ted Hart is CEO of Hart Philanthropic Services, (http://tedhart.com) a global consultancy to nonprofits, providing serious solutions to nonprofit challenges. He is also Founder of the international ePhilanthropy Foundation (http://www.ephilanthropy.org).

Hart has served as CEO of the University Maryland Medical System Foundation, and before that as Chief Development Officer for Johns Hopkins Bayview Medical Center. He has been certified as an Advanced Certified Fund Raising Executive (ACFRE) by the Association of Fundraising Professionals (AFP).

Hart is author to several published articles, an editor and author of the books, "Major Donors – Finding Big Gifts In Your Database and Online", "Nonprofit Internet Strategies Best Practices for Marketing, Communications and Fundraising Success" *Fundraising On The Internet: The ePhilanthropyFoundation.Org's Guide To Success Online*, a contributing author to *Achieving Excellence in Fund Raising Second Edition*. You can reach Ted at tedhart@tedhart.com.

NOTES

1. Kellogg Foundation Report on e-Philanthropy v2.001.
2. http://www.wkkf.org/DesktopModules/WKF.00_DmaSupport/ViewDoc.aspx?
   fld=PDFFile&CID=2&ListID=28&ItemID=20661&LanguageID=0.
3. "Wikis" is shorthand for Wikipedia users; is common usage among internet users.

Introducción

Ted Hart
tedhart.com

People to People Fundraising: Social Networking and Web 2.0 for Charities es un libro lleno de estrategias de vanguardia, datos y técnicas propuestas por los principales expertos del mundo en ePhilanthropy.

Web 1.0 típicamente no era más que una versión en línea de materiales y contenido fuera de línea—los artículos serían impresos en línea de la misma manera que fuera de línea. En la mayoría de los casos, simplemente era una versión en línea del contenido fuera de línea. Algunas organizaciones benéficas prepararían contenido que palabra-por-palabra reflejaría lo que usted encontraría en las campañas de correo directo.

En resumen, Web 1.0 era la red que le hablaba a la gente. Web 2.0 es una red en donde los usuarios generan ellos mismos el contenido, crean comunidades, unen gente alrededor del mundo—gente que probablemente nunca se conozcan pero que se pueden unir para causas que apoyan colectivamente.

Los verdaderos poderes de los métodos basados en ePhilanthropy radican en su habilidad para poder hacer más que simplemente funcionar como una causa noble para procurar fondos. Radican en las áreas de comunicación y en la promesa de construir relaciones de Web 2.0. De hecho, estos son los verdaderos conductores del éxito de la procuración de fondos tanto fuera de línea como en línea. El Internet es una plataforma ideal desde la cual se puede contactar, informar y captar donadores potenciales, muchos de los cuales pueden estar más allá del alcance de los canales habituales de procuración de fondos.

Dándole a los donadores la oportunidad de participar y contribuir con el éxito de una organización no lucrativa más allá del donativo en línea está demostrando ser exitoso para las organizaciones sin fines de lucro. Mientras demuestra una gran área de crecimiento, **el uso de estas nuevas técnicas desafía** a las relaciones tradicionales de control desde arriba; de pedir-dar que las organizaciones benéficas tradicionalmente han tenido con las personas que las apoyan.

Aprovechando a los defensores y donadores apasionados, las organizaciones no lucrativas pueden desarrollar comunidades de apoyo en línea más allá de sus listas de correo directo o inclusive de sus listas de correo electrónico. Las técnicas para establecer redes sociales en Internet se han convertido en una de las diferencias más fuertes e importantes entre lo que es práctico tradicionalmente fuera de línea y lo que ahora las organizaciones no lucrativas pueden alcanzar en línea.

Junto con estos cambios en la manera como una organización no lucrativa interactúa con un donante, vienen más demandas de los donantes para tener transparencia y revelación. ePhilanthropy es una fuerza transformadora que está impulsando a las organizaciones no lucrativas en todo el mundo hacia una nueva manera de hacer negocios caracterizada por la participación de los donantes, la revelación abierta y total y el establecimiento de redes sociales en Internet.

Primero, las organizaciones no lucrativas deben usar el Internet como una herramienta de comunicación y administración y después como una herramienta para procurar fondos. Un procurador de fondos avezado le dirá que cuando usted puede entablar y fomentar una relación con un posible donador, usted tiene una oportunidad mucho mayor de solicitar exitosamente un donativo.

En marzo de 2001, el profesor de Harvard, James Austin, escribió, "no cometa errores; la revolución de ePhilanthropy llegó para quedarse, y transformará la donación benéfica de una manera tan profunda como la tecnología está cambiando al mundo comercial. Las organizaciones no lucrativas que han descartado a ePhilanthropy como una moda pasajera, o que han huido de ella por confusión, tarde o temprano deberán reconciliarse con ella. Si no lo hacen, se arriesgan a perder contacto con donantes y a poner en peligro la vitalidad de su trabajo."[1]

El escrito del Dr. Austin en 2007 agregaba "Los beneficios de ePhilanthropy han sido probados por sus primeros adoptadores y la tecnología de apoyo ha avanzado significativamente, reduciendo por lo tanto los riesgos y haciendo aun más robusta la recompensa de la adopción." El Dr. Austin nos recuerda que las organizaciones benéficas "se arriesgan a perder contacto con donadores y a poner en peligro la vitalidad de su trabajo."[2]

Ahora podemos decir que Web 2.0 y las técnicas para establecer redes sociales en Internet de ePhilanthropy no son una moda pasajera, son herramientas y técnicas que ya han cambiado y seguirán cambiando la manera en cómo las organizaciones no lucrativas se comunican con las personas que las apoyan en el mundo en línea.

Cada organización no lucrativa aprenderá, ahora o más tarde, que estas técnicas son importantes para su habilidad para permanecer como beneficencias, para su habilidad para alcanzar a las personas que las apoyan y darles la oportunidad para que se unan a causas importantes. Si no lo hacen, cómo renunciar al control absoluto es una de las premisas de Web 2.0, invitar a las personas que las apoyan y a las comunidades de gentes a que comenten y se vuelvan parte de la causa en lugar de apoyar simplemente a la causa con un cheque. Para las organizaciones sin fines de lucro que les gusta mantener las riendas cortas sobre todos los comunicados, Web 2.0 puede crear un escenario incómodo, pero cada vez más las organizaciones benéficas entenderán el poder y la necesidad de estas herramientas.

Como ejemplo de una organización no lucrativa que llegó a este extremo es Wikimedia Foundation, Inc., una organización sin fines de lucro dedicada a fomentar el crecimiento, desarrollo y distribución de contenido multilingüe, gratis, y a proporcionar al público el contenido total de estos proyectos basados en wiki, sin costo alguno.

"Wikis"[3] son otro "resultado" de Web 2.0, siendo lo más impresionante de ello que las aportaciones aquí están totalmente mantenidas por los usuarios del sitio. No hay ningún propietario dominante del contenido en este sitio. Cualquiera puede entrar y contribuir y también corregir el contenido que se ahí encuentra. La comunidad de Wikipedia está dotada con una función de edición de historia que le permite a la comunidad de usuarios de Wikipedia ver quién ha hecho las actualizaciones.

Una de las grandes historias de éxito del Internet ha sido YouTube.com de Google. Algunas organizaciones benéficas incluyendo a Greenpeace cuentan con la gran afluencia de personas en ese sitio y con la facilidad de uso para promover ahí su contenido. Por ejemplo, al momento de imprimir, Greenpeace había colocado un video de los populares comerciales de televisión de IBM/Mac (busque "*Hi. I'm a Mac [Hola. Soy Mac]*—la parodia de Greenpeace Apple"), sin embargo la versión de Greenpeace promovía un iPOD "más verde," desde septiembre de 2006 hasta febrero de 2007 más de 41,000 personas habían visto este video. A Greenpeace no le costó nada colocar el video en YouTube.

Sin importar la causa, las personas que apoyan a las organizaciones sin fines de lucro suelen estar apasionadas por sus causas, a muchos se les puede llamar fácilmente para que vuelvan defensores de la causa, reenviando y recomendando el contenido a sus familiares, amigos y colegas. Esta importante realidad forma la base para entender la gran oportunidad que se puede tener al aprovechar la pasión de las personas que las apoyan.

Un sitio de red es el defensor y centro educativo 24/7 de las organizaciones no lucrativas, pero son las legiones de personas que las apoyan y las redes del Internet a las cuales representan, las que convierten la promesa en realidad.

En este libro usted encontrará muchas ideas creativas, técnicas y sugerencias que le pueden ayudar a aprovechar el establecimiento de redes sociales en Internet y de Web 2.0 para su organización. El momento para comenzar es ahora.

NOTAS

1. Reporte de Kellogg Foundation sobre e-Philanthrophy v2.001.
2. http://www.wkkf.org/DesktopModules/WKF.00_DmaSupport/ViewDoc.aspx? fld=PDFFile&CID=2&ListID=28&ItemID=20661&LanguageID=0
3. "Wikis" es forma corta para usuarios de Wikipedia; es el uso comién en tre usuarios de Internet.

Introduction

Ted Hart
tedhart.com

People to People Fundraising: Social Networking and Web 2.0 for Charities est un livre exposant les stratégies, données et techniques d'avant garde offertes par les meilleurs experts mondiaux en ePhilanthropy.

Le Web 1.0 n'était en fait rien de plus qu'une version online des outils et du contenu off-line, présentant ainsi les mêmes articles online que off-line. Pour quelques associations caritatives, le contenu online était mot pour mot identique à ce que l'on pouvait retrouver dans leurs campagnes de mailing papier.

En résumé, le Web 1.0 était le Web qui parlait aux gens. Le Web 2.0 est une version qui permet aux utilisateurs de générer eux-mêmes du contenu, de créer des communautés et de tisser des liens entre des personnes du monde entier qui ne se rencontreront probablement jamais mais qui soutiennent les mêmes causes.

La véritable puissance de l'ePhilanthropy se situe dans sa capacité à faire plus que collecter de l'argent. Son intérêt se situe tant en communication qu'en développement d'une relation.

Internet est une plate-forme idéale qui permet d'atteindre, d'informer et d'amener des donateurs potentiels à s'engager aux côtés d'une cause, au-delà des canaux traditionnels de fundraising. Communiquer et développer la relation sont les éléments clefs assurant le succès de ces techniques.

Donner la possibilité au donateur de participer et de contribuer à la réussite d'une association, par le don online, est la garantie du succès pour une organisation caritative. L'utilisation de ces nouvelles techniques rend obsolète la traditionnelle relation ⟨⟨top-down⟩⟩ (demande induisant un don) qu'utilisent jusqu'à présent les associations avec leurs sympathisants.

Grâce à la sollicitation online des amis, des sympathisants et des donateurs, les associations peuvent désormais atteindre et développer des communautés virtuelles qui vont bien au-delà de leurs propres bases d'adresses email. Les outils internet de mise en réseau sont l'une des différences les plus marquantes par rapport à ce qui se fait traditionnellement offline.

Avec ces mutations qui permettent une meilleure interaction entre les associations et leurs donateurs, il est, en contrepartie, exigé transparence et éthique. La ePhilanthropy a le pouvoir de propulser n'importe quelle association vers une nouvelle façon de faire sa collecte caractérisée par la participation du donateur, la transparence et l'élargissement du réseau de relations.

Les associations doivent d'abord appréhender Internet comme un outil de communication et de construction de la relation, puis en second temps comme un outil de la collecte de fonds.

N'importe quel professionnel de la collecte de fonds sait que lorsqu'une association développe une relation particulière avec un donateur potentiel, elle se donne toutes les chances de faire donner ce dernier.

En avril 2001, un professeur d'Harvard, James Austin, a écrit, ⟨⟨ne vous trompez pas; la révolution de la ePhilanthropy est là et va transformer l'acte de don aussi profondément que cela a été le cas dans le monde du commerce. Les associations qui ont appréhendé la ePhilanthropy comme un effet de mode, ou quelque chose de confus, auront du, tôt ou tard, se réconcilier avec elle. Si elles ne le font pas, elles risquent de perdre le lien avec les donateurs et mettre en péril la vitalité de leur travail⟩⟩.[1]

Le Docteur Austin a ajouté en 2007, ⟨⟨les avantages de la ePhilanthropy ont été prouvés par les "early-adopters" et la facilité des outils s'est développée de manière significative, ainsi les risques ont été réduits et la fiabilité des "early-adopters" donne de meilleurs résultats⟩⟩. Le Docteur Austin nous rappelle que sans cela, les associations ⟨⟨risquent de perdre le lien avec les donateurs et mettre en péril la vitalité de leur travail⟩⟩.[2]

Nous pouvons désormais dire que le Web 2.0 et que les techniques de mise en relation ne sont en aucun cas un effet de mode, mais sont des outils qui vont continuer à changer la façon dont communiquent les associations et leurs sympathisants.

Les associations vont apprendre au fur et à mesure que ces techniques sont essentielles si elles veulent continuer à susciter la générosité des sympathisants, et à les fédérer autour des causes qui leur sont chères. Si elles ne font pas cela, elles vont finir par perdre le contrôle et ne faire qu'encaisser de moins en moins de chèques de leurs sympathisants, tandis qu'avec le Web 2.0 elles vont inviter les partisans et leurs communautés à commenter et à prendre parti pour des causes. Pour les associations qui aiment garder un certain contrôle, le Web 2.0 peut générer le sentiment de ne plus maîtriser sa communication, or, une bonne partie d'entre elles comprendront petit à petit les enjeux et la nécessité de ces outils.

La Fondation Wikimedia est un exemple d'association à but non lucratif qui consacre son activité à encourager la croissance, le développement et la distribution gratuite de contenu libre et multilingue au grand public.

Les ⟨⟨wikis⟩⟩[3] sont une autre forme du Web 2.0. Leurs particularités: les contenus sont ici entièrement rédigés par les utilisateurs du site. Il n'existe pas réellement d'auteurs du contenu du site dans la mesure où tout le monde participe. Chacun peut en effet se connecter, améliorer ou encore corriger le contenu du site. La communauté wikipedia possède une fonction d'historique des modifications permettant aux utilisateurs de wikipedia de savoir qui a écrit quoi.

Un des plus gros succès Internet a été le site de YouTube.com. Beaucoup d'associations, comme Greenpeace par exemple, profitent de la simplicité d'utilisation de ce site pour déposer du contenu et ainsi faire leur promotion. Un des exemples les plus frappants est celui de la parodie de la publicité d'IBM/MAC, sur les iPod, déposée par Greenpeace sur YouTube.com. Six mois plus tard, plus de 41 000 personnes l'avaient visionnée.

Indépendamment de la cause, les sympathisants d'une association ont tendance à être passionnés par ce qu'ils soutiennent, et sont susceptibles de relayer le message auprès de leurs familles, amis ou collègues. Cette réalité est une opportunité à saisir.

Un site Web est un outil de sensibilisation fonctionnant 24 heures sur 24 et 7 jours sur 7 pour les associations, mais ce sont les partisans et les réseaux qu'ils représentent qui permettent d'atteindre cette réalité.

Dans ce livre, vous trouverez de nombreuses idées créatives, des techniques et des suggestions qui vous aideront à exploiter les différents outils relationnels et le Web 2.0 au profit de votre organisation. Il est le temps de s'y mettre aujourd'hui!

Traduction par Frédéric Fournier—CEO Optimus

NOTES

1. W. K. Kellogg Foundation. e-Philanthropy V2.001: From Entrepreneurial Adventure to an Online Community, April 2001.
2. http://www.wkkf.org/DesktopModules/WKF.00_DmaSupport/ViewDoc.aspx? fld=PDFFile&CID=2&ListID=28&ItemID=20661&LanguageID=0
3. "Wikis" is shorthand for Wikipedia users; is common usage among internet users.

Community Building/Advocacy

The Changing Nature of Community: Leveraging the Internet to Build Relationships and Expand the Reach of Your Organization

Steven R. MacLaughlin

Blackbaud

THE ESSENCE OF COMMUNITY

The group has gathered together once again from distances far away and nearby. They have come together for the annual gathering on the lake shore; a traditional reunion to renew their connection to one another and to reminisce about days gone by. It has continued more years than one can count. Going by so quickly, can one truly grasp its significance in the moment?

The elders of the group enjoy themselves amid the buzz and activity that surrounds them. Their children are now parents themselves who are caught between moments of relaxation and frenzied activity. The youngest of the group are up early each morning and seem to have tapped the rays of the sun to fuel them through the day. There is food and drink and festivities in full swing, until the sun dips just below the horizon.

As everyone in this budding community draws closer together around a fire, stories are shared from days gone by. The intensity of the fire is rivaled only by the warmth generated by a community brought together by common bonds.

This scene could have taken place 3,000 years ago or three days ago. It is a scene that reminds us of the communal bonds we have between family members. But it also invokes the spirit of community between people. This is the kind of close community feeling individuals and organizations strive to capture.

At its core, the Internet, like any community, is a group of people linked by shared relationships, experiences, beliefs, or goals. Such a broad definition is important to note because communities are all around, us whether we realize it or not. A community is also a reflection of its members and can be very fluid and dynamic. Like physical communities, Internet communities are untethered organic entities that change shape, size, and other characteristics over time.

This in part explains why physical corporations or organizations struggle with understanding and creating communities. Communities often subvert authority not of their own making. This can be a force for good, but obviously there is always the potential for ne'er-do-wells.

Given all of these characteristics, it should come as no surprise that "communities" have taken up root on the Internet. The climate with its nonlinear amorphous space is a perfect new homestead for communities. Over time, the Internet has been settled by different kinds of communities, and it continues to grow at a rapid pace.

Still, some important questions remain for nonprofit organizations. How do we transcend the limitations of distance, geography, age, language, disability, and culture to build an online community among our supporters? How do we rekindle the flame of familiarity and spark interaction for the greater good? How do we stand out in a sea of choices for our constituents? These questions, and many more, will be explored as we seek to understand the changing nature of community. Let us first start with understanding the link between community and philanthropy.

COMMUNITY BUILDING IS CENTRAL TO PHILANTHROPY

A fundamental reality of fundraising is that people give to people with causes, not to organizations. Buildings and brochures may in some ways influence people, but they cannot hold a conversation. People need to feel a personal connection to the causes and initiatives they choose to donate to. The power of personal content, communication, and collaboration all combine to create a sense of community.

In that sense, community building is fundraising—you cannot separate the two. They are intertwined in their creation and growth over time. However, building a community is no simple feat, and there are no magic wands, silver bullets, or shortcuts to doing it effectively. Many organizations believe that their communities will appear spontaneously with little or no effort. This is simply not the case.

The reality is that you have to remind people of the communal connections they have to your organization. Their memories might be a bit hazy. Their vision might be a bit blurry. Their focus might be a bit fuzzy. You need to put the wheels in motion to make these connections more front and center.

Aristotle famously wrote in 328 B.C. that "man is by nature a social animal." Thankfully, you do not have to be a Greek scholar or philosophy expert to understand the truth in that statement. People have a natural desire to be connected to others. This is true of family members, friends, neighbors, coworkers, and anyone else in their relationship circle.

People connect in part through shared unique experiences and information. That is the common denominator in the equation of their relationships. Perhaps they are family members, attend the same school together, belong to the same club or organization, attend the same events, read the same publications or blogs, cheer on the same sports team, are colleagues in the same profession, or worship together in some way.

People also connect through helping others and making a difference in the world. This connection may be made primarily by an individual, but certainly there is a larger group of other supporters present where there is a connection. Many individuals get involved through volunteering, serving on boards, or participating in events. Their individual contributions of time and talent help both the organizations and the world around them. The people they meet along the way help to build a tight-knit community. These interactions create lasting connections long after they take place.

Finally, people connect by interacting with others in a personal way. This might be in person, in writing, over the telephone, on radio or television, or online. It is this shift to the online medium that is becoming a catalyst for change among nonprofit organizations. Never before have people been able to transcend the physical boundaries of location, language, or other limitations to connect with one another in such powerful ways.

THE INTERNET CONTINUES TO TRANSFORM THE NONPROFIT WORLD

As the Internet continues to change how businesses interact with their customers, it also transforms how nonprofits interact with their constituents. Organizations continue to increase their use of Web content, e-mail, and other Internet communication vehicles to extend their reach.

Online fundraising generated through the online channel also continues to increase steadily. Studies and surveys consistently indicate that online donations are growing at a higher rate than offline giving. Although the dollar amounts do not yet exceed traditional fundraising, they are certainly no longer something to be scoffed at or ignored.

While the use of the Internet continues to grow by nonprofit organizations, their use of more sophisticated online fundraising techniques remains largely under-developed. This slow adoption trend is in sharp contrast to the growth of commercial use of the Internet as a trusted place for financial transactions. Aside from sites such as Amazon.com and eBay, there is a range of services online that includes banking to car insurance, groceries to gaming, in addition to medical sites, computer buying, veterinarian services, zebra safari excursions, and everything in between.

If it is obvious that the Internet is a place where commerce abounds, then the obvious cannot be overstated enough: People have an expectation that the organizations they interact with also offer a host of online services. If Bank of America is doing it, then the local food bank should be doing it too. If Amazon.com can tell me what I have purchased in the past, then groups working to save the Amazon rain forests should be able to tell me how much I have donated to them. Nonprofits may have reason to distinguish the two but your constituents will not.

This is not to say that nonprofits are still Stone Age inhabitants of the Internet. Clearly many organizations have invested countless time, resources, and money to better promote their organization and meet the needs of their constituents. They serve as a beacon of what is possible for other organizations to follow. And there are clear signs that a shift to using the Internet is in full swing.

The State of the Nonprofit Industry 2006 survey noted that 75 percent of the organizations plan to increase their use of e-mail to communicate with constituents and 60 percent plan to increase the use Web content for the same purpose.[1] This is compared with only 32 percent of organizations planning to increase their use of traditional mail and 34 percent planning to increase telephone-based communication. This type of channel switching will only increase over time.

The traditional forms of fundraising are tried and true but can also be very expensive to maintain for many nonprofits. The cost savings of sending 50,000 e-mails versus the expense of sending a printed direct mail piece to the same group are substantial. These kinds of hard cost savings will get the attention of even the most ardent Internet skeptics. This logic extends to other forms of communication that nonprofits continue to use because it is what they have always done. What does it cost to produce an elaborate annual report, mail it out, and store all the unused copies for years and years versus placing it online as a downloadable or interactive document?

Using the Internet for these kinds of activities is a straightforward and effective way to communicate with constituents. And continuing to push the increase of online activities will no doubt continue. Soon just doing the occasional e-mail blast or posting content to the Web will not be enough to meet the demands of constituents. They will expect more frequent, personalized, and interactive communication from the nonprofit organizations they support.

The future of nonprofit communication will involve using multiple channels, both online and offline, to reach constituents. And a single campaign may mix different channels at varying intervals to have maximum impact. This future will also demand more responsiveness to the wants and needs expressed by individuals. This is because constituents expect to have this kind of choice and, perhaps more important, because they expect better stewardship.

This brings us to the important topic of understanding the purpose for your online endeavors. Here, too, we see more basic usage of the Internet to connect with constituents. Many organizations have chosen to limit their perception of the Web at best to a one-way communication vehicle or at worst just a brochure gussied up with spinning graphics and HTML (see Exhibit 1.1).

This is symptomatic of a Web site ownership problem that has plagued many organizations. Traditionally, an organization's Web site has been under the control of either information technology (IT) or marketing. Whereas their goals and objectives may be well intended, it is fair to say that their core focus is not development oriented. Marketing views the Web through a traditional lens focused on the message not the medium; IT views the Web through a different lens focused on another system that must be maintained and supported.

These may be overgeneralizations, but that does not mean there is not a ring of truth to them. Development has been and continues to be shut out from many of the Web conversations. The organization's wide-angle lens should be focused on relationship management, stewardship, and working to secure the capital to serve the organization's mission.

The usage of the Internet is often broken down to the three C's: content, commerce, and community. A marketing-controlled Web presence leverages content to meet its objectives. An IT controlled Web presence relies on commerce to automate information and financial transactions that require little to no attention to

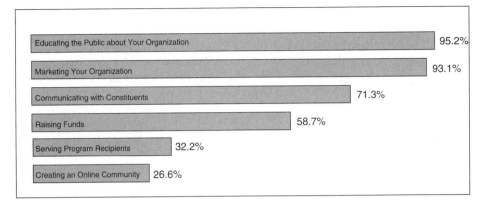

EXHIBIT 1.1 What Purposes Does Your Organization's Web Site Serve?
Source: *State of the Nonprofit Industry 2006*[4]

maintain. A development-controlled Web presence seeks to build online community and affinity to establish lasting and meaningful relationships with constituents. An effective online presence includes all of these elements—an organization that is able to get all three to play well together will be successful online.

Nonprofit organizations need to take a much more holistic focus of who controls and contributes to the overall online presence. Keep in mind that marketing, IT, and development are just three of the contributors. The needs and roles of operations, finance, advocacy, stewardship, volunteers, and staff should also be taken into account. They are important stakeholders in helping to drive both offline and online success.

Getting these elements all to move in the same direction takes planning. It also takes compromise and coordination. The Web site should not be just a brochure or a reproduction of the organizational chart or a combination of unstructured links or poorly designed donation forms; it has the potential to be so much more to your organization and your constituents with the right plan in place. This is another area where nonprofits appear to struggle with taking the next big leap forward.

Only 17 percent of the *State of the Nonprofit Industry 2006* survey respondents indicated that they have a written Web strategy, although 26 percent did note that they are working on one. The fact that neither of these statistics has changed substantially from past surveys is troubling. The importance of a well-thought-out strategy that has the input and buy-in of both stakeholders and constituents cannot be underestimated.

It would also be fair to say that many organizations have focused on more tactical initiatives instead of developing a comprehensive strategy to drive their online efforts. There is merit to getting on with things rather than getting caught up in strategic planning meetings intent on boiling the ocean. But very few nonprofits will venture very far outside their nearby surroundings without an atlas or road map to guide them to where they want to arrive.

This result in part explains why the adoption of more progressive online tools and techniques has been slow among nonprofit organizations. The lack of solid short- and long-term strategies has limited the means put in use toward an uncertain end. The basic use of Web content, e-mail, and rudimentary online transactions potentially fulfill first- and second-tier status online, but not much more.

A first-tier presence on the Web is limited to one-way communication. Such Web sites are mostly static online presences that communicate content and information to visitors. They may also combine the use of e-mail communication to inform constituents about information that is relevant and meaningful to them. Many organizations have started and stopped their Web site development with this kind of basic presence.

A second-tier presence on the Web adds the element of two-way communication. This means that constituents can not only receive online information but can also interact with different online services. For example, they might be able to choose the types of content they want to view, control their subscriptions to various e-mail newsletter lists, view and update various pieces of key information about themselves, and participate in other online activities that are conversational in nature.

A third-tier presence on the Web adds multidirectional communication. Not only can the organization communicate with constituents, and constituents can communicate with the organization, but constituents can communicate among themselves. These kinds of online community and social networking experiences are much more effective at attracting, retaining, and growing relationships with constituents. They also reflect the direction of where the Web is heading, and most constituents will expect these kinds of capabilities.

The use of e-mail and Web content in more meaningful ways is just the beginning. Much more is possible than many nonprofit organizations have chosen to implement, including the use of online distributed fundraising, online advocacy, recurring giving programs, discussion boards, blogs, and other Web 2.0–type functionality.

"Web 2.0" refers to second-generation Web-based services that emphasize online collaboration and sharing among users.[2] The term was originally used by O'Reilly Media in 2004 to describe the idea that the Web will become a platform that decentralizes content generation and distribution. This concept has since taken on a much broader scope to include all sorts of social networking, personal publishing, and enabling technologies that drive participation online.

These kinds of innovations are becoming more widely adopted by more progressive nonprofit organizations. Like the adoption cycle of most technological innovations, there are already early adopters using these tools, and each new innovation is trying to cross the chasm into more mainstream use.

What tier does your organization occupy? How long have you been there? What did it take to get there? What will it take to get to the next level? How committed is the organization to getting there? Who are the key stakeholders who can lead or influence change to get there? What is the price of doing something, and what is the cost of doing nothing? These are questions nearly every nonprofit organization has or will face at some point.

THE NEXT MAJOR EVOLUTION IN ePHILANTHROPY

Revolutions happen in an instant—a single moment, event, or breakthrough idea that changes both perceptions and realities in our world. Revolutions are rare, though many happenings are mistaken for revolutionary moment. The Internet is not revolutionary but, instead, an evolving medium that continues to change over time.

Online content publishing was being done before blogs. Online personalized content existed before Yahoo! and Google. Online audio and video existed before podcasts and YouTube. Online gaming existed before the multitude of online poker tournaments or Second Life. Online file sharing existed before Napster and iTunes. Online communities and social networks existed before Facebook, LinkedIn, and MySpace.

This evolving nature of online technology also applies to Internet-based giving. Although online fundraising occurred before 9/11, the Asian tsunami, and Hurricane Katrina, for example, it took one of these events to capture the attention of a mainstream audience. In general, technology races forward, more intent on the journey than any single destination. The speed of this evolution is often controlled by two key factors: cost and distribution.

To understand how online communities have evolved, let us first start by understanding how content publishing has evolved over time. Both content and communities have traveled different paths before combining to transform how the Internet is being used today.

The transformation of content publishing has been a process shaped over several hundred years. The first printed book was published in China around 868. The Chinese later invented movable clay type around 1041. In the 1440s several Europeans, including Johannes Gutenberg, Laurens Janszoon Coster, and Panfilo Castaldi, claimed to have invented the printing press.[3]

So why do historians give Gutenberg, a goldsmith by trade, credit for the invention? First, because he combined wooden and metal movable type with oil-based ink for his printing press. His approach drastically reduced the cost of setup and printing. Gutenberg's knowledge of the materials he chose also produced highly durable books. Second, his best-known printed work was the Bible, and there was a large community focused on making sure it was widely distributed across Europe and the world. Gutenberg solved the cost and distribution problem, and the rest is history.

Fast forward a few hundred years and there is little conceptual difference between Gutenberg's printing press of the 1440s and Web content publishing. The cost of publishing online is substantially lower and the distribution capabilities are now instantaneously global. No other medium can claim that ability. Coincidentally, one of the most popular software applications for publishing is called Movable Type. Evolution, not revolution.

The transformation of online communities also illustrates that they are not something that appeared out of thin air in recent years. The early days of the Internet were used primarily by government and academicians as a means to communicate and collaborate. This "networks of networks" created to survive nuclear Armageddon quickly become a highly trafficked place for scientists, researchers, and technology tinkerers.

E-mail first appeared in 1965 and initially allowed users on the same system to communicate with one another. By the late 1970s e-mail was prevalent in different governmental, academic, scientific, and business sectors. Around the same time bulletin board systems (BBSs) began to spring up and brought the wonders of electronic communication to a broader audience.

A BBS allows users to dial into the system over a phone line and perform functions, such as file sharing, reading news, and exchanging messages with other users. Some of these BBSs were free, and others were fee-based services. They were tidal pool communities that grew larger or dried up over time. They might be considered the first true online communities because of the discussion forums and other messaging formats that allowed members to interact with one another.

Some of these tidal pools became larger seas throughout the mid-1980s and into the 1990s. Online services like CompuServe, GEnie, and Prodigy offered a range of online content and community features through dial-up service for a monthly subscription fee. America Online began as an online gaming service that avoided bankruptcy by switching to a mega-BBS format in 1985. These online communities were just as robust in dialogue and engaging in conversation as anything currently taking place online. The main difference once again was their cost and their limited distribution to users of that particular system.

These communities were highly segmented across a variety of interest groups. You name a topic and it probably had a discussion forum, listserv, or chat room full of active discussion. Anthropology, car repair, comic books, Gaelic football, gardening, politics, religion, toy trains, quiltmaking, and a host of other unique subjects prevailed. The value in these communities came from the active participation of and the shared interests among its members.

As BBSs reached their peak in the mid-1990s, the World Wide Web opened up the floodgates to Internet access. The tidal pools became seas and the seas became an ocean. Suddenly the barriers of proprietary dial-up systems and costly connectivity begin to disappear. Access transforms the size of the Internet's user base and more user friendly tools help nontechnical people engage with one another.

A little-known fact is that the first Web browser, (called WorldWideWeb and later renamed Nexus) could not only browse the Internet but also publish content. The proliferation of desktop publishing software in the late 1980s also helped to fuel the distribution of content online. Suddenly the Web became a vibrant and dynamic place not only to view content but to contribute to the conversation as well. And the cost to produce meaningful content is significantly less than using traditional media.

The blogging, podcasting, and social networking growth that have exploded in recent years are the next steps along the Internet's journey. The value of all of these technologies comes in the information they help share and the number of people that choose to participate. Being able to instantaneously attract large numbers of people from across the globe to an important cause or just for fun has fundamentally changed how we interact with one another.

This phenomenon is often referred to as a "network effect." The theory is that the more people who use a particular resource, the more valuable that resource becomes. The Internet allows for network effects on a massive scale. Think about how the local garage sale has been transformed by something like eBay. Think about how the want ads in the local newspaper have been transformed by something like Monster.com. Think about how grassroots politics has been transformed by the ability for organizations to mobilize supporters online.

As nonprofits adopt more Web 2.0 kinds of technologies, the value of network effects will become very important to their success online. Organizations that embrace online social networks like MySpace, utilize video-sharing sites such as YouTube, and distribute content via Really Simple Syndication (RSS) can cast a wider net to reach their constituents. These other online sites are simply nodes on the network: nodes which attract millions of visitors that nonprofits can route back to their own Web sites.

Successful organizations will have a presence on these larger sites to interact with both new and current constituents. Co-opetition, a neologism coined to describe cooperative competition, will be a key strategy employed by these organizations to get themselves present at as many possible contact points on the Internet as possible. Getting people to visit your space is much more likely using this approach.

Communities of all shapes and sizes have this same kind of potential. They have the ability to bring together people with common goals, interests, and motivations for the greater good. Nonprofits that can move beyond static online sites or even basic transactional sites to more dynamic online communities have the best chance for long-term success.

WHAT THE INTERNET MEANS TO NONPROFITS

The Internet is now a ubiquitous presence in our lives. It is in our homes and office buildings, and the miracle of wireless fidelity (WiFi) has brought it to almost every other location. This ease of contact has been extremely helpful for increasing access in the developing world as well as reducing the cost of wiring older structures. Like electricity and running water, the ability to tap into the Internet from almost anywhere changes how we live and work.

This degree of access matters a great deal to nonprofits for a number of reasons, including the abundance choices made possible by the Internet. Constituents can now interact with organizations at 3 PM or 3 AM. They can use search engines and nonprofit information sites like GuideStar.org or CharityNavigator.org to find like-minded organizations. An abundance of choices also means that one organization's site is just a few clicks away from another one.

This translates into what is known as a low switching cost for constituents. Economists have devoted countless amounts of research into how consumers of goods, services, and information deal with switching costs. Often what prevents people from changing in the offline world are things such as cancellation fees, installation and training costs, or potential financial or social risks for doing so.

The Internet has extremely low or in some cases no switching costs. If an organization's Web site does a poor job of meeting a constituent's needs, then finding and using one that does involves very little effort or risk. This fact reinforces the importance of developing more robust online communities. Constituents have come to expect a better online experience, and nonprofits that can meet or exceed those expectations will be the most successful in the future.

Many nonprofit organizations cite their smaller size as one reason why they have chosen not to build an online community. Do not forget that on the Web size means nothing. The largest and smallest organizations are all made equal. Perception carries a tremendous amount of weight and influence on the Web. Some thoughtful work to present your organization can go a long way toward building your online image and reputation.

What is your organization's story? How are you trying to meet your goals? What are different ways to support the organization? What kind of impact does someone's financial support make? Your ability to clearly articulate the answers to these kinds of questions can quickly tell a visitor some very valuable information. Never underestimate of the importance of getting your message right and getting it in front of the right people.

Other nonprofit organizations may say that their physical location deters them from taking the next big leap online. Location on the Web also means nothing. It doesn't matter if your constituents are down the street, across a border, or around the world. Every Web site is a global destination that doesn't take vacations, doesn't call in sick, and is always open for visitors. Many organizations would be surprised to find just how interested people would be to visit their sites if only they knew they existed.

More than ever, organizations need to expand the reach of their organization beyond their four walls. More than ever, organizations need to find ways to overcome new challenges and seize on new opportunities. This is true across a broad spectrum of organizations focused on different missions. For example:

- Education institutions need to involve alumni more closely, on a more regular and sustainable basis, and build lasting relationships along the way.
- Museums and cultural institutions need to increase memberships, add ticket sales, and make constituents want to renew those commitments on a regular basis.
- Healthcare and human services organizations need to be mindful of privacy and confidentially concerns but also must be able to connect and communicate with a diverse group of constituents.
- Cause-based organizations need to share information with an ever-increasing critical mass of people and empower them to be advocates.
- Religious and other faith-based organizations need to communicate in more meaningful ways to their constituents without overmessaging them in the process.
- Associations need to provide value-added benefits and services to members in an environment where options abound and retention is a critical factor to growth and success.
- Foundations and grant-making institutions need to provide more transparency and accountability into how they operate.

In a landscape of increased competition for funding and support, all fundraising organizations need to build and strengthen relationships. Many nonprofit organizations do not see themselves as competitors with other groups. This perception by no means diminishes the reality that they are oftentimes courting the same constituents.

The key is greater involvement on a broader and deeper scale—without blowing out the budget. I do not mean to endorse or suggest that purchasing all the latest greatest technology will solve all of these issues overnight. Once again, the need to have a strategy and plan in place is the best way to get things moving in the right direction.

Any amount of strategic planning begins with determining the needs and goals of your organization. It is also important to understand what has kept you from meeting these objectives in the past. Do these barriers still remain? What is different about this situation than in the past? What key stakeholders can help you to move things forward? Which key stakeholders still need convincing?

Incremental improvement can also be just as effective as giant leaps and bounds. Forward momentum can be one of the most powerful forces in the universe. Far too many organizations believe they need to be doing everything immediately rather than just doing something. One way to get moving in the right direction can be through looking at the traditional fundraising model versus the online fundraising model and the online community model (see Exhibit 1.2).

The traditional fundraising model is based on a tiered structure. Prospects are acquired through a variety of acquisition activities including marketing, direct mail, and other initiatives. The sheer volume of constituents in this tier makes it difficult for high-touch and personal interaction. The goal is to get enough mutual interest to convert these prospects into donors, event attendees, or members.

The donors tier allows for more interaction once supporters can be slotted into an annual fund, giving circle, membership group, or other kind of contributor program. Organizations begin to cultivate donors with the capacity and inclination to give. Groups of donors are assigned to fundraisers, which still means little to no personal attention. The goal is to maintain consistent giving year after year while identifying individuals interested in investing in the organization.

The investors tier accounts for individuals that have, or plan to make, a major gift or a planned gift. At this point a tremendous amount of time, resources, and personal attention are put into the relationship. Here we find the culmination of a donor cultivation process that maximizes giving and emphasizes stewardship (see Exhibit 1.3). Getting to this critical level depends on how well the relationship has been built over a long period of time. The goal is to make the constituent a significant investor based on his or her interests and for the organization to show the impact of that gift.

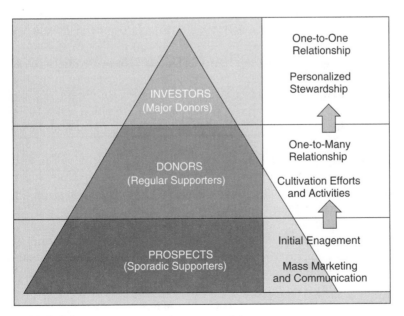

EXHIBIT 1.2 Traditional Fundraising Model

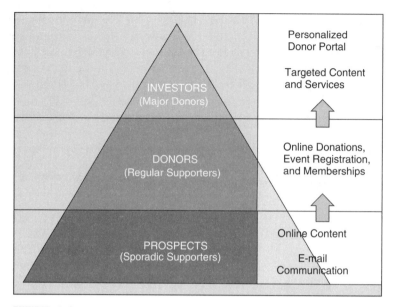

EXHIBIT 1.3   Online Fundraising Model

The online fundraising model can also be based on a tiered structure. Prospects are acquired through lower cost channels such as online content and e-mail communication. A key difference is that the Web can begin to treat them with personalized attention on a mass scale. The goal is to provide a compelling story and multiple ways to contribute to the organization.

The donors tier can streamline and simplify online giving, allow event registrations, and simplify membership programs for constituents that prefer to use the Web. Giving programs can be targeted based on a constituent's individual interests or suggestions based on their previous giving history. This allows for a much more focused relationship management program that uses donor behavior to help shape the relationship. The goal is to identify their areas of interest and capacity to further personalize their online experience.

The investors tier takes stewardship to the next level (see Exhibit 1.4). Technology allows for greater accountability through online reporting and showing the effect of gifts made than realistically feasible by traditional means. An online donor portal that is driven by historical information, self-reported preferences, and targeted services helps to increase the points of contact with the constituent. The goal is to provide meaningful interaction and guidance during the final steps in the development process, but also to encourage a more robust ongoing stewardship program.

The online community model can work in conjunction with both traditional fundraising and its Web counterpart. Prospects begin their relationship by participating in activities that only require an Internet connection. Online advocacy, viral marketing, and other interactions allow them to build greater affinity with the organization. The goal is to get prospects to take an action that provides enough information to take the relationship to the next level.

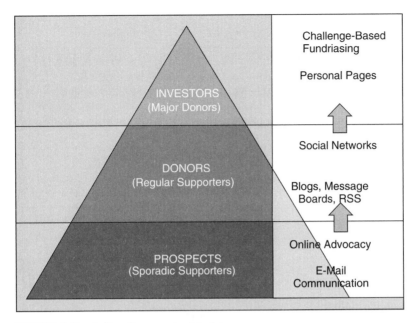

Challenge-Based
Fundriasing

Personal Pages

INVESTORS
(Major Donors)

Social Networks

DONORS
(Regular Supporters)

Blogs, Message
Boards, RSS

Online Advocacy

PROSPECTS
(Sporadic Supporters)

E-Mail
Communication

EXHIBIT 1.4 Online Community Model

The donors tier can be enriched by providing more value-added online services. Allowing donors to participate in more social networking, communication channels between constituents and interactive features helps to strengthen their bonds to the organization. The advent of new technologies, such as RSS, can be a powerful tool in keeping in touch with constituents. RSS allows organizations to publish news and information that can be read on other sites and through other software applications. Organizations now have a tool to distribute content besides just using Web pages and e-mail. The goal is to provide an online experience that allows constituents to interact in multiple ways with like-minded people toward the organization's goals.

The investors tier allows these special constituents to extend the reach of the organization is some exciting new ways. The Internet allows these individuals to issue fundraising challenges to other constituents, which can help to increase overall fundraising. This type of approach also allows investors to gain recognition among peers in a more personal fashion. Additional online services that allow investors to get updated personal information about the impact their investment helps with accountability and stewardship. The goal is to give these key constituents a way to remain involved and engaged long after the fundraising process has matured.

Looking at the traditional fundraising process in comparison to online fundraising and community-building activities is an important step in moving an organization's online strategy forward. Examining how current offline efforts are being handled, and how they might be improved through the use of the Internet, is something organizations need to act on.

Nonprofits need to look at how they currently interact with constituents and how that interaction could be enhanced in more meaningful ways. Every organization

Vertical	Key Business Drivers	Online Tools
Associations	■ Promote the organization and benefits of membership ■ Offer services that allow for greater scalability ■ Reduce costs through online communication	■ Member services on a fee or free basis ■ Communication through Web and e-mail content ■ Access to resources, documents, and shared tools
Cause Based	■ Raise awareness for a cause ■ Reduce costs through online communication	■ Advocacy and volunteer capabilities ■ Special online membership and giving program levels
Cultural	■ Maintain and grow membership ■ Promote interest in performances, exhibits, artists/personalities ■ Reduce costs through online communication	■ Ticketing and special offers for community members ■ Membership benefits that can be used online ■ Express event and exhibit preferences and interests
Education	■ Maintain and deepen engagement with alumni ■ Provide channel for a variety of constituents to interact with one another ■ Reduce costs through online communication	■ Class notes and news published by alumni ■ Online chapters and clubs ■ Directories and social networking capabilities ■ Student, parent, faculty, and staff communities
Faith Based	■ Communicate with members ■ Provide an alternative channel for communication ■ Reduce costs through online communication	■ RSS feeds to syndicate events, announcements, and blog posts ■ Event registrations and calendars ■ E-mail communication and newsletters
Healthcare	■ Provide information and resources ■ Connect members with specialists and other members ■ Support mission of the overall organization by providing care and supporting research	■ Blogs and message boards—interactive, asynchronous communication ■ Resource directories and online chat ■ "Care Pages"—allow grateful patients and caregivers to post and share information

EXHIBIT 1.5   How Companies Leverage the Internet

has a community of constituents who have a vested interest in the success of the mission. Recognize that the strength and reach of the community can be greatly enhanced by leveraging technologies such as the Internet. Seek to find and engage the community of stakeholders for the long-term success of your organization.

ONLINE COMMUNITIES IN ACTION

One proven way to help understand ways to leverage the Internet is to look at how other organizations have been successful (see Exhibit 1.5). Often looking at the common threads between similar organizations reveals a deeper understanding of the possibilities.

CONCLUSION

Communities are an essential part of our lives. They have existed throughout the course of human history. They are powerful drivers of connectedness between people and groups that share common bonds. Communities are emotion-driven groups that make a meaningful impact on the people, places, and organizations they interact with.

They are also an essential part of fundraising. Building communities is all about the personal relationships that organizations build over the course of time, and these are person-centered sets of activities. Nonprofit organizations spend countless amounts of time, resources, and finances to turn these constituents into investors. The convenient reality is that may of the tried-and-true concepts of traditional fundraising apply on the Internet.

Communities continue to be an evolving way that people use the Internet. The Internet is a personal medium and continues to exhibit this development in many new ways as communities and social networks continue to become a larger part of people's interaction on the Web.

Nonprofit organizations also continue to increase how they leverage the Internet to meet their organization's goals. Their level of online sophistication largely depends on who in the organization controls or influences the Web site and whether a clear strategy has been defined.

People have much greater expectations than in the past. They expect both businesses and nonprofit organizations to offer a variety of online options. They do not make a major distinction between the two when it comes to meeting their needs but want rewarding online experiences. They also want more rewarding online experiences with the organizations they support.

When it comes to the organizations they interact with, people have a multitude of choices. Those choices will continue to be influenced and shaped by how accessible, interactive, and transparent these organizations are online. Technology is no longer a limiting factor in the ability to develop thriving and successful online communities.

Communities and the people that drive them blur the lines between online and offline. In many respects there is no difference between how both places are perceived, with the exception that on the Internet space, distance, size, and location no longer matter. Nonprofit organizations that embrace the opportunity to build an online community for their stakeholders and constituents will be making a valuable investment in their own future. The organization they help may be their own.

ABOUT THE AUTHOR

Steven R. MacLaughlin, is the practice manager of Blackbaud *Interactive* and is responsible for leading how Blackbaud delivers Internet solutions for its clients.

Steve has spent more than a decade building successful online initiatives with a broad range of Fortune 500 firms, government and educational institutions, and nonprofit organizations. Steve earned both his undergraduate degree and a Master of Science degree in interactive media from Indiana University.

NOTES

1. *State of the Nonprofit Industry 2006*, Blackbaud, Inc., Available at: www.blackbaud.com/files/resources/industry_analysis/12-06_NonprofitIndustrySurvey_Results.pdf
2. http://en.wikipedia.org/wiki/Web_2.0.
3. John Man, *Gutenberg: How One Man Remade the World with Words* (Hoboken, NJ: John Wiley & Sons, 2002).

CHAPTER 2

Web Site Benchmarking: Six Criteria for Measuring Effectiveness Online

Ted Hart
tedhart.com

Adrian Melrose
Giving Matters

WHEN YOU ONLY HAVE 10 SECONDS

A centerpiece to any nonprofit organization's online strategy is its Web site. It is a landing page for content, interaction, and donations. As this book seeks to focus attention on the use of online services to build strong social networks, and to use Web 2.0 strategies to seek broader participation, it is the Web site that is the hub for content and interaction, and therefore is the focus for this chapter.

You have 10 seconds to engage your Web site visitor to take some action you desire on the Web site: to click somewhere to explore the site. The criteria for measuring effectiveness will help you enhance your chances of success. Working closely with Giving Matters, a research-focused consultancy, in the United Kingdom, we present six criteria that can be used to evaluate any charity Web site. The benchmark study of UK Charity Websites[1] developed by Giving Matters compares how well charities engage with donors, volunteers, and other stakeholders in the online environment. It also evaluates how the organization's presence on the Internet adds value or insight to its proposition.

We evaluated Web sites using six criteria grouped in the following categories: usability, communication, responsiveness, housekeeping, transparency, and accessibility. Following review of the criteria, readers are urged to browse the top five Web sites we review and compare our notes, regarding what works and what does not.

This criterion is used to measure aspects of, and to better understand, the online presence of charities. It seeks to discover how successfully they use the power of the internet to engage, share and network.

We selected criteria and subcriteria for each category on the basis of their applicability to charity Web sites, and the value they added. In this evaluation, we emphasize a charity's social media activities and stated environmental stance for the first time, reflecting the growing influence and relevance of these factors. We took special care to balance the criteria, to ensure that they were relatively equally weighted. In each category, the scores range from 0 to 5, with 0 being the worst and 5 being the best.

An evaluation of 120 charity Web sites by Giving Matters found the following general trends:

1. They score highest in the Usability category.
2. They do well in Responsiveness and Communication.
3. Their scores are weak in Housekeeping and Transparency.
4. Their accessibility scores are very low showing a general lack of consideration in this area.

Exhibit 2.1 presents the results by category and criterion, with comparisons to a similar study completed in 2006.

#	Categories and Criteria	Average 2006	Average 2007	Difference	% of 2006
0	Overall Score	2.67	2.50	(0.17)	−6
1	**Usability**	**2.89**	**3.31**	**0.42**	**15**
1.1	Homepage	3.31	3.55	0.24	7
1.2	Navigation Structure	4.76	3.22	(1.55)	−32
1.3	Links	2.79	3.18	0.39	14
2	**Accessibility**	**1.41**	**1.60**	**0.19**	**14**
2.1	Standard HTML	0.03	0.28	0.25	1000
2.2	Homepage Accessibility	0.59	1.11	0.52	89
2.3	User Control	3.61	3.42	(0.20)	−5
3	**Communication**	**1.26**	**2.73**	**1.46**	**116**
3.1	E-Newsletter	1.13	1.38	0.25	22
3.2	Communication Channels	0.73	2.22	1.49	206
3.3	Up-to-Date Information	2.06	3.89	1.83	89
3.4	Interaction	2.38	3.42	1.04	44
4	**Transparency**	**2.29**	**2.22**	**(0.07)**	**−3**
4.1	Charity Number and Purpose	4.03	4.28	0.26	6
4.2	Financial Information	2.61	1.92	(0.70)	−27
4.3	Corporate Social Responsibility	0.13	0.83	0.71	567
4.4	Trustees	2.39	1.84	(0.55)	−23
5	**Responsiveness**	**2.97**	**2.70**	**(0.27)**	**−9**
5.1	Giving	3.88	3.70	(0.18)	−5
5.2	Tools for Giving	2.83	3.11	0.28	10
5.3	Volunteers	3.21	2.27	(0.95)	−29
5.4	Volunteering	1.96	2.02	0.05	3
5.5	Fundraising (new)		2.39	2.39	
5.6	Corporate Involvement (new)		2.73	2.73	
6	**Housekeeping**	**4.30**	**2.45**	**(1.85)**	**−43**
6.1	Home Page Rank	3.26	2.73	(0.54)	−16
6.2	Ad Words/Meta Tags	4.04	3.80	(0.24)	−6
6.3	Social Networking (new)		0.81	0.81	

EXHIBIT 2.1   Overall Scores by Categories and Criteria

A REVIEW OF BENCHMARK CRITERIA

Charities that have been reviewed should carefully review the categories in which they score best and then consider where they performed worst, comparing this to their own Web site review. Each category is compared to the corresponding result from 2006. When evaluating the Web site we considered:

1. Usability. Is the site easy to use?
2. Communication. Can users communicate with the charity and each other?
3. Responsiveness. Are giving, volunteering, fundraising, and corporate involvement encouraged and supported?
4. Housekeeping. Does the charity put search engine optimization (SEO) into practice and does the site support and work in harmony with social networking sites?
5. Transparency. Is the charity open with its information?
6. Accessibility. Can everyone access the site?

1. Usability

Usability is the measure that shows how easily people can use a charity Web site, to achieve a particular goal, in a satisfying way. A usable site should be easy to use and understand, efficient, effective, satisfying, and enjoyable.

The Charity Matters study sought to simply evaluate whether the site helps users to understand its purpose, and to navigate through the content. The study found that the average charity Web site has a very good home page, provides sufficient navigational support, and has satisfactory links as shown in the following.

Home Page
- A typical home page:
  - Most of the time: Says or illustrates what the charity does; presents some information, usually news and announcements.
  - More rarely: Appeals for giving, fundraising, and volunteering. In 35 percent of cases, users have to scroll down to see or get to this important content.

Navigation Structure
- Getting to the home page is not always easy:
  - Only 72 percent (62 percent in 2006) of the sites place a link to the home page on the logo.
  - Only 85 percent (79 percent in 2006) provide an explicit Home link or button.
  - Two of the sites have neither, which is an improvement from last year's four sites with no link to the home page.
- The user's current location isn't well indicated:
  - The menu properly represents the location in 62 percent of the sites.
  - Breadcrumb navigation (a path) exists in 42 percent of the sites.

Links
- Links are relatively easy to recognize and use, yet basic guidelines for links aren't well observed:
  - 13 (8 in 2006) sites have links that meet all evaluation criteria.
  - 5 (15 last year) sites do not meet a single criterion.

- The lack of differentiation between visited and unvisited links remains the most common failure, and the only criterion for which we see a year-on-year reduction in the score:
  - In 2006, 25 percent of the sites differentiated visited from unvisited links.
  - In 2007, only 18 percent of the sites make the distinction.

2. Communication

Communication refers to the exchange of information between the Web sites and their users, as well as between users. In our study, Communication indicates how prepared charity Web sites must meet the informational needs of users by providing different channels for active and timely information exchange.

Charity Web sites are now adopting technologies for dynamic communication and maintaining content on a more regular basis.

E-Newsletter
- The e-newsletter remains the most common communication feature:
  - Offered by 58 percent of the Web sites.
  - Charities rarely send subscription confirmation. Of those that do, only half provide information on how to unsubscribe.

Web 2.0 Content
- Charities have started blogging, and using other communication technologies:
  - We have identified some form of a blog or diary on 42 charity Web sites—a big step forward compared to 2006.
  - Many charities are also using forums and message boards; some are offering video and audio as podcasts and webcasts; very few are offering chat rooms.

Interaction
- Most charities allow users to connect in a number of ways:
  - Most provide an e-mail address, or an online form to complete.
  - Virtually all provide mailing addresses and phone numbers.
  - Contact information is usually anonymous; Web sites rarely provide the names of people to be contacted.

Up-to-Date Information
- Content on Web sites should indicate how current it is:
  - The content is dated on 89 percent of the sites. In more than half of those sites, the information has been updated within a week.

Blogs   Short for Web logs, blogs are the communication tool of contemporary online communities. In essence, they are journals or diaries that the author(s) intend(s) to be read by the general public or by a particular interested group.

A blog represents the personality of the author or the Web site. It is usually regularly updated, offers chronological access to data, and links to related content. In the 2006 study, we were disappointed that no charities had started a blog, but this year we see that charities are catching up with the trend:

- 33 charity Web sites (almost one-third) have some form of a blog and nine have online diaries.

Forums Forums (or discussion boards) are places where users discuss various topics. Message boards are similar to forums and allow users to post personal announcements and messages (although answers and discussions are not expected). As the two forms of communication are similar, we combined them in one criterion.

Last year, we found one of the two on eight Web sites; this year the number is considerably higher:

- 47 charity Web sites (39 percent) have a forum or message board.
- 1 site has both a forum and a message board.
- 4 sites have a peculiar form of message board, allowing users to make their own pages (or subsites) for fundraising or other purposes.

Chats enable real-time exchange between users, and are very popular with younger people in particular:

- Last year, we found only one charity Web site with a chat room. This year, we found three.
- We also found one site that has discontinued the use of chats, and one site that mentioned chat rooms but didn't provide the service (or it could not be found).

Podcasts and Webcasts These forms of communication are the latest, popular online communication tool. We were looking for live video or audio too.

- We found podcasts on 18 sites; this seems to be the most popular way of offering audio content.
- On one site, we even found a "petcast."

Combining Communication Channels Some Web sites use two or more communication channels to interact with their users:

- 50 sites offer at least one of the channels.
- 24 sites use two channels.
- 7 sites have three channels (the missing channel is chat for all seven).
- 1 has all four channels.
- 38 sites do not use any of these communication technologies.

Updated Data in Communication Channels The data in the various communication channels is not always updated. Some diaries dated back to 2005 and 2004. Overall, the channel with the most up-to-date information is the forum.

- 23 sites maintain the information quite regularly; data had been updated within a week of the day of evaluation.
- 24 sites had updated the data within a month of the day of evaluation.
- 35 sites included the data in the communication channels older than a month.

3. Responsiveness

Charities make good use of their Web sites for collecting donations, and for providing information to donors and volunteers on various options and activities.

Giving

- 68 percent of charity Web sites have a dedicated page or section where they list the available giving options and provide explanations on how to donate or leave a legacy.
- 73 percent provide testimonials or stories about beneficiaries.
- The most commonly used forms of giving are online donations (89 percent of sites), and leaving a legacy (85 percent of sites).
- 42 percent of sites generate revenues via an online shop.

Volunteering

- 59 percent of sites state how they work with volunteers. Only 25 percent provide stories about people who have volunteered.
- 41 percent provide contact information (telephone number and e-mail address) for volunteers. Occasionally, the name of the charity's contact employee is provided.
- Volunteering online is only possible on 42 percent of charity Web sites (51 of 120 sites assessed).

Fundraising and Corporate Involvement

- 50 percent of sites have information on how to organize an event; 61 percent include a list of events; only 18 percent post stories of people who have participated in fundraising events.
- 69 percent of charities indicate an interest in working with companies, providing information on how companies can help. Most sites offer contact information, but rarely include the name of the person to contact.

4. Housekeeping

Charity Web sites do well at basic housekeeping.

Home Page Ranking and Search Engine Optimization (SEO)

- Home pages are well prepared and maintained with the proper use of page titles, keywords, and descriptions.
- The Web sites are well optimized for search engines:
  - 83 percent of Web sites have a Google page rank for their home pages of between 4 and 6. The average rank is 5.61.
  - Two sites have a rank of 8. The maximum Google page rank is 10.

Page rank relies on the uniquely democratic nature of the Web by using its vast link structure as an indicator of an individual page's value. In essence, Google interprets a link from page A to page B as a vote, by page A, for page B. But, Google looks at more than the sheer volume of votes, or links a page receives; it also analyzes the page that casts the vote. Votes cast by pages that are themselves "important" weigh more heavily and help to make other pages "important."

Social Networking

- 55 charity Web sites have profiles in social networking sites. This indicates positive thinking toward taking users' interaction beyond the Web site, and the uptake in participation of social media. Participation is encouraged in social networking sites (myspace.com, bebo.com, and facebook.com) and links to images and video on youtube.com and flickr.com.

5. Transparency

Transparency instills public confidence, and is a measure of the willingness of charities to show inside information. Transparency is important because charities usually collect significant sums of money, so people on both the giving and receiving ends are interested in how these funds are managed and distributed.

Corporate Social Responsibility (CSR) is an emerging business trend. Even so, the term is useful shorthand for a range of socially responsible activities that have now progressed beyond the commercial world and into the charity arena. CSR policies can incorporate a number of different issue areas that can be categorized more generally fewer than three headings (hence the term triple bottom-line): economic, environment, and social. Even more broadly, CSR activities could include any of the following:

- Environment
- Workplace or Health and Well-Being (Occupational Health & Safety)
- Human Rights and Diversity
- Supply Chain
- Community Investment or Social Issues
- Corporate Governance
- Marketplace

Those organizations that take CSR seriously look to the GRI (Global Reporting Initiative, www.globalreporting.org) to get an idea of the scope of the issues they should cover.

In the authors' opinion, charities don't appear to be very open about what they are doing. They readily state their charity number and purpose but more reticent about sharing information regarding finances and management.

When it comes to overtly stating their practices in terms of social responsibility (as the commercial sector is doing with explicit Corporate Social Responsibility policies and activities), charity Web sites rarely offer any information.

Charity Purpose
- Virtually all (95 percent) state their purpose and explain what they do (98 percent).

Financial
- More than half of the Web sites, 56 percent (67), provide a financial report in sections, such as About Us or Finance. A few more provide reports elsewhere, and are therefore harder to find and more likely to remain unseen.
  - Most financial reports contain information on management and staff expenses.
  - Most charities continue to present this information as a PDF file to download.

Trustees
- Charities have become more secretive about their management and trustees:
  - 58 percent present lists of management and trustee names (68 percent in

2006). Most charities rarely provide some detail or insight about these people with overall responsibility.

Corporate Social Responsibility

- The likelihood of finding social responsibility-related content on a charity Web site has increased:
  - 17 percent of the Web sites state a policy, interest, or involvement in CSR.
  - 40 percent claim that they engage in CSR-related activities (e.g., recycling and environmentally friendly actions), which is higher.

6. Accessibility

Accessibility is about providing everyone with equal opportunities for accessing a site. It is a measure of how easy it is for people to get to, use, and understand things. Our focus is on the technical aspects of providing people with access to Web sites, so the scores in this category indicate how well the charity Web sites meet these technical criteria.

Evaluating the "soft" aspects of accessibility in a heuristic manner (i.e., through trial and error, or with only loosely defined rules) is not possible without having access to real users and their needs, desires, disabilities, or constraints. So, accessibility and usability always go together, and complement each other, with usability being the factor that shows whether users can do their jobs or accomplish their tasks.

Accessibility is now a legal requirement in the United Kingdom, because creating more accessibility has been shown to also increase search engine visibility and also ensures that the site complies with the disability discrimination legislation. Even if charities were not bound in this way, the fact that they exist to help people in need would probably encourage most users to believe that their Web sites would be compliant.

This category is generally the biggest disappointment in evaluation of a charity Web site. Very few charity Web sites comply with accessibility standards. (Quick Tips on making your Web site accessible are at: www.w3.org/WAI/quicktips/Overview .php.)

Conformance to HTML

- In most cases the HTML coding of charity Web sites does not comply with accessibility standards:
  - 105 sites (88 percent) score zero when checked for valid HTML.

Homepage Accessibility

- 43 percent of home pages (52) meet the basic accessibility requirements
- Only two sites have home pages that meet the strictest accessibility requirements. Last year, there were four sites.
- Only two Web sites score zero in accessibility, meaning that they do not meet even a single criterion.

User Control

- Most charity Web sites do provide meaningful, descriptive alternative texts for images. They also allow users to control the size of texts, avoid using flash and frames, and use meaningful and understandable addresses for their pages.

TOP FIVE CHARITY WEB SITES

Exhibit 2.2 lists the top five charity Web sites evaluated in 2007.

Website	2007	2006 Score	2006 Diff	2006 Rank
Cancer Research UK, www.cancerresearchuk.org	4.02	3.52	0.50	5
WaterAid, www.wateraid.org.uk	3.53	3.60	(0.06)	4
Royal National Institute for Deaf People, www.rnid.org.uk	3.51	3.35	0.15	12
Oxfam, www.oxfam.org.uk	3.48	3.68	(0.21)	2
Marie Curie Cancer Care, www.mariecurie.org.uk	3.46	3.12	0.34	24

EXHIBIT 2.2 Top Five Web Sites

The top-ranked site, Cancer Research UK, scored significantly higher than the others—Cancer Research UK outscores WaterAid by almost half a point—0.49. The scores of the other four sites are very similar—the difference between the second and the fifth is just 0.07. Thus far, there has been no such thing as a perfect charity Web site.

However, while similar in value, the scores of these four sites are composed and distributed quite differently across the criteria. For example, some sites score well in Usability, while others have good results in Communication, and so on.

The details of the sites individual scores are shown by category, using spider charts. Spider charts (also known as radar charts) graphically show the size of the gap in the evaluation criteria. The charts have an axis for each criterion, and the data is plotted along each one. Points close to the center of an axis indicate low values; points near the outer edge are high in value. The overall size and shape of the area (achieved by connecting the values for all criteria) shows how well the evaluated Web site satisfies the criteria for that category. A large area indicates high scores, while an area spaced regularly around the center point indicates balanced scores across all criteria. Exhibit 2.3 shows the scores of these top 5 sites compared to the overall report averages.

> *When interpreting the charts, pay attention to each axis to identify concentrations of strengths and weaknesses.*

1. Cancer Research UK, www.cancerresearchuk.org In the benchmark study created by Giving Matters, the Cancer Research UK's site received the highest score (Exhibit 2.4).

Usability
The site shows full compliance with all criteria and has the top score in the category.

Accessibility
This is the weakest point of the site.

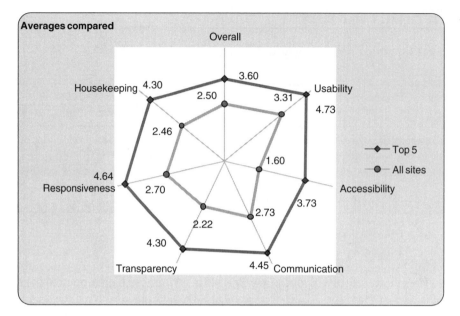

EXHIBIT 2.3 Top 5 Averages Compared to Overall Averages of All Web Sites

1. The site meets all criteria for user control.
2. The home page meets the basic (priority 1) accessibility requirements.
3. Its HTML does not pass the validation check.

Communication
1. A newsletter is available and a confirmation e-mail is sent to subscribers. However, information for unsubscribing is not contained within the message.
2. Communication channels used: online diaries (although the service is temporarily stopped), message board, and podcasts. They are regularly updated.
3. Content is dated and up to date.
4. Contact information doesn't include e-mail addresses or any named individuals. The site seems to prefer online forms as a means of getting in touch.

Transparency
1. Detailed information on the charity's work and purpose.
2. Detailed information about its trustees.
3. A financial report with information on management and staff remuneration. However, an overall financial summary is missing.
4. Some mention of CSR, although a clear statement was not found. The charity is involved in recycling activities.

Responsiveness
1. Full compliance with giving criteria—the site uses all of the tools for giving evaluated in the study: online donations, legacies, direct debit, and online shops.
2. Great support for volunteers, although details for volunteering offline and a named contact for volunteering requests are not included.
3. Full compliance with fundraising criteria: information on organizing fundraising events is provided, a calendar of events is available, and stories of people who have participated in such events are presented.

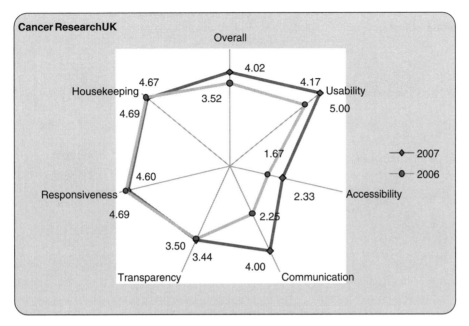

EXHIBIT 2.4 Cancer Research U.K.—Scores by Category

4. Information on corporate involvement is available, but without contact information being provided alongside.

Housekeeping

1. Great home page rank = 8.
2. Full compliance with search optimization criteria.
3. High social media channel adoption, with profiles on three social networking sites (myspace.com, bebo.com, and facebook.com) and links to images and video on youtube.com and flickr.com.

2. WaterAid, www.wateraid.org.uk (Exhibit 2.5)

Usability

1. The home page is rich in information and meets all criteria.
2. The navigation structure is very good and also meets all criteria.
3. Links are recognizable and have good anchors. However, visited links are not distinguished from unvisited.

Accessibility

1. The Web site meets all criteria for user control, but does not have descriptive alternative texts for images.
2. The home page does not meet the basic (priority 1) accessibility requirements.
3. The HTML does not pass the validation check.

Communication

1. Full compliance with newsletter criteria.
2. Communication channels used: blog, forum, podcasts. Information is outdated.
3. Content on the basic pages of the Web site is dated and up to date.

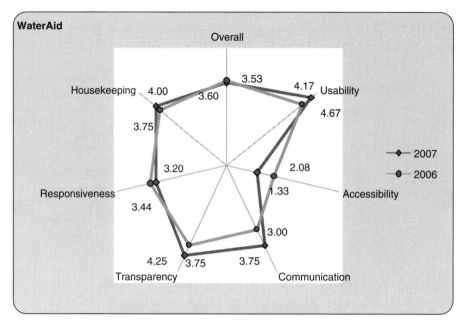

EXHIBIT 2.5 WaterAid—Scores by Category

4. Contact information is missing e-mail addresses and names. Preferred contact method is probably online forms.

Transparency

1. Detailed information on the charity's work and purpose.
2. Detailed information about trustees.
3. Full financial information: full report and a separate financial summary.
4. No formal social responsibility statement, although involvement in recycling and sanitation activities mentioned.

Responsiveness

1. Excellent compliance with giving criteria—the site uses all of the tools for giving evaluated in the study (except shop-giving through physical retail outlets).
2. Only adequate information for volunteers—no volunteer stories provided to share experiences and entice new volunteers. Neither a contact phone number nor a name is provided in the context of volunteering, although an e-mail address is available.
3. A calendar of fundraising events is available. However, the Web site offers no information on organizing fundraising events or stories about people who have participated in such events.
4. Information on corporate involvement is available with contact information (except name).

Housekeeping

1. Very good home page rank = 6.
2. Full compliance with search optimization criteria.
3. A good adoption of social media, with profiles on four social networking sites (myspace.com, youtube.com, facebook.com, and flickr.com), but no profile on bebo.com.

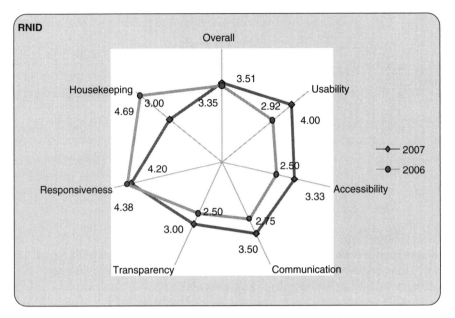

EXHIBIT 2.6 Royal National Institute for Deaf People—Scores by Category

3. Royal National Institute for Deaf People, www.rnid.org.uk Royal National Institute for Deaf People is the third best Web site in our 2007 benchmark study (it was ranked 12 in 2006), just 0.02 points behind second place. This Web site's score has improved in Usability, Accessibility, Communication, and Transparency. However, there's been a very noticeable decrease in Housekeeping (Exhibit 2.6)

Usability
1. The home page is good: it presents the Web site well and contains useful content, but unfortunately requires users to scroll down to see more content. The home page does not contain any information on donating.
2. The navigation structure is very good and meets all criteria.
3. Links meet all criteria too.

Accessibility
A relative strength of the site.

1. The Web site meets all criteria for user control (although it does not use descriptive alternative texts for images).
2. The home page meets the basic (priority 1) accessibility requirements.
3. The HTML code is good, although some errors are observed.

Communication
1. A newsletter is available, but no confirmation is sent for subscription.
2. Communication channels used: forum.
3. Content is dated and up to date.
4. Contact information is extensive, but no names are provided.

Transparency
1. Detailed information about the charity's work and purpose, as well as on trustees.

2. Financial report is provided, with info on management and staff remuneration (but no financial summary).
3. No social responsibility statement, and no evidence of involvement in CSR-friendly activities.

Responsiveness
1. Good compliance with giving criteria—the Web site uses all of the tools for giving evaluated in the study (except shop-giving and online shop).
2. Great support for volunteers. The only missing information is a named contact person for volunteering requests.
3. Information on organizing fundraising events, and a calendar of such events, is available. Stories about people who have participated in such events are missing.
4. Information on corporate involvement is available with contact information, however, name of contact person is missing.

Housekeeping
1. Excellent home page rank = 7.
2. Full compliance with search optimization criteria.
3. No obvious social media adoption, since we found no profiles on social networking sites, and no links to content on such sites.

4. Oxfam, www.oxfam.org.uk   Oxfam is second best in Transparency and third best in Housekeeping (Exhibit 2.7).

Usability
1. The home page is good: it contains useful content, but doesn't state what the charity does. The home page does not contain any content on donating.
2. The navigation structure is very good, except it doesn't indicate the current location of users.
3. Links are a relative weakness: no-link texts use the same color as links, possibly causing confusion; visited links are not differentiated from nonvisited.

Accessibility
1. The Web site meets all criteria for user control but one: font size is fixed, so some users may be unable to enlarge the texts if needed.
2. The home page does not meet even the basic (priority 1) accessibility requirements.
3. The HTML does not pass the validation check.

Communication
1. A newsletter is available, but no e-mail confirmation is sent for subscription.
2. Communication channels used: blog, forum, and podcasts. All are regularly updated.
3. Content on the basic pages of the site is dated and up to date.
4. Contact information is provided, except for names. No feedback/enquiry form is available.

Transparency
1. Detailed information on the charity's work and purpose is provided, as well as on trustees. There is no management listing.
2. Financial report is provided, with information on management and staff remuneration, but no financial summary.
3. CSR is part of what the charity does; it is incorporated excellently within the site.

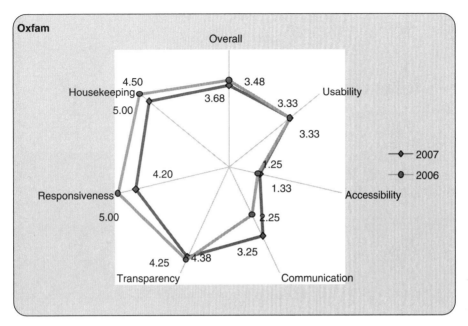

EXHIBIT 2.7 Oxfam—Scores by Category

Responsiveness

1. The Web site uses all of the tools for giving evaluated in the study, and even includes stories about people who have been helped. There isn't a single page detailing all the giving options.
2. Great support for volunteers, although volunteering online is not possible.
3. Full compliance with fundraising criteria, since information on organizing fundraising events is provided, calendar of events is available, and stories of people who have participated in such events are presented.
4. Full compliance with corporate involvement criteria.

Housekeeping

1. Excellent home page rank = 7.
2. Full compliance with search optimization criteria.
3. Profiles on four of the social networking sites (myspace.com, bebo.com, facebook.com, and flickr.com), as well as links to youtube.com.

5. Marie Curie Cancer Care, www.mariecurie.org.uk   This site is fourth in Communication and fifth in Responsiveness (Exhibit 2.8).

Usability

1. The home page is good: it presents the Web site and contains useful content, although it does not contain any content on volunteering.
2. The navigation structure is very good and meets all criteria.
3. Links are a relative weakness: visited links are not differentiated from nonvisited ones, and some link anchors are poor.

Communication

1. Full compliance with newsletter criteria.

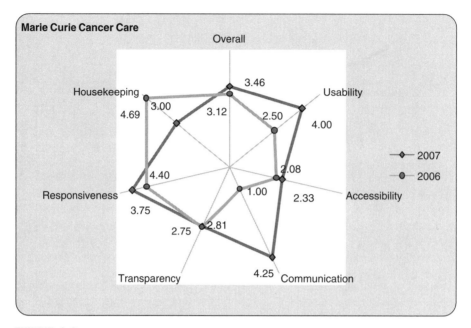

EXHIBIT 2.8 Marie Curie Cancer Care—Scores by Category

2. Communication channels used: personal fundraising pages—enabling users to create their own fundraising pages within the site.
3. Content is dated and current.
4. Contact information includes names, but no e-mail addresses.

Responsiveness
1. Full compliance with giving criteria—the Web site uses all of the tools for giving evaluated in the study.
2. A lot of information for volunteers, but volunteering online is not possible, and there's no information on volunteering offline available.
3. Full compliance with fundraising criteria, with information on organizing fundraising events provided, a calendar of events available, and stories of people who have participated in such events presented.
4. Acceptable level of compliance with corporate involvement criteria, but phone numbers and contact names are missing.

Housekeeping
1. Excellent home page rank = 7.
2. The home page does not use meta keywords and description.
3. Profiles on two of the social networking sites (myspace.com and facebook.com).

Transparency
1. Detailed information on the charity's work and purpose is included. Management and trustee biographies are missing.
2. Financial report is provided, with information on management and staff remuneration. However, a financial summary is missing.
3. A formal social responsibility statement was not found. The charity is involved in recycling activities.

Accessibility
1. The Web site meets all criteria for user control.
2. The home page meets the basic (priority 1) accessibility requirements.
3. The HTML does not pass the validation check.

CONCLUSION

Charities are relying more and more on their Web sites as a means of initiating relationships, social networking, marketing, fundraising, communication, and interaction.

Many charities regard their Web sites as merely a one-way information flow; rather like a corporate brochure. While this continues to be basically true, there are signs that charities are slowly breaking away from this traditional use of the Web:

- The home page is becoming richer and more focused.
- Content is being updated on a more regular basis.
- There is more communication with users—we see increased use of newsletters, blogs, and discussion forums, as well as podcasts.
- Some charities are early adopters of social responsibility statements.
- A few charities are early adopters of social media.

Although some small improvement is noticeable, especially in meeting the accessibility guidelines set by the Web Accessibility Initiative (WAI), charities are still far from compliant with accessibility legislative regulations. Scores in Accessibility continue to be extremely low.

General Recommendations for Charities:

1. In the online dimension of their work, charities need to be more open to change and innovation. The Internet is developing quickly, offering new possibilities on an almost daily basis.
2. Charities must make it an urgent priority to pay more attention to the varying requirements of users who have different constraints, needs, and preferences.

Most charity Web sites have a long way to go before they meet even the minimal guidelines used in this report. Attention to these guidelines (and many others) could improve the experience offered by charity Web sites to their users.

Any charity that invests time and effort into increasing the compliance of its Web site to these six criteria will improve the user experience, increase its community outreach and interaction, and increase its online presence.

ABOUT THE AUTHORS

Ted Hart is CEO of Hart Philanthropic Services (http://tedhart.com), a global consultancy to nonprofits, providing serious solutions to nonprofit challenges. He is also Founder of the international ePhilanthropy Foundation (www.ephilanthropy.org), which is headquartered in Washington, DC. Ted has served as CEO of the University Maryland Medical System Foundation, and Chief Development Officer for Johns Hopkins Bayview Medical Center. He has been certified as an Advanced Certified Fund Raising Executive (ACFRE) by the Association of Fundraising Professionals (AFP) and an ePhilanthropy master trainer by the ePhilanthropy Foundation. Hart is author to several published articles, as well as an editor and author of four books.

Adrian Melrose is a South African born entrepreneur who now lives in the UK. He is qualified as a Chartered Accountant but has spent the last ten years in management consulting and technology roles.

In 2003, Adrian co-founded 2B Reputation Intelligence, which was sold to Factiva (a Dow Jones company) two-years later. 2B Reputation Intelligence's solution provision spanned technology, communication, and data analysis. He is currently the Chief Executive of Webface Technology Ventures (www.webface.com), a company that provides seed capital and growth management to online businesses largely operating in the social software space.

Through Webface's investment in Giving Matters (blog.givingmatters.co.uk), a Venture Philanthropy business, Adrian is actively involved in the UK Charity sector (known as the Third Sector in the UK). He is a trustee of several Charities and has served on the judging panel of the Third Sector Excellence Awards (thirdsector.co.uk/).

NOTE

1. We selected the charities with the help of the list of "The Top 100 UK Charities by Voluntary Income Source," as quoted in *The Major Charities: An Independent Guide* by Fitzherbert and Becher, Directory of Social Change, 2002).

CHAPTER 3

Advocacy 2.0: Leveraging Social Networking to Further Your Organization's Mission

Sheeraz Haji
Convio, Inc.

Emma Zolbrod
Independent marketing consultant

H ow does a nonprofit organization earn 2 million media impressions, identify 200 key activists in 37 states, and convince each of them to invite friends and family to a house party to watch the State of the Union Address? And do so in a way that builds a community of supporters and grows the organization's list? Ask Sojourners—whose online advocacy efforts led to these impressive results. It is just one of many nonprofit organizations across the nation that leverages peer-to-peer communications to further its mission by taking advantage of the convergence of online advocacy, social networking tools, and Web 2.0 applications.

CHANGING LANDSCAPE OF ONLINE ADVOCACY

Most nonprofit organizations have recognized the benefits of online advocacy tools and have moved their organizing onto the Internet. The ease of Web-based communications has generated a huge increase in the number of citizen communications to Capitol Hill, local government, and other decision-making targets. Capitol Hill itself receives over 300 million electronic messages sent each year—ten times the volume of print, fax, or phone communications. Online advocacy has become even more sophisticated with the advent of Web 2.0 applications and social networking tools, both of which have empowered constituents and introduced new and unique ways of organizing.

In its various forms, online advocacy is used by membership organizations of all types and sizes—including charities, public interest groups, associations, and educational institutions—to recruit supporters and to mobilize constituencies quickly and effectively. Like any organizing campaign, online advocacy is as much about constituent relationship building and engagement as it is about urging political change. By leveraging technology in conjunction with organizing campaigns, organizations

SOJOURNERS: "THE STATE OF OUR VALUES" CAMPAIGN

We use advocacy as messaging. The goal is for people to take up an idea and then repeat it in a focused way.
—David J. Allen, associate director of individual giving, Sojourners/Call to Renewal

Organization: The mission of Sojourners/Call to Renewal is to articulate the biblical call to social justice, inspiring hope and building a movement to transform individuals, communities, the church, and the world.

Situation: In January 2006, Sojourners/Call to Renewal launched an innovative campaign to encourage people to host State of the Union watch gatherings in churches and activists homes across America.

Solution: Sojourners/Call to Renewal empowered their supporters and extended their reach by providing constituents with the tools they needed to organize, promote, and host a house party.

Four weeks before the official State of the Union Address, Sojourners/Call to Renewal sent out an e-mail blast to list members with the message "Host a party, download a toolkit." The downloadable Organizers' Toolkit included tips on how to organize a house party, rookie tips for generating earned media, and a sign-up sheet to manage the attendee list. A reminder e-mail was sent out a week later, and more toolkits were downloaded. Once they reached a critical mass of hosts (about 100), Sojourners/Call to Renewal organized conference calls with Executive Director Jim Wallis and Press Secretary Jack J. Pannell Jr. In addition to specific details to help hosts execute a successful party, emphasis was placed on generating earned media. Community building quickly took place as event hosts exchanged ideas and provided each other with feedback. The final two weeks before the State of the Union Address, a weekly e-mail blast was sent to the organization's supporters with an important message "Attend a watch party near you, or organize one." Recipients were then able to search by zip code and radius to find a nearby watch party. The final reminder e-mail, which went out the day before the event, was an effective tool that prompted last-minute registrations and maximized turnout.

Results: The campaign results were impressive:

- Two hundred watch parties in 37 states
- Estimated 2 million earned media impressions
- Identification of 200 key activists
- Community building
- List growth

provide constituents with easy ways to get involved while simultaneously furthering their mission. Web-based advocacy efforts can engage the unaffiliated, recruit new supporters, and convert those supporters into donors.

At the basic level, online advocacy can include a number of different engagement techniques, such as gathering petition signatures or sending messages to legislators and other targets via e-mail, fax, and Web form. These techniques can be facilitated by online tools that are affordable, technically easy to deploy, and simple for advocates to use. Some online advocacy tools have sophisticated filtering capabilities for strategic targeting as well as comprehensive tracking capabilities that measure usage and response rates to determine an activist's desired level of involvement so that the organization can better serve those interests and boost the overall effectiveness of future campaigns.

Recipients of advocacy-related e-mail messages can respond quickly to urgent appeals and take action at their convenience by clicking on links in the e-mail messages they receive. With online advocacy, the "viral marketing" effect of friends forwarding an e-mail to like-minded peers can quickly promote a campaign (for free) at an accelerated pace that otherwise would have been impossible. In comparison, phone campaigns and direct mail (e.g., postcards, letters) are much more complex, time-consuming, and expensive, offering less opportunity to spread the word. Web 2.0 applications, such as user-contributed content and the increased adoption of social networking tools, further magnify the effect and importance of peer networks.

HANDING OVER THE REINS TO YOUR CONSTITUENTS: THE ROLE OF USER-CONTRIBUTED CONTENT AND SOCIAL NETWORKING IN ONLINE ADVOCACY

The nature of digital communications, coupled with the introduction of Web 2.0, lends itself to user-driven marketing activities. These activities fall into two camps:

1. **Constituent-led content.** Encourage constituents to create and pass along content that resides on your organization's Web site.
2. **Live in your supporters' worlds.** Take your content to the place where current and future constituents already spend time.

Organizations with successful online advocacy campaigns are doing a combination of the two. By using their own networks to promote an issue, constituents can distribute information, organize house parties, and encourage action within their own communities at a faster pace than ever before. Web sites that encourage user-contributed content, as well those that facilitate social networking, have changed the way in which people communicate with each other and the way in which constituents communicate with organizations. The key benefit of this approach is the increased degree of constituent engagement. Instead of broadcasting a message one way, organizations can now engage in two-way conversations and then expand that dialogue to a community of their most active supporters.

User-contributed content, one of the important aspects of Web 2.0, is founded on the premise that Web site visitors should actively participate in the generation of new content or the improvement of existing content. Examples of user-contributed content include discussions; blogs; comments (the ability to append comments to other content, e.g., "Tell us what you think of this story"); ratings (where users can assign a rating to content); tagging (where users can append tags to any item on a Web site in an attempt to better describe it from the user's perspective); and the creation of user-authored content (where a user edits or adds to existing content on a Web page).

The value of user-contributed content is better content. From the viewpoint of constituent-based organizations, user-contributed content presents an opportunity to break down barriers that currently separate an organization from its Web site visitors and encourage a passive observer to become an engaged participant. Of course, the type and desired level of engagement can vary from one organization to the next, but may include participating in a survey, commenting on an article, rating content, posting images, taking action, and making a donation. This new model requires an organization to take a large leap of faith and to willingly relinquish control of its content. Unlike the old model, where an organization creates and controls the content, tone, and message on its Web site, the new model empowers the visitors to modify and create content, instead of simply consuming it. Although there are obvious risks associated with such a transfer of power, the potential to create a flourishing and engaged community often outweighs the risks. The new model leverages user-contributed content to allow visitors to take a certain degree of ownership over the content itself, to become active participants in the community, and to promote an organization's mission and related causes. Once users participate in the content creation process, they have a vested interest in that content and in the community, and will be more inclined to promote it to friends and encourage others to comment on their content. This higher level of engagement within the new model decreases the likelihood that users will leave the community.

The process of getting users to describe, rate, and contribute content is only half the battle; the organization must then leverage those contributions in a meaningful way that promotes further engagement. Leveraging user-contributed content opens up potential opportunities to:

- Maintain a list of "Top-Rated Items" on the Web site's home page. Environmental Defense uses this form of user-contributed content to gather feedback from recipients of its e-newsletter. Individuals are asked to rate the contents of each e-newsletter. The feedback loop created by these interactions provides Environmental Defense with additional insight into the interests of its audience, as well as the appeal of certain topics.
- Offer Really Simple Syndication (RSS) feeds of content that is either contributed by users, has received high ratings from visitors, rated most highly, or is tagged to a certain category. RSS makes it simple to provide a consolidated list of the latest information from your organization, so that supporters can track the issues and topics that they care about without having to go to your organization's Web site. For example, North Shore Animal League America maintains an updated list of stories, updates, tips, and more on its home page and distributes these through

RSS feed as well. The Humane Society of the United States also distributes an RSS feed of its press releases so that interested parties can automatically receive the organization's latest news. RSS feeds on its Web site act as an additional channel to get the right information to the right people at the right time.

- Allow users to maintain personalized spaces where they maintain lists of their contributions (blog/discussion posts, comments) and other information that they deem of interest (e.g., favorite Web pages, favorite writers, etc.).
- Segment lists and send targeted messages to members based on contribution activities (e.g., most active members who have contributed ratings).
- Develop a better understanding of the organization's content development, site structure and design, as well as ad buys, based on an analysis of user-contributed content.

User-contributed content can be taken to an entirely different level with Web sites such as MySpace and YouTube, in which the majority of content (in the form of text, images, music, videos, etc.) is contributed by visitors. MySpace, the fastest-growing social networking Web site, presents a unique opportunity for individuals to post information about themselves, share this content with others, and build a network within the MySpace community. More and more nonprofit organizations recognize the potential universe of like-minded constituents who exist within the realm of MySpace and are identifying ways to incorporate the site into their campaigning efforts.

YouTube also leverages online communities and user-contributed content, but in a different way from MySpace. YouTube, with its tagline "Broadcast Yourself," has fundamentally changed how content is delivered to people over the internet. As of the end of August 2006, the site hosts more than 6.1 million videos, with over 1.73 billion views at that time.[1] YouTube serves more than 70 million videos per day, and the growth of its unique audience continues to increase at an unprecedented rate (a 297 percent increase between January 2006 and July 2006 alone).[2]

Like Flickr, a photo-sharing site, YouTube offers people a place where they can upload, share, view, and comment on original videos. Previously, one had to invest a significant amount of money to produce a sophisticated video that would attract attention. With YouTube, this is no longer the case. People's expectations of video quality have shifted as their interest in creating and sharing video content with each other has increased. With YouTube, anyone with the means to record a video can contribute content. As a result, the ways in which one can organize online has gone in a new direction. Peer-to-peer communications of the latest advocacy issues are accelerated on a global scale through YouTube, which also serves as an effective means to educate people about important issues. This evolution presents an exciting opportunity for nonprofits to create and use video as a medium to further their organizations' mission.

Visitors of MySpace, YouTube, or other social networking Web sites are not necessarily an organization's current donors or activists, but they are people who could potentially become involved in the organization in the future. The extent of an organization's investment in sites that focus on user-contributed content is heavily dependent on its mission, resources, and risk aversion. As Mark Ruben from M+R

OXFAM: LAUNCHING THE "ROCK FOR DARFUR" CAMPAIGN WITH MYSPACE.COM

Oxfam employs Web 2.0 tools in order to reach a broader audience. These tools allow us to build a stronger sense of community among our supporters, which is critical as we work to end poverty, hunger, and injustice.
— Tim Fullerton, eAdvocacy coordinator, Oxfam America

Organization: Oxfam America is a Boston-based international development and relief agency and an affiliate of Oxfam International. Working with local partners, Oxfam delivers development programs and emergency relief services and campaigns for change in global practices and policies that keep people in poverty.

Situation: In the summer of 2006, MySpace.com contacted Oxfam to propose the launch of a joint campaign to raise awareness about the situation in Darfur, Sudan. Oxfam saw this as a great opportunity to bring Darfur's need of aid and peacekeeping efforts to the forefront of the minds of Americans.

Solution: MySpace, in partnership with MySpace bands across the United States, and Oxfam, launched "Rock for Darfur" in October 2006. The campaign raised awareness and funds for the humanitarian crisis in Sudan. Part of the campaign included a 20-concert event, a public service announcement featuring Samuel L. Jackson, and interactive components found on the "Rock for Darfur" MySpace profile at www.myspace.com/RockForDarfur.

The campaign included a downloadable "Host Your Own Darfur Dialogue" toolkit that included a collection of videos, articles, and ideas of easy ways for individuals and their friends to get involved and end the crisis. People were encouraged to meet up at any convenient location—their home, school, work, church, or synagogue—to learn more about the crisis and then take action by sending elected officials a message that encouraged them to support aid and peacekeeping efforts in Darfur.

Results: The campaign was featured in more than 200 media outlets and raised more than $16,000. More important, the campaign raised awareness about the situation in Darfur. As a result of the campaign, Oxfam America doubled the average monthly number of new sign-ups in October and added 200 new donors to its list, with donations larger than the organization's average. Oxfam America also created its own MySpace page and added more than 15,000 friends to its page with little effort or promotion.

Strategic Services noted in a recent article about using MySpace for advocacy, "Prepare to lose control. If you or your lawyers are not comfortable with the fact that you're going to lose some control over content, MySpace isn't right for you."[3] Moreover, unlike e-mail action alerts where the success of a campaign can

NARAL PRO-CHOICE AMERICA: "THE AMBER AND JEN PROJECT"

We have used online advocacy in some form for more than five years and recently reached a point where we need to get more creative to extend our reach and target a younger group of supporters. Using innovative tools, like YouTube, allows us to communicate with a different audience in a way that resonates with them. It's all about adapting your online tools to meet your targets' interests.
    —Kristin Koch, deputy director of communications for online
                                        strategies, NARAL Pro-Choice America

Organization: For more than 30 years, NARAL Pro-Choice America has been the nation's leading advocate for privacy and a woman's right to choose. The organization's work: electing pro-choice federal candidates, lobbying Congress, conducting research and analysis of state bills and laws, organizing, and supporting a network of affiliates in 25 states.

Situation: With many years of experience using traditional online advocacy tools to engage supporters, NARAL Pro-Choice America decided that it was time to take an innovative approach to reach out to the next generation of supporters.

Solution: In its first attempt to use YouTube as a means to further its advocacy efforts, two of NARAL Pro-Choice America's employees, Amber Wobschall and Jen Moseley, created a two-part series of homemade videos that detailed how to become a pro-choice activist and elect pro-choice lawmakers to Congress.

Results: Within two months of posting the videos, they had been viewed 7,500 times and received positive comments from a number of viewers. One of the videos shows a step-by-step process for viewers to follow in order to get involved and have an impact on the 2006 congressional elections. Activists are encouraged to print flyers and post them in various locations within their community.

be measured within a reasonably short time frame after the campaign is launched, social networking Web sites build momentum over time and thus require patience.

The introduction of Web 2.0 and social networking has put additional, rich-media tools in the hands of people at the local level. Empowered by the ability to have an impact in their local community quickly and effectively, more and more people are beginning to leverage these tools to implement change. Local advocacy is a growing channel that allows organizations to expand their effectiveness of grassroots organizing to affect policy issues. It is much easier to influence the political situation by mobilizing resources within your immediate community than it is to directly change the mind of the highest level of elected officials within the U.S. government, namely the president. The 2006 election cycle provided a perfect example of this shift to advocacy at the local level with organizations such as MoveOn.org and Equality Ohio encouraging citizens to come together and drive change in their communities with a big-picture goal of changing the state of the national government.

UNFORESEEN HURDLES AND CHALLENGES IN ONLINE ADVOCACY

Whereas the Internet has revolutionized the way in which organizations communicate with constituents and, in turn, how citizens communicate with members of Congress, this paradigm shift has not been without obstacles. The most prominent challenges to date have centered on deliverability of e-mails to constituents and the online delivery of constituent messages to Congress.

Nonprofit organizations of all sizes are facing considerable challenges as they reach out to their supporters using e-mail. The advantages of this communication method—instant, low-cost access to an organization's audience, with personalization and tracking capabilities unavailable via direct mail or telemarketing—remain compelling, but are being undermined by spam concerns. According to the messaging management firm Postini, more than 73 percent of all e-mail is spam. Therefore, it is increasingly important for all nonprofit organizations to adhere strictly to permission-based messaging, pay attention to all spam complaints, and partner with an e-mail provider that understands the landscape. The combination of these factors will maximize an organization's ability to deliver messages to their supporters' in boxes.

Constituents are not the only ones who complain about the tidal wave of digital communications. These communications overwhelmed Congress to the point where, beginning in the summer of 2006, many members of Congress would accept digital communications only if they are submitted through Web forms (custom Web pages that collect citizens' contact information and comment and then submit it to an office's correspondence management system). Although the switch from e-mail to Web forms provides a variety of benefits to politicians, it creates significant communication barriers between citizens and elected officials. Elected officials can choose to restrict these inbound communications only to constituents who live within a legislator's district.

CONVERTING ACTIVISTS TO DONORS

The true power of the Internet is evidenced when a wide range of organizational staff (i.e., communications, advocacy, membership, and development staff) can work collaboratively to schedule, create, send, and measure all of their constituency messaging. This cooperative approach can help organizations tap into potential new sources of revenue and other means of support. Online advocacy tools allow organizations to easily identify individuals who are most likely to become donors and communicate with them through targeted fundraising appeals. Individuals who take part in advocacy campaigning (both online and offline) are more likely to be long-term supporters of an organization and its mission.

MOVEON.ORG: "TAKING BACK THE HOUSE"

All that hard work paid off. Here we are, with an important victory. It's not the end of this story. It's more of a beginning. But in 2005 and 2006, we laid the foundation on which we can finally begin to build a more progressive America.
 —Eli Pariser, executive director, MoveOn.org

Organization: The MoveOn family of organizations brings real Americans back into the political process. With over 3.3 million members across America—from carpenters to stay-at-home moms to business leaders—they work together to realize the progressive vision of our country's founders. MoveOn is a service—a way for busy but concerned citizens to find their political voice in a system dominated by big money and big media.

Situation: In the days after the 2004 election, taking back the House in 2006 seemed like a stretch. However, for MoveOn's members—many of whom were new to political action in 2004—it seemed like the only hope to put our nation back on its path. And so, trusting in the wisdom of crowds, MoveOn set its sight on the House for 2006.

Solution: MoveOn built a national, volunteer-powered grassroots campaign to win back the House. With thousands of teams around the country, the organization ran a massive, neighbor-to-neighbor drive to mobilize opposition to the Republican leadership's conservative policies and promote progressive candidates. MoveOn reached millions of people at their homes and many more through the media.

In key swing districts where conservative incumbents were vulnerable, MoveOn publicly held them accountable for each and every vote they cast against the public interest. Instead of launching a field campaign three months before the election, in January 2005, MoveOn started to recruit leaders, persuade voters, and build a grassroots base for victory. In addition, MoveOn's efforts to mobilize voters had an even larger impact in a lower-turnout congressional election than they did in the presidential election.

Results: In the end, MoveOn exceeded all of its targets:

- 7,492 house parties were attended by 46,790 volunteers.
- 51,719 supporters made calls from home.
- 7,001,102 total calls were made across 61 targeted districts.
- 250,000 members contributed $3.6 million to individual House candidates and over $2.8 million to fund MoveOn's TV ads in targeted districts.
- More people volunteered in 2006 than in 2004.
- MoveOn's membership grew by 450,000.

Source: http://pol.moveon.org/2006report/

EQUALITY OHIO: "TURNOUT OHIO" CAMPAIGN

Over the past five years, the country has witnessed a dramatic shift of power from the federal government to state legislatures. As a state chapter of the Equality Federation, Equality Ohio organizes at the state and local levels to advance a proactive legislative agenda in communities throughout the entire state.
                    —Andrea Wood, manager of New Media and Engagement,
                                                           Equality Ohio

Organization: Equality Ohio, an affiliate of Equality Federation, serves as an advocate and champion for fair treatment and equal opportunity for lesbian, gay, bisexual, and transgender citizens. The organization facilitates a greater understanding of our common humanity through education and outreach efforts. It engages and empowers individuals, families, organizations, businesses, and institutions in Ohio's urban, suburban, and rural areas and collaborates with local, regional, statewide, and national organizations, and government agencies.

Situation: In 2006 Equality Ohio launched "TurnOUT Ohio," a five-month campaign focused on two strategic objectives: increase political power of lesbian, gay, bisexual, and transgender Ohioans in the 2006 election cycle and build a foundation for continued momentum through the 2008 elections and beyond.

Solution: Online, Equality Ohio created a TurnOUT Ohio "hub" Web site and regularly sent out campaign updates to members. It also recruited volunteers using MySpace, and launched several online advocacy and fundraising campaigns targeted at local communities. Offline, the organization's staff coordinated direct-mail fundraising letters to members; managed a 40-line, computer-assisted phone bank; sent flyers; reached out in person to community groups; tabling events; and went door-to-door canvassing in targeted precincts throughout the state.

Results: During the three months that followed the launch of the campaign, Equality Ohio recruited 58 new volunteers, knocked on 516 doors in Ohio neighborhoods, and raised nearly $10,000 through coordinated direct mail and online fundraising campaigns.

In an attempt to convert activists into donors, many organizations are turning to peer-to-peer events to engage their list members and supporters. The Humane Society of the United States, for example, hosted "Walk for the Animals" in the fall of 2006. The local event registered more than 900 participants and raised over $65,000. Covenant House California (CHC), an organization that serves homeless and at-risk youth ages 13 to 24 in the Bay Area, also found success in such events. In September 2006 it launched a Yoga-thon, its first peer-to-peer

EARTHJUSTICE: TURNING ACTIVISTS INTO DONORS

We have generally been reluctant to ask activists to also support us financially, thinking that maybe we'd turn them off. But that's not the case. Folks who care about our issues want us to succeed, and they welcome the chance to write us a check. Our relationship with our online supporters is more complicated than we thought.
  —Allison Kozak, director of online strategy, Earthjustice

Organization: Earthjustice is the nation's largest environmental law firm using the courts to protect people's health, air and water quality, wild places, and wildlife. Founded as the Sierra Club Legal Defense Fund in 1971, the organization enforces and strengthens environmental laws on behalf of hundreds of organizations and communities free of charge.

Situation: In 2005 the Bush administration repealed the popular Roadless Area Conservation Rule, put in place to protect the last unspoiled national forest land from commercial logging, road construction, and other damaging activities. Earthjustice immediately went to court, but also needed the public to speak out, letting the administration know Americans supported the rule and that it was wrong to repeal the rule without regard for public commentary.

At the same time, Earthjustice was curious to know more about the people who took action on the organization's behalf. Could these advocates be convinced to provide financial support as well?

Solution: The repeal of the Roadless Rule was an important message communicated throughout 2005 and 2006 in multiple integrated campaigns. Two online campaigns were developed, one at the end of 2005 and another a year later. The 2005 campaign emphasized advocacy, asking supporters to sign a petition and pass it along to friends. The campaign included five messages, concluding with a soft request for donations. The emphasis in the 2006 campaign, however, was on fundraising. Though supporters were asked to send a letter to the Bush administration, this four-message campaign included several specific requests for donations. In addition to targeting the existing list of online supporters, in both cases Earthjustice acquired e-mail addresses from a major online environmental portal to include in the campaign.

Results: As expected, the 2005 campaign, which emphasized advocacy, generated more actions, while the 2006 fundraising campaign raised over $5,000, about six times the 2005 results. More interesting was the performance of the names acquired through the environmental portal. Earthjustice expected the names to perform well on advocacy but not well on donations. In fact, the acquired names performed about the same as the existing supporters in each campaign. Those targeted in 2006 for fundraising also donated much more than those from 2005, indicating that asking for donations yields more donations, even from those typically considered "only activists."

fundraising event. Over $15,000 was raised by 60 individuals who solicited dona-
tions from within their personal networks. In addition to the impressive amount
raised, CHC's list grew by 100 people. CHC drove participation through an e-mail
campaign to an initial list of 1,000 constituents. Esti Iturralde, CHC development
coordinator, explains, "We planned the e-mail campaign to engage constituents
through personal stories about the kids Covenant House has 'saved from the
streets.'" The personal element of the stories attracted the interest of a surprising
number of list members, many of whom had never made donations before.

INTEGRATING ONLINE ADVOCACY INTO COMMUNICATIONS PLANS

Far too many constituents have had this experience: They attend a dinner or other
event in support of their favorite nonprofit organization. While there, they make a
generous donation. Days or weeks later they then receive a "generic" e-mail—with
no reference to their recent gift—asking them to take action and to support the
organization financially. Instead of feeling good about a recent donation, constituents
are now left wondering if their favorite organization knows them at all.

This occurs because an organization's data and communications are in discrete
silos. Online advocacy campaigns should be closely coordinated with all other communication programs (i.e., direct mail, advertising, phone campaigns, canvassing,
and lobbying). In the process of coordinating its advocacy efforts, an organization
must keep in mind that activists view the organization as a single entity, even if
internally it functions as individual departments with separate initiatives and goals
that may reach well beyond advocacy into fundraising, education, and awareness.
Nonprofit organizations need to be aware of activists' perceptions in order to successfully cultivate relationships with each individual. To this end, attempts must be
made to ensure interdepartmental coordination of outbound communications. This
coordinated approach to reaching out to constituents will not only lead to improved
productivity within an organization, but will also help maintain the organization's
brand identity that represents the group's mission, values, initiatives, and activities in
a way that appeals to the target audience. A unified effort that represents the interests
and goals of different departments will allow an organization to leverage its brand
identity, which can then serve as a differentiator and help keep the organization top
of mind.

National organizations with affiliates and single organizations with multiple
departments find it difficult to create a single brand that is consistent across all
communication channels. For national organizations, it is difficult to give affiliates
autonomy while maintaining a single brand, particularly as these organizations
expand their presence online. Within an organization, each department often uses a
unique voice as well as a separate look and feel for its outbound communications,
which leads to a fragmented public image made up of several silos. This challenge
grows exponentially when organizations allow enthusiastic constituents to advocate
on their behalf.

Internet-based solutions help organizations of all sizes achieve brand consistency across all of their communications. Unified online constituent relationship
management (eCRM) platforms can integrate online advocacy efforts with the

organization's Web site, database, and other online communications.[4] These tools allow organizations more control over their image and the ability to facilitate consistent branding in all constituent-facing communications. By integrating online outreach and Web site content in such a way that encourages supporters to take action, organizations can create an activist-friendly environment that maximizes participation and increases the likelihood of ongoing involvement.

Because online advocacy is an activity that is very much in the public's eye, it is important to consider marketing and branding issues when designing and conducting campaigns The easiest and most effective way to leverage online advocacy to strengthen your mission and reinforce your brand is to coordinate outreach to your activist and donor base through cross-departmental communication, including e-newsletters and fundraising appeals that promote advocacy campaigns. It is critical to maintain consistency across all branding elements that make up the organization's identity (e.g., logos and images) in order to effectively build and leverage your brand to further your organization's mission.

EVER-GROWING ONLINE TOOLKIT

The once somewhat basic online toolkit available to organizations has expanded significantly over recent years. User-contributed content and new online functionality that delivers customized content in online communications now enables organizations to leverage the interests, previous actions, and demographic of their constituents in new and exciting ways.

In order to maximize results of online efforts, an organization should strategically integrate its Web site with all of its other advocacy initiatives. Long gone are the days when a Web site was merely "brochureware." Now, in order to attract and maintain the interest of a visitor, a Web site must be a lively tool that reflects the organization's latest initiatives—from advocacy and fundraising to education and awareness. When visitors land on your Web site, they should be served content that is relevant to their interests, past interactions, and potential opportunities for involvement. No longer should an organization design its Web site for the potential universe of visitors; it must be addressed to an individual. There is an increased need to invest in the personalization of content within a Web site in the form of donation and action requests, subscription opportunities, and recruitment options. Visitors should seamlessly move throughout an organization's Web site and view context-rich Web pages that are designed to keep them involved and engaged.

For many organizations, improving their online communications means leveraging multiple applications to achieve a constituent engagement goal. The increasing desire for "openness" within the world of online tools has dramatically increased the number of application programming interfaces (APIs) available to organizations. Nonprofits can use many applications available on the Web easily, but the resulting data from these specialized applications must become part of a constituent's existing online history in order for the information to be used effectively for future targeted outreach efforts. At their most basic level, APIs allow organizations to compile data from multiple sources to meet their engagement goals. Using APIs, organizations can consolidate external activities and constituent information from a combination of Web-based eCRM software and specialized third-party applications. Nonprofits

UNIVERSITY OF CALIFORNIA: MOBILIZING CONSTITUENTS ACROSS MULTIPLE CAMPUSES WITH A CONSISTENT MESSAGE

For our alumni, there is a huge appetite to be informed and engaged. Almost immediately after we launched our online advocacy program, we had 4,000 advocates. After so much talking and consensus-building, here was something that was actually created and quickly brought results.

—Trey Davis, director of special projects, University of California

Organization: Founded in 1869, the University of California system includes more than 209,000 students and 170,000 faculty and staff, with more than 1.4 million alumni living and working around the world.

Situation: All ten UC campuses—Berkeley, Davis, Irvine, Los Angeles, Merced, Riverside, San Diego, San Francisco, Santa Barbara, and Santa Cruz—and the systemwide Office of the President needed to share content in an efficient and timely manner that would easily allow them to reach out to their target audience in a coordinated yet independent way.

Solution: The entire UC system now uses the same online tools that allow them to share the content, and even the graphical branding, of e-mail messages and advocacy campaigns with one another. With their online advocacy tool, one location can create an e-mail message or advocacy campaign, and all of the other campuses are able to use the content as is or customize it to fit their specific campus and regional goals. Each campus has control over its own list.

Results: Since the first campus implemented GetActive tools in November 2003 under the umbrella "UC for California" campaign (www.ucforcalifornia .org), UC has sent hundreds of thousands of e-mails to students, parents, faculty, alumni, and community supporters of each school. Through its online advocacy campaigns, UC can quickly identify its most effective campaigns across all campuses, and administrators can easily share campaign successes and constituent activities across the institution. UC has transformed the way in which it communicates with its constituents. In doing so, it has dramatically increased the effectiveness of its advocacy efforts and protected its budget and advanced its legislative agenda.

can leverage a wider range of engagement options while continuing to benefit from the integration features of the online tools that they have in place. Integration APIs and Web services provide additional methods for storing and retrieving data from a central online database. Tools for building "mash-ups" (i.e., a Web application that combines data from more than one source into an integrated experience) of

POLLY KLAAS® FOUNDATION: GENERATING ENGAGEMENT OPPORTUNITIES FOR ACTIVISTS

The ability to coordinate online and offline campaigns in real-time is critical for the safe return of a kidnapped child, and is essential to the overall execution of our organization's mission.
—Glena Records, director of communications & education,
Polly Klaas Foundation

Organization: The Polly Klaas Foundation (PKF) is a national nonprofit that helps missing children, prevents children from going missing, and works with policymakers to pass laws that help protect them.

Situation: Due to its static Web site, PKF had limited online outreach in 2002 and felt that it was missing significant opportunities to recruit and engage supporters.

Solution: PKF expanded its online efforts to include advocacy and fundraising. Several years later it integrated its Web site with its other online initiatives. In doing so, the organization has quickly grown its community of supporters and extended its universe of online donors, activists, volunteers, and concerned parents.

Results: Interested parties can now engage with the organization in a number of different ways:

- Learn how to educate children about abduction prevention and Internet safety
- Participate in safety fairs conducted in conjunction with law enforcement and local citizens
- Tell a friend about PKF's downloadable child safety information kit
- Send letters to elected officials online
- Donate to PKF to help fund the organization's various initiatives
- Become an eVolunteer who prints and distributes posters of missing children in the local area

The eVolunteer program alone has proven to be an effective means of administering and executing a large-scale campaign online. Within 48 hours of the launch of the volunteer recruitment campaign, more than 600 eVolunteers had responded.

third-party services, such as Flickr and Google Maps APIs, are actively shared online, for free, as companies, nonprofits, and individuals post and share code that they developed. This openness within the online community fosters a new, unprecedented degree of peer-to-peer networking.

AFSCME: LEVERAGING MASH-UP TECHNOLOGY TO LAUNCH THE "ACT NOW!" CAMPAIGN

The recent ActNow.org project for AFSCME merged Google maps with an online petition campaign to create an interactive map displaying participants' virtual yard signs. With additional APIs and the opportunity to pass activities from other applications directly into AFSCME's online database, we can be even more innovative and effective in taking our clients' campaigns into new spaces and catching the attention of constituents.

—Michael Cervino, vice president and cofounder of Beaconfire Consulting

Organization: American Federation of State, County, and Municipal Employees (AFSCME) is the nation's largest and fastest-growing public service employees union.

Situation: In late 2005, Congress put forth a budget and tax cut proposal targeting a range of public programs that support low-income and working Americans. In response, AFSCME and the Emergency Campaign of America's Priorities—a coalition of organizations—turned to Beaconfire Consulting to quickly launch a campaign focused on creating an activist network to stop those proposed cuts. AFSCME and its partners needed a venue to create solidarity among opponents of the proposal and to deliver a swift and unified message to Capitol Hill.

Solution: Beaconfire worked with AFSCME and its partners to deliver a full-scale nationwide public awareness campaign—within a short two-week time frame. ActNow.org, the Web site for the Emergency Campaign for America's Priorities, which launched in October 2005, united concerned citizens from across the country through "mash-up technology"—a powerful combination of tools allowing Web site visitors to map their advocacy actions on a large Google map and send customized activist messages right to the in boxes of members of Congress. The result? The campaign was successful in changing the minds of a dozen U.S. Representatives who otherwise would have voted in support of the cuts.

How did the campaign work? Activists were encouraged to plant virtual "yard signs" containing unique campaign slogans on a giant interactive Google map. Constituents then were able not only to virtually survey their neighborhoods to learn about the concentrations of activists there, but also were able to share the Web address of their personalized maps with others.

Results: Within just a few days after launch of the campaign, the effort had generated 20,000 signs posted on Google maps.

Another innovative strategy continued to fuel the growth in number of campaign participants: an iPod contest. Beaconfire developed the contest to award an iPod to the activist responsible for getting the most signs planted as a result of sharing his or her campaign URLs with friends. This contest drummed up support to the tune of more than 10,000 additional participants—an average rate of four friends taking action and planting signs upon learning about the campaign. The heavy pass-along component continues to pull in activists—so far 30,000 Americans have planted virtual yard signs. Source: Beaconfire Consulting (http://beaconfire.com/clients/stories/marketing/afscme.php)

LOOKING FORWARD

The Internet continues to offer nonprofit organizations a myriad of opportunities for deepening their engagement with current and future constituents. The increasing role of social networking Web sites, user contributed content, peer-to-peer events, and application mash-ups are fundamentally shifting the landscape in which non-profits interact with their constituents. New companies focused on Web 2.0 surface each day, all striving to build community and encourage social networking. For example, MapBuzz (www.mapbuzz.com) recently launched its community Web site that makes it easy for people to share information about where they live through online maps. As the proliferation of such tools continues, it becomes increasingly challenging for nonprofits to vie for the attention of their target audience; organizations must take a two-pronged approach to their online engagement efforts:

1. **Constituent-led content.** Encourage constituents to create and pass along content that resides on your organization's Web site.
2. **Live in your supporters' world.** Take your content to the place where current and future constituents already spend time.

Not only must nonprofits become more vigilant in developing attention-grabbing stories and clever campaigns to garner the attention of their supporters, but they need to engage these supporters in content creation and a two-way dialogue. In addition, nonprofits must continue to intercept current and future supporters in places where they are most likely to be found. Social networking sites provide exciting opportunities to engage with like-minded individuals. As Madeline Stanionis, chief executive officer and cofounder of The Watershed Company (a consulting company), states: "Organizations need to become a part of their constituent's world instead of making the constituents become part of theirs. Focus on a way to become relevant to the whole of people's lives, instead of just a piece of it, and remain nimble to the way that technology changes and evolves."

Online advocacy's impact will continue to expand across the globe. SMS (short message service) or Text technology are embedded into most cell phones, providing an additional media channel for one-to-one and also one-to-many communication. Eight million voters in Venezuela used SMS technology to find their polling place, casting votes for a radically new government, while Montenegro election officials used SMS to provide real-time election monitoring. The evolution of online tools will continue to gain momentum. Web 3.0 is just around the corner and will offer new ways to leverage geospatial data for virtual activism at the local and global levels. Finally, as the technology landscape continues to evolve, nonprofit activists must stay true to the mission of their organization. Genuine passion for a just cause will inspire through all media.

ABOUT THE AUTHORS

Sheeraz Haji, as president of Convio, Inc., former chief executive and cofounder of GetActive Software, is leading the integration of the two foremost eCRM software and services vendors within the nonprofit sector. In addition, he heads the company's partner program.

Under Sheeraz's leadership, GetActive become a leading provider of relationship management software for membership organizations. His management of GetActive resulted in the attainment of over 800 clients.

Sheeraz is an active member of the board of directors for Nonprofit Technology Enterprise Network (N-TEN), the ePhilanthropy Foundation, and the Association of Fundraising Professionals—Washington, DC, chapter. He is an expert presenter at multiple industry events sponsored by such organizations as Politics Online, NTEN, PBS, NPR, National Council for Nonprofit Associations, and Association of Fundraising Professionals. Before GetActive, Sheeraz led a product management team at Digital Impact, a provider of online direct marketing solutions for enterprises. He has also worked as a strategy consultant for McKinsey & Company, where he served both nonprofit and for-profit organizations. Sheeraz has a BS from Brown University and an MS from Stanford University.

Emma Zolbrod is an independent marketing consultant. She provides consulting services to companies interested in increasing their results through strategic marketing. As the former director of marketing of GetActive Software, Emma's expertise spans communications, sales tools, product marketing, strategy, public relations, and events. Prior to joining GetActive, she led CRM marketing initiatives at Corio, an enterprise application service provider, and was a senior consultant at Ventaso, a sales and marketing software company. Emma holds a BA from the University of Victoria in Canada and an MBA from INSEAD, with a focus on marketing and strategy.

NOTES

1. WSJ Online: http://online.wsj.com/public/article/SB115689298168048904-5w WyrSwyn6RfVfz9NwLk774VUWc_20070829.html?mod = rss_free.
2. www.youtube.com; Nielsen/NetRatings report released July 21, 2006.
3. www.mrss.com/news/Ten_Commandments_of_MySpace_Advocacy.pdf.
4. www.convio.com/site/PageServer?pagename = sol_ecrmApproach.

CHAPTER 4

Peer-to-Peer Fundraising and Community Building

Phil King
Artez Interactive

Nicci Noble
The Salvation Army

As of December 30, 2006, there were approximately 6,499,697,060 people on our planet. Of those, 16.8 percent, or 1,091,730,861, were on the Internet, according to information presented at www.internetworldstats.com.

The Internet is big, and growing bigger every minute.

Charities across the globe are now realizing they need more than just a Web site to keep up with this growing Internet population. In the late 1990s, the focus of most e-philanthropy conversations was the tremendous transactional efficiencies brought by the Internet. Contributions made through the medium of Web-based donation forms were superior in so many ways to other channels: They were immediate, they were secure, they could be e-receipted, and they could be made at any time of the day or night. Thank-you e-mails and update newsletters could be sent at the click of button ... no paper, no stamps.

Organizations such as the Salvation Army have seen tremendous growth in the numbers and value of all donations received online. The Salvation Army received more money via the Web during Christmas 2005 (November 1, 2005 to December 31, 2005 and December) than in the first four years it accepted Internet gifts (for November 20, 2000 to December 31, 2004):

First four years of Web-based giving	$6,013,311
2005 Christmas	$7,150,140

Sounds great, doesn't it? But before you get too comfortable that all you need to do is set up an online donation button, consider this. The Internet is not only growing rapidly, it is changing dramatically. In December 2006 *Time* magazine announced that the Person of the Year was "You" (see Exhibit 4.1). It is "you" when you write a blog, load a video on YouTube, add your photos to Flickr, update

EXHIBIT 4.1 *TIME* Person of the Year
Source: Photo illustration for *TIME* by Arthur Hochstein, with photographs by Spencer Jones-Glasshouse.

an entry on Wikipedia, or share personal information on MySpace. It seemed that overnight the power had shifted from *them* to *you*.

To be successful in this new Internet, in this Web 2.0 world, leaders need to embrace the individual "you" and all of the powerful tools an individual has at his or her fingertips. This chapter explores how some leading charitable organizations are dealing with individual Internet users, how they are creating online communities catering to them, and how organizations continue to leverage this most dynamic medium on the globe.

CREATING COMMUNITIES OF FUNDRAISERS, NOT DONORS

If you ask fundraisers how they spend their time, you're likely to get a pretty standard response: "I search for donors" quickly followed by " . . . of course!" In fact, during the early days of our experimentation at both Artez Interactive and the Salvation Army (the respective organizations of the authors), our focus was very much on finding donors and getting that online gift. Much energy was spent optimizing donation buttons and donation pages, adding lots of flexibility to encourage donors to make one-time, monthly, quarterly gifts, with or without electronic tax receipts and with or without e-cards . . . you get the picture.

We are not suggesting this was resource and energy misapplied. We were focused on the unbelievable transactional efficiencies of the Web. The time and cost to send thousands of e-mails, which asked people to click back to a secure online donation form where they could make a donation using their credit card, was astoundingly better than a comparable paper-based campaign using the postal system.

What we had not focused on, however, was the more potent characteristic of the Web as a two-way communication medium and community of interwoven communities—hence, the name "world wide web." It was primarily in the arena of pledge-based special events where we started getting a glimpse of what would thrill us in 2007.

Years ago, pledge-based, special event organizers had realized that it was far more fruitful to search for fundraisers than to search for donors. A good pledge event would recruit an army of volunteer fundraisers, all armed with their trusty pledge forms, and unleash them into their own social networks. The simple math of these types of campaigns really tells the story of how money is raised in a pledge event:

# of participants × % who fundraise × # of people they ask × # who give ×

average gift/sponsor = $ raised

The Internet does not fundamentally alter this equation; it simply provides amphetamines to it. Now we can sit on our couch, watch the evening news, and ask 100 people by e-mail to support our fundraising efforts. Those people can be down the street or across the globe. We can receive instant feedback about who has given, and event organizers working at the charity can identify us at any point in time as a "good" fundraiser or a fundraiser "in need of support" and communicate with us appropriately.

One of the many challenges that arise from this new world of Internet peer-based fundraising is recognition. In a simpler model, where we simply search for donors, it is relatively easy to create recognition circles, programs, and honors based on the amount each person gives. But what about the amount each person raises? Using our couch-potato example, let's imagine that from the 100 e-mails we sent, we get a 75 percent response rate, and our average gift is $50. That means that, in addition to catching up on the nightly news, we raised $3,750! Let's also assume that we pull out our own credit card and make a $50 gift to bring our total to a nice round $3,800.

How will that charity steward us? If it pulls our record from its database, it will show, quite accurately, that we are a $50 donor. However, more and more charities in search of fundraisers (not just donors) will treat us with the gratitude due to a $3,800 fundraiser.

What if you do not have any pledge-based, special events? As we mentioned earlier, our first glimpse of the Internet's ability to find fundraisers (not just donors) happened in the area of pledge events. Fast forward to 2007 and witness an explosion of peer fundraising online that is unrelated to special events, many examples of which we will provide in this chapter.

GETTING YOUR SUPPORTERS TO *DO MORE THAN GIVE*

Hurricane Katrina was among the strongest hurricanes ever to strike the United States, according to scientists at the National Oceanic & Atmospheric Administration (NOAA) in Asheville, North Carolina.

The American public's exposure and response to the hurricanes and floods of 2005 was as unprecedented as devastation caused along the Gulf Coast. More money was given online in response to Hurricanes Katrina and Rita than any other natural disaster in history. The American Red Cross was reported to have received more than $450 million online for the 2005 Gulf Coast natural disasters.

The Salvation Army was challenged with a relief and recovery effort unparalleled to any other in its history, despite its experience providing for the aftermath of many of the country and world's significant disasters of the last century.

The public overwhelmingly supported disaster work by giving five times more money through the Web in the 18 days after Katrina hit land than in the Salvation Army's first four years of receiving online gifts combined.

People across the country wanted to get out and help Gulf Coast residents and the victims of the flooding in New Orleans. America's disaster relief organizations, mass care agencies, and nonprofits could not register, train, and deploy walk-up or casual volunteers at the rate they were available. The Salvation Army was no different from the other disaster relief agencies in this respect (see Exhibit 4.2). People wanted to be engaged in the relief effort no matter where they were at that moment.

We wanted to empower these would-be volunteers by providing a vehicle to do more than give of themselves, by raising much-needed funds for the relief effort by their ability to reach their family, friends, colleagues, and customers.

The "Do More Than Give" campaign provided an opportunity for the public to get involved from the comfort of their keyboard. E-mailing their social and professional contacts to either make a gift and/or join them as volunteer fundraiser creating personalized online giving page of their own in support of the ongoing relief effort along the ravaged Gulf Coast.

The Salvation Army learned from previous Web-based campaign testing that many of its online donors were comfortable with peer-to-peer fundraising although, until that time, it had not tested any broadcast e-mail strategies announcing a peer-to-peer online giving campaign.

Approximately 11,000 of the Salvation Army's Western Territory donors, who had indicated they wanted to receive more information were sent a message announcing the Do More Than Give campaign.[1] These recipients were asked make a donation or become a volunteer fundraiser by hosting a personalized Web page with 100 percent the funds going towards the Gulf Coast disaster relief effort.

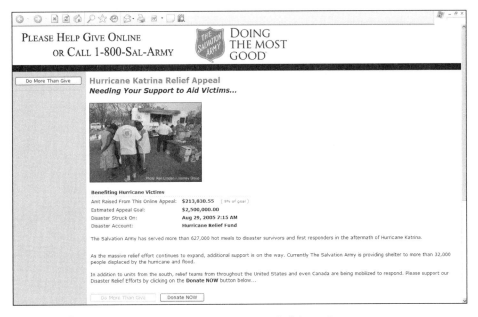

EXHIBIT 4.2   Salvation Army Hurricane Katrina Relief Appeal

- 10,951 e-mails sent to Western Territory donors
- 375 gifts in 72 hours, totaling $73,191
- 1,476 gifts in two weeks, totaling $217,968

This campaign had no marketing or media budget and took less than two days to configure, design, and deploy (see Exhibit 4.3). These figures illustrate the power of a peer-level ask.

2005 "Do More Than Give" Campaign	
No. of online donors opting in	171,015
Acquisition ratio	39%
No. of gifts to "Do More Than Give"	1,476
"Do More Than Give" national $ amount	$217,968
Average gift amount	$194

This experiment in peer-to-peer fundraising worked quite well. We must explain, however, that not every attempt has gone well. As we receive more internal and external pressures there is a need to provide more sophisticated and flexible tools. Being open to new ideas and new tools will help expand fundraising opportunities on the Web. The charge to keep learning from experimenting with and testing new electronic initiatives is important. Like our staff, our donors are becoming

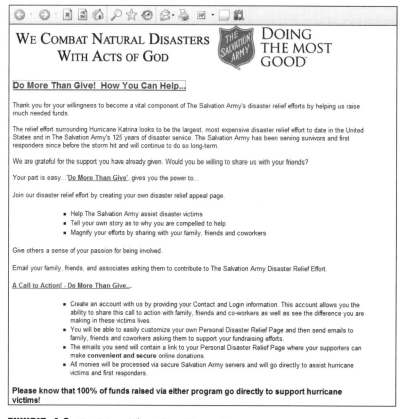

EXHIBIT 4.3 Do More Than Give Campaign

increasingly Web savvy. Having a benchmark or foundation to build on is a critical to sustainable progress.

LEAVE YOUR OFFICE TO FIND YOUR SUPPORTERS (AKA "YOU WON'T BE THEIR HOME PAGE")

We noticed something fascinating in 2006. Participants in charitable events and fundraising campaigns started turning their noses up at the technology being offered by their chosen charity. We had seen this type of behavior before, but certainly not to the extent it occurred that year—the same year *Time* selected "You" as Person of the Year.

It was not that the tools being offered by the charities were getting weaker. It was because the tools being offered on the Web in general were getting that much stronger! Sites such as Blogger, Flickr, MySpace, Second Life, and YouTube were exploding with new users and new features, and those users happened to be the very same people who were walking, running, and biking for their favorite charity.

We took a screen shot (see Exhibit 4.4) of a prime example of this type of behavior. Jodi Rice is the type of supporter any charity would cherish. In this

EXHIBIT 4.4   Example of Personalized Web Site Appeal

case, she was taking part in the eighth annual Friends for Life Bike Rally, which would have her cycle from Toronto to Montreal from July 23 to 28, 2006—that's approximately 100 kilometers per day. What intrigues us about this example is not that she raised over $3,000 from 58 sponsors but rather how she used technology to support her fundraising efforts.

Had she been an "average" online fundraiser, she would have set up her personal fundraising page inside the technology provided to her by the Toronto People with AIDS Foundation. That technology allows her to add a photo and some personal text, set a fundraising target, and then e-mail her friends and family for support. But Jodi was not average. She had established a personal space on the popular Blogger Web site in January 2005. This technology allowed her to load as many photos as she wished, link to her online videos, and maintain interactive maps of her progress as she cycled from Toronto to Montreal.

Blogger was her online community of choice. She had already established relationships with other Blogger users; she had already cross-linked to their sites and their blogs. So, what Jodi decided to do could technically be called a "mash-up." She created an account using the charity's technology so all funds would flow to the proper bank account and electronic e-receipts would be generated in accordance with the charity's standards. But she directed her peers to her Blogger site, where she had lifted elements of the charity's technology—the fundraising thermometer, for example—and added them.

Some of you reading this example will inhale through your teeth as you image your head of marketing asking "But how are we going to control our brand?" We believe this genie is already out of the bottle, this cow is already out of the barn, and this cat is already out of the bag; the more appropriate question should be: "How are we going to share our brand with her brand?" Yes, Jodi Rice has a brand. It's all about her (at least, it's all about "her" to the friends and family who are donating on her page).

Some in the fundraising technology community were also threatened by this behavior: "I can't believe she's *stealing* our tools and using them on her page." In the face of an unstoppable tide we, the creators of fundraising technology, have admitted we cannot possibly compete with the likes of YouTube and Flickr. So let's join them! Let's fashion our technology in a manner that encourages borrowing and mashing up and widgets and whatever else Jodi Rice wishes to do in the future. The tools many of you will use in 2007 and 2008 will integrate video from YouTube, photos from Flickr, and blogs from Blogger.

Which brings us back to the title of this section: "Leave Your Office to Find Your Supporters." Imagine the Web as a physical community. Your charity's Web site is your office; their Blogger space is their home. If you wanted to create an offline community, would you wait for supporters to visit you in your office, or would you pound the pavement in search of them? I think we all know the answer to this question. Rather than dreaming that one day your supporters will bookmark your Web site and make it their home page, wouldn't it be more practical to understand what home page they currently have and what your role in that page could be?

PEOPLE GIVE TO PEOPLE

It almost goes without saying, but it is so critical to grasp that we'll risk telling you something you already know: People give to people, even online!

We think most of us have experienced this in our "real" offline world. A paid canvasser rings your doorbell and asks for a gift to a very legitimate charity. The answer, however, is "Not right now, we're just in the middle of dinner." On a different evening, the doorbell rings again, but this time it is the elderly neighbor who lives a few doors down—who has negotiated her walker up our front porch steps—asking on behalf of the *same* very legitimate charity. "Of course, let me just find my wallet."

We believe this human behavior holds just as true on the Internet. To test this hypothesis, one of our authors, Philip King, conducted a controlled experiment during the summer of 2006. He had just started working with a terrific charitable organization based in London named Comic Relief. Comic Relief was founded in 1985 by comedy scriptwriter Richard Curtis in response to famine in Ethiopia, and now raises money for Africa and for disadvantaged people in the United Kingdom.

Comic Relief organized a pledge-based special event named "Sport Relief Mile," which would in the end involve more than 423,000 people across the U.K. and make it one of the biggest mass participation events in the country's history (see Exhibit 4.5). On the topic of fundraising, a concern some of the organizers expressed to Philip could be summed up neatly: "But we're only running a mile. How willing will people be to give for just a mile?" For context to the reader: Much charitable

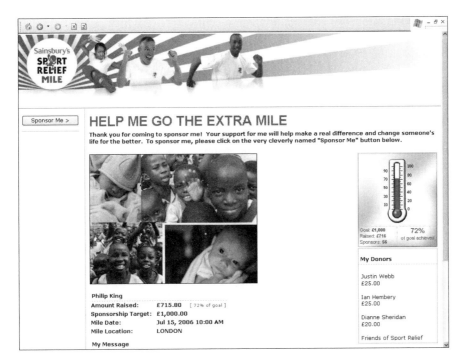

EXHIBIT 4.5   Go the Extra Mile Campaign

fundraising does exist in the United Kingdom, but typically involves running a marathon or similar strenuous physical challenge.

In order to prove his hypothesis that people give primarily to people (not due to the cause or length of the run, in this case), Philip created a Canadian fundraising team and vowed to raise funds from friends and family outside of the United Kingdom—most of whom are not at all familiar with Comic Relief. To make matters worse, the donation would occur in British pounds (the site was sending all donations through the U.K. site), and no personal tax benefit would accrue to the donors.

Sounds like an uphill battle, right? Wrong. The "Canadian, Eh?" team composed of four Canadians and one American raised over $4,000 (£2,000) from 124 donors. Philip later followed up with many of the generous people who donated through his online giving page and asked them why they gave. Generally the response was "Philip, if you're supporting it, that's all I need to know."

Of course, we're not suggesting that the cause is unimportant or that the specific type of activity the fundraiser chooses to perform is unimportant; what we are suggesting is that these are not the *primary* drivers of getting the peer-to-peer online gift.

POWER OF INCENTIVES IN BUILDING COMMUNITIES

People will become online fundraisers and attract other online fundraisers to create communities of online fundraisers because they have an *incentive* do so. It may sound too easy to believe, but all you have to do, per se, to create a successful online fundraising community is understand which incentives drive which people and then invite them to participate.

Imagine you run a charity and want to create a community of online fundraisers for your cause. Imagine your cause is a worthy one—Alzheimer's disease, stroke and depression research—but it certainly does not have the broad appeal of, say, breast cancer research and prevention. To add to the challenge, select your target demographic as men ages 30 to 55 years old.

This was precisely the challenge the Baycrest Foundation took on in the spring of 2006. Their answer: the Baycrest International Pro-Am Hockey Tournament. The idea was brilliantly simple: Encourage men in Canada to create hockey teams that would compete in a tournament held March 23 to 25. If you have not been to Canada lately, we will give you a cultural insight: Canadian men love to compete while playing ice hockey.

So what could be better than getting together with your fellow Canucks to play a little competitive hockey? How about the ability to draft a real National Hockey League pro to your team? The charity set forth very clear rules: Each hockey team would be allowed to fundraise through the Internet. At 5 PM on the evening before the tournament was to begin, the team that had raised the most donations would be allowed to pick first from the roster of 20 hockey stars, the team that had raised the second most would pick next, and so on.

As you can see from screen shot of that event in Exhibit 4.6, the top individual fundraiser raised over $84,000; the top team raised over $105,000.

EXHIBIT 4.6 Individual Fundraiser Tally

What this charity understood was the power of incentives. In this example, the incentive was not a T-shirt or a set of golf balls or a free flight; it was the opportunity to play hockey along side a hero, which, as the saying goes, is priceless. By the end of this campaign, this group of 30- to 55-year-old men raising money online for Alzheimer's research collected more than $800,000. They also had a terrific time playing hockey with their heroes.

POWER OF CELEBRITY IN BUILDING COMMUNITIES

How do you create an online community overnight? It sure helps if you have access to celebrity.

Allow us to return to the fundraising event in the United Kingdom in support of Comic Relief. By July 4, 2006, our author, Philip, had raised several hundred pounds and was feeling rather good about the progress he was making through his personal online giving page. On that same day, a well-known British comedian, David Walliams, suggested he would do more than just run a mile for Comic Relief; he would swim the English Channel.

Less than ten and a half hours later, Walliams emerged exhausted in northern France—and had attracted almost $2 million through his personal giving page.

Around the same time but on the other side of the Atlantic, Rick Reilly was writing a column in *Sports Illustrated* about malaria, challenging each of his

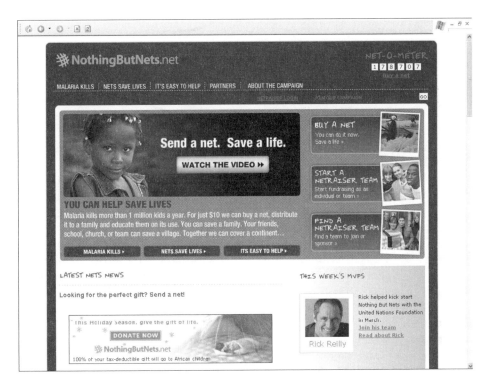

EXHIBIT 4.7　Nothing But Nets Campaign

readers to donate $10 for the purchase of an antimalarial bed net (see Exhibit 4.7). Due to the incredible response from thousands of Americans, the United Nations Foundation created the "Nothing But Nets" campaign. On its campaign site at www.nothingbutnets.net, visitors are encouraged to purchase a net for $10, start a Netraiser team, or join an existing Netraiser team. To help donors answer the question "Where does my $10 go?" there are links on the site to YouTube videos documenting a recent trip Reilly took to Nigeria, where he traveled to see how the first 150,000 bed nets were being used. At the time of publishing this book, the Net-o-Meter registered at over 398,000 nets, and the Bill and Melinda Gates Foundation had agreed to match dollar for dollar any funds raised through the site.

ALLOW COMMUNITIES TO EMERGE

Do you know who your most enthusiastic supporters are? Many organizations are becoming more sophisticated in their application of donor relationship management techniques. However, most of these techniques focus on individual behaviors, such as how many times a Mr. Foley has donated over a certain period of time, or how large his gifts have been.

In contrast, the Internet is exploding with technologies that focus on *collective* rather than individual action. YouTube is a modern version of a television network broadcaster, but is based on the collective digital video contributions of millions of subscribers. The individual video is not what makes YouTube exciting; the collection of videos provides the juice. And this collective- or community-based approach can be leveraged by charitable organizations to identify their most enthusiastic supporters.

Adrian Bradbury and Kieran Hayward first heard the stories of the night commuters of northern Uganda in the spring of 2005. They were so struck by the plight of the children there that they vowed to create what they later called a "GuluWalk." Every evening in July 2005, they walked 12.5 kilometers downtown to sleep in front of city hall. At sunrise, after about four hours of sleep, they make the trek home. Both men continued to work full time and attempted to maintain their usual daily routine, to mimic the lifestyle endured by the Acholi children of northern Uganda.

Based on unprecedented media coverage and interest, Bradbury and Hayward decided to invite the public to join them the following year. On October 21, 2006, over 30,000 people, in 82 cities and 15 different countries, took to the streets to urge the world to support peace in northern Uganda, collectively raising more than $500,000. If you visit www.guluwalk.com, you'll find a thriving, global online community that exists in MySpace, YouTube, Wikipedia, and Flickr (see Exhibit 4.8).

How do Bradbury and Hayward identify their most enthusiastic, committed supporters? They have a cornucopia of digital community actions to interpret: who posted the most photos to Flickr, who ranked the YouTube videos highest, who raised the largest number of donations through their online giving system? There was little way for them to predict ahead of time that the "Beijing Dragons" would form a team and raise significant money in China, or that the students at Boston College (led by Captain Meghan Battle) would attract over 120 donors, or that Caity Sackeroff would put up her hand to lead a group in Vancouver, British Columbia.

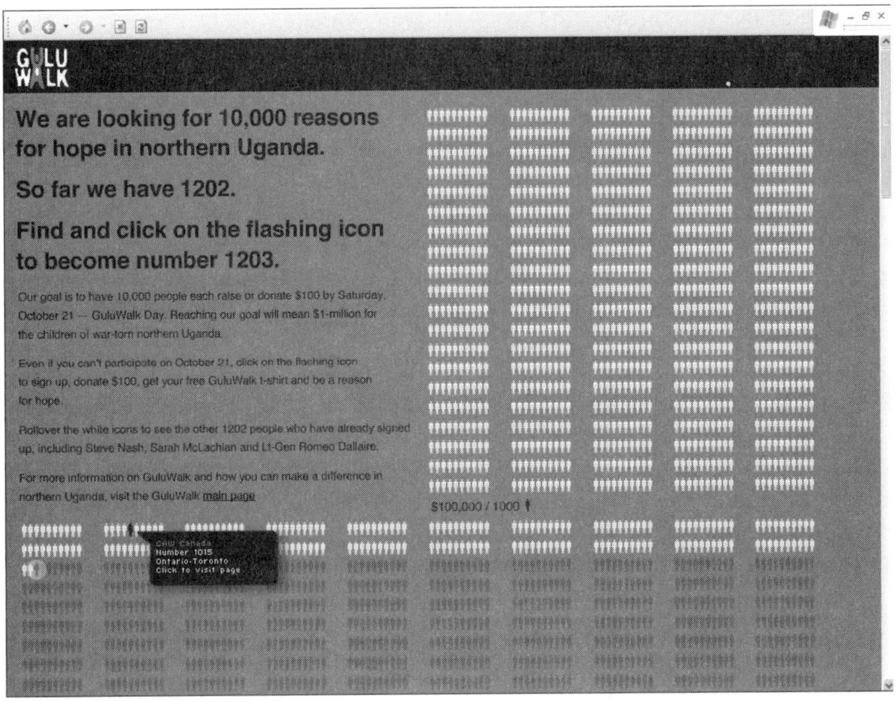

EXHIBIT 4.8   Gulu Walk

Because Bradbury and Hayward used technologies effectively, they allowed their social network to emerge from the global Internet.

45 PERCENT EFFECT OF ONLINE COMMUNITIES

When it comes to online communities, not all participants are equal. This is particularly evident in online fundraising communities.

The Canadian Breast Cancer Foundation manages the largest single-day fundraising event in Canada, the CIBC Run for the Cure. Because the foundation is one of the first charities to use personal fundraising pages online, it has a wealth of data to mine spanning many years. One glimpse of the statistics paints an interesting picture, which we call the "45 percent effect."

Year	$ Online	No. Online Fundraisers	Top 10%	$ from Top 10%	% Online $
2004	$ 4,054,644	18,344	1,834	$1,811,494.00	44.7%
2005	$ 6,468,929	25,923	2,592	$2,918,249.00	45.1%
2006	$ 8,278,544	29,589	2,959	$3,757,575.00	45.4%
Totals	$18,802,117	73,856		$8,487,318.00	

In each of the years from 2004 to 2006, approximately 45 percent of all online funds were raised by exactly the top 10 percent of online fundraisers.

Let's compare this to a very different online community of fundraisers: the GuluWalk community described earlier. Unlike the Run for the Cure, GuluWalk had its first year in 2006. The top 10 percent in GuluWalk Canada raised 43 percent of all funds; in GuluWalk USA, 45 percent; and in GuluWalk International, 39 percent.

Returning to the Run for the Cure example, let's look further into this 10 percent group of influential and successful online fundraisers. Of the 2,592 fundraisers in the year 2005, 45 percent had been in the elite club in the previous year. Of the 2,959 in year 2006, 48 percent were returning.

This fundraising concentration provides instruction for anyone trying to build and nurture online communities: Focus on the radical minority and the influential few. Current community and social fundraising systems provide us with the ability to identify this minority not only after the fundraising campaign has concluded but during its evolution. Monitor leading indicators carefully, focusing on individual funds raised but can also include other behaviors, such as the number of e-mail solicitations sent and the total number of individual donations received. If teams are involved, understand which teams have the most team funds raised and which teams have the most members.

Once you have identified your influential few (either during or after your campaign), treat them like any VIP should be treated. You want them back next year; you *need* them back next year. Just because they are part of an Internet-based community does not mean they would not appreciate a phone call from the president of your charity or maybe someone who has been helped by the funds they have raised.

CREATING COMMUNITIES OF INTEREST: CASE STUDY OF THE SALVATION ARMY ONLINE RED KETTLE

Creating an online community of volunteer fundraisers for your organization depends on a multitude of factors and varies greatly by organization and mission.

Five years ago the Salvation Army did not solicit funds via the Web, nor could it dynamically assign codes to online gifts tracking specific appeals or campaigns. Today the Salvation Army solicits by way of e-mail, tracks specific campaigns, interfaces with third-party vendors to leverage online giving tools like peer-to-peer applications, and processes 36 currencies in more than 111 countries through the Internet.

Oftentimes our best ideas are inspired by challenge. Replenishing the decreasing number of traditional Kettle locations across the country is a challenge but also an opportunity to create a community of Salvation Army supporters online.

The traditional Salvation Army Red Kettle's "career" as a fundraiser began 116 years ago in San Francisco. Traditional Kettle locations are usually found near shopping malls and busy street corners. Passersby toss cash and change into the Kettles.

Online Red Kettles offer a reduced need for coordination of volunteers to stand for hours and finance departments to count and audit cash and change; managing such things online means there is no risk of theft of cash and change, and is less costly overall.

According to Major George Hood, Community Relations Secretary, Salvation Army national headquarters: "Online donations are becoming an ever-increasing part of successful fundraising, and we were eager to merge the Internet with our Red Kettle campaign to extend the reach of the Red Kettles and The Salvation Army."

Building communities of volunteer fundraisers on the Web that are committed to your organization's mission can augment the overall success of the nonprofit's fundraising objectives. These volunteer fundraisers, building their personally "endorsed" community of donors and supporters, are your best online community members.

The same rules apply for *all* donors, no matter through which medium they contribute to your organization. The cultivation process for a donor who gives online and meets your organizations criteria for a "major donor" should be the same as if they came to you through any other channel: Find out what their preference is and listen to them.

The Giving USA Foundation has consistently reported that individuals give more than corporations and foundations. We know major gifts are generally made by donors who have a real-world relationship with their favorite organizations. The evolution of this new medium provides another direct response vehicle to identify, acquire, and cultivate relationships with donors.

Each donor, especially one who is a major donor by your organization's standards, should be treated as such. Online donors should not be viewed as transactional; they are still donors. Peer-to-peer gifts can be seen not only as fundraising but as volunteer friend-raising. Continuing to engage these constituents electronically is vital to furthering their relationship with the organization. Volunteer Web-based fundraising events raise money and those who donate when asked by a peer are the best donors among the organization's emerging electronic communities.

As the sophistication and comfort levels rise in our Web-based communities, so should the number of giving options available.

As with any fundraising campaign, we learned that we should start planning earlier than normal. Things will come up, no matter how well you plan. Focus on recruiting more volunteers/hosts and engage them to fundraise. Retain and entice past volunteers/hosts to do so again. The Salvation Army is creating and cultivating communities of interest online by recruiting Online Red Kettle Campaign veterans to further promote and recruit involvement from all levels and constituents is how (see Exhibit 4.9).

For example, out of the more than 4,429 Online Red Kettle gifts totaling $482,317, 20 online community members raised $92,481 themselves. Volunteers like these, who self-identify at this level, are not just donors but should be considered allies in your organization's mission.

	Top Group Kettles	Amount Raised		Top Personal Kettles	Amount Raised
1.	Metro Denver Advisory Board Ringers	$18,733	1.	Jim Cummings	$9,593
2.	The Salvation Army of Wake County	$4,440	2.	Susan Tucker	$7,100
3.	Kansas City Advisory Board	$4,150	3.	James White	$6,145
4.	Legally Appealing	$3,925	4.	Dick Manteuffel	$5,000
5.	Intermountain DHQ	$3,900	5.	Michael Woodruff	$3,750
6.	Nicci's Band of Bellringers	$2,925	6.	Lacy Hennessy	$3,560
7.	SDM head QUARTERS to KETTLES	$2,781	7.	Anonymous Kettle Host	$3,050
8.	KTVI FOX 2	$2,740	8.	Stephanie Gustafson	$2,535
9.	No Perfect People	$2,250	9.	Kim Moeller	$2,125
10.	Lexington SA Advisory Board	$1,770	10.	Daniel Roe	$2,009

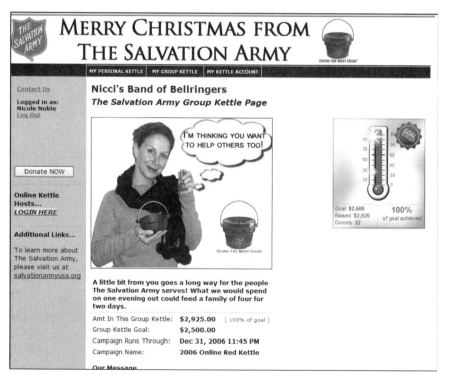

EXHIBIT 4.9   Red Kettle Campaign

Secure high-profile corporate partners and sponsors, including advisory organizations, boards, and sound cause-related marketing partnerships. Obtain buy-in from leadership, advisory organizations, boards, national and local staff, and public relations contacts. This is critical: Get the right message out, at the right time, to the right people.

We learned that maintaining consistent ongoing communications with Online Red Kettle hosts is key, but not overloading them; the aim is to encourage them to focus on specific actions and desired results. Make sure your message suits the audience you are addressing.

	2005 Campaign	2006 Campaign	% Increase
Total Dollar Figures	$130,813	$482,317	268%
Personal/Group Kettles	$88,157	$414,224	370%
Business Kettles	$24,492	$30,033	23%
Wal-Mart*	$17,964	$35,772	99%

*Wal-Mart made a traditional cash donation to help fill its Online Red Kettle in the amount of $250,000 that is not reflected in this table.

There is new contingency of volunteers that are using their time wisely on the Web helping their charity of choice. The Salvation Army has experienced a great deal of success using Web-based people to people fundraising applications. The evidence of these ever growing social networks is illustrated in the increase of the number of Online Red Kettle hosts, donors, and average gifts.

In addition to these statistics, the average online gift in 2005 was $82.69 and 2006 the average online gift was $102.23.

HOW DO YOU LOOK ON YOUTUBE?

During a recent presentation, we mentioned the popular online video Web site YouTube. The group started snickering and looking sideways at each other; we were clearly not in on this joke. When pushed to divulge the reason for the reaction, the group urged us to fire up YouTube on our browser and type in the name of their charity "Kids Help Phone" (see Exhibit 4.10).

We were suddenly faced with over 50 video clips that had been tagged using the charity's brand. What was going on? We clicked on one of the videos and quickly got the point. Kids Help Phone provides a terrific telephone counseling service to teens facing a variety of issues, from homosexuality, to bullying, to suicide. What these videos showed were kids using their cell phones to videotape prank calls to the service.

We asked the group what they thought of this. Comments ranged, but the consensus was "This is terrible; we have to stop this; this threatens our brand in the community." The only challenge is ... they cannot stop this. "Hey, look on the bright side," we encouraged them. "At least you are *on* YouTube!"

EXHIBIT 4.10   Kids Help Phone Campaign

Like it or not, you will share control of your brand with your donors, volunteers, and other supporters much more in the next ten years than you did in the last ten. The risk of not embracing this new self-expression is that you and your organization will be left completely out of the conversation. Portal sites such as www.justgiving.com, www.chipin.com, and www.givemeaning.com are creating new opportunities for communities of Internet-savvy donors…and new options and challenges for traditional charities attempting to develop direct relationships with their supporters.

CONCLUSION: WHAT GETS US EXCITED

The ever-changing culture of how we utilize the Internet in response to our community's needs and charitable intent, both locally and globally, is exciting. Do you recall the moment in time when direct mail came of age? Would you say that the Internet, as a fundraising channel, was born on September 11, 2001 and has continued to grow as swiftly as the magnitude of our most recent natural disasters?

The fluidity of the Web is unlike other traditional fundraising media or disciplines. Its cost effectiveness allows us to give the public a platform that is easy to use and that they can personalize.

Web-based fundraising can be seen as another facet of direct response fundraising; the standards of direct mail can apply for prospecting and acquiring new donors by means of this new medium/channel. But there are significant differences with the Web, primarily in the fact that it is a two-way medium that encourages user-generated content and allows the creative combination of many different sets of tools and technologies.

Each year the public becomes more generous and socially responsible with their charitable dollars. It is up to us, the ethical fundraisers and online practitioners, to continue to engage and cultivate the ever growing philanthropic public by using tools that are secure, flexible, and effective. It is our challenge to become increasingly comfortable and imaginative as the focus of control shifts from *us*—the charities—to *them*—our supporters.

ABOUT THE AUTHORS

Philip King is president and chief executive officer of Artez Interactive. He spends his time at Artez working with Canadian charities to envision and create the online fundraising campaigns of tomorrow. Prior to joining Artez in 2002, Philip served as vice president of e-Business with United Way of Greater Toronto. He has served on various not-for-profit boards and advisory panels including a federal task-force, the Voluntary Sector Roundtable for Information Management/Information Technology. He holds a BA from Harvard University as well as an MBA from the University of Toronto and lives in Toronto with his wife, Leta, and their two sons, Sam and Adam.

Nicci Noble was born in New Orleans and raised in the South, she has been volunteering with nonprofit organizations since the age of ten, when she first collected donations for Buddy Poppies on behalf of the Veterans for Foreign Wars.

Nicci is the electronic fundraising specialist for the Salvation Army's National Headquarters. She has expanded the nonprofit's Web presence and pioneered its electronic fundraising and communication efforts. In addition, she has created and implemented the first national online giving programs for the Salvation Army. As a result of her efforts, the Salvation Army has seen an increase in Web-based revenue and number of donors giving online.

When she is not busy raising money for the Salvation Army via the Internet, Nicci serves as a sustaining member of the Junior League of San Francisco after seven years of active volunteer service with the Association of Junior Leagues International. Nicci is currently the president of the Golden Gate Chapter of the Association of Fundraising Professionals.

NOTE

1. The Salvation Army Western Territory comprises the West and now includes the 13 western states as well as the Marshall Islands, Guam, and Micronesia. The territory has more than 300 corps community centers (churches) and numerous social service units.

PART TWO

People-to-People Fundraising

CHAPTER 5

Crafting the Marketing Strategy to Make It Happen

Katya Andresen
Network for Good

Bill Strathmann
Network for Good

INTRODUCTION

Once a year, in December, our organization, Network for Good, sends the people who have used our giving system their donation histories for tax purposes and to encourage year-end giving. Last year, after a friend got his, he was mystified.

"There was some charity I didn't recognize in there. I had no idea what the charity was, yet I'd supposedly made a donation," he told us.

While we inwardly panicked about the prospect of faults in our computer system generating thousands of false giving records, he finished the story.

"I wracked my brains. Then I vaguely remembered a friend asking me to give to some charity because he was running a race. That was the donation. Here was some charity that I'm sure is worthy, but I have no knowledge of it or relationship to it. But my friend did, and that was what mattered."

He is right; that is what matters. It is what matters to the donor, and it is what matters to us as fundraisers.

In fact, whenever we get a group of fundraisers together in a room for a workshop, we ask them about the last time they gave money to a cause other than their own. This gets everyone to step out of their role as fundraisers and into the role of an audience, which is an important perspective to retain as fundraisers. Even more important, without fail, everyone in the room says they gave because they felt a personal connection to someone or something. Their stories illustrate once again what matters: the personal relationship between the person who asks for donations and the donor.

In the following pages, we deconstruct why this is the case for our friend, the people at our workshops, and donors in general. Both of the authors of this chapter happen to be the progeny of psychiatrists, but we are not undertaking this exercise solely out of an urge to analyze motivation. We are looking into the topic because it is useful to know the social psychology and marketing principles behind the potent people-to-people fundraising concept. It helps us to tap its power.

Next, we will apply these psychological principles to conducting effective people-to-people fundraising online. We provide five rules for getting your donors to effectively fundraise for your cause, using interesting case studies to illustrate those rules.

By the time this chapter goes into print, the Internet inevitably will have changed. Some of the examples here will seem old school. Fortunately, though, as we emphasize in these pages, both the psychology and rules of personal fundraising are unchanging. Apply them consistently with the mind of a marketer and you'll be an effective fundraiser online, whether you're operating in Web 1.0, 2.0, or beyond.

PUTTING PERSONAL FUNDRAISING ON THE COUCH

So why does personal fundraising work—online, offline, across cultures and borders? Four principles influence our giving.

1. It is based on a two-way relationship, not one-sided promotion.
2. The personal fundraiser is an authentic and authoritative messenger.
3. People-to-people fundraising is based in story.
4. People-to-people fundraising translates impulse into action online.

It Is Based on a Two-Way Relationship, Not One-Sided Promotion

The traditional model of marketing is one-sided: The person selling something (or seeking donations) makes a case to an audience and hopes people will listen and act. This model can be somewhat effective if you know your audience and target the message accordingly. It is less effective if you simply broadcast your message to a wide audience and hope someone listens. Marketers call the latter a spray-and-pray approach. It is like turning on the proverbial firehose: spraying your message to the masses with a billboard or conduct untargeted e-mail blast and praying that someone, somewhere, gives money as a result.

By contrast, people-to-people fundraising is based on two-way communication; it is a conversation between individuals rather than a speech from an organization. It puts your message in the mouth of the person most likely to prompt a donation: someone the audience knows.

There are two useful social psychology theories at work here: liking and reciprocation. In a great book on these theories, *Influence: Science and Practice*, Robert Cialdini explains: "People prefer to say yes to individuals they know and like." He says we like people who are similar to us, who praise us, who are in frequent contact with us, who share common connections to us, and—shallow as it is—people who are physically attractive.[1]

Pair this idea of liking with the principle of reciprocation, which states that "People give back to you the kind of treatment they have received from you." It is no mistake, says Cialdini, that a synonym for "thank you" is "much obliged." When we like someone and perceive they have treated us well, we are likely to return the favor.

Here is a very personal example of what we mean. Bill's mother passed away from cancer in 1996, and this is what he wrote friends about the experience in 2004.

This year I am running the Chicago Marathon for Leslie Strathmann, my mom. If you know me, you know my mom died of cancer on April 13, 1996. You also know what an incredible person she was. She originally had colon cancer which ultimately took over her liver and took her life. The year she died, I ran my first marathon in DC. Then, in '98, I ran the NYC Marathon on her birthday, November 1st. Now I have the chance to actually raise money for the American Cancer Society in her name by running my fifth marathon and my first Chicago Marathon. My goal is to raise $750 and finish in under 3 hours or in the top 3% of the runners. I would really appreciate your support."

Of course, his family and friends wanted to help, because they liked Bill, had positive memories of him, and wanted to do something in memory of his mother. The effort raised $1,765, and Bill finished in the time he wanted. Bill also found the experience transformative on another level—he ended up changing careers and becoming chief executive officer of Network for Good.

That result is interesting because of what happens in direct "conversation" that is the underpinning of personal fundraising. The person asks for help because he or she cares about a cause. The donor helps because he or she cares about the person—either directly or through a shared friend or experience. And then two more things happen: The person who asked for help is inclined to say yes to requests from the people who contributed as well as yes to requests from the charity to fundraise again.

In our example, Bill will always support the causes of his friends and family members, who supported him, and he is a longtime advocate for the American Cancer Society as well as the head of an organization that helps all charities fundraise online.

The moral of the story? Personal fundraising is not only based in relationships; it also deepens them. This is far from the world of spray and pray. It is more like an approach of "concentrate and inundate" with people with a shared history and sense of friendly obligation.

Cialdini tells an intriguing story that illustrates just how deep those relationships—and personal obligations—become. He tells the story of how, in 1985, the Ethiopian Red Cross, based in a country ravaged by drought, war, and starvation, sent a $5,000 donation to victims of earthquakes in Mexico City. A journalist, intrigued by the reasons behind the poor nation's gift to Mexico, learned that in 1935, Mexico had sent aid to Ethiopia when it was invaded by Italy. The Ethiopians had remembered.

The Personal Fundraiser Is an Authentic and Authoritative Messenger

In the age of relentless marketing messages, "reality" shows, and false personas on MySpace, authenticity is a rare commodity. Stephen Colbert, a television comedian, has captured the erosion of genuine with the word "truthiness."

People crave what is true and credible, and in a world of truthiness, they listen to those genuine voices with special care. The messenger has become as important as the message. People listen to other people. They look to human beings, not corporations or causes, to communicate and connect with. Messengers from outside our organization are probably far more credible than we are.

Or as online fundraising expert Mark Rovner of Sea Change Strategies puts it, "There is something inherently more credible about a friend or neighbor telling you something or raising money. You already trust that person."

Information from personal contacts generates twice as much impact than information that is company-led, according to Millward Brown in a Word of Mouth Influence Study in 2005. Subsequent research from Cone Inc. shows that over three quarters of people cite friends and family as most influential in their giving (2006 Cone Nonprofit Research).

It is not hard to see why this is the case from a psychological perspective. Which is more believable: Bill and Katya telling you that Network for Good (where we both work) is a fabulous resource for nonprofits, or a colleague from another charity? What is more compelling: the American Cancer Society's Web site or Bill's personal story? Your colleague, in the first case, and Bill, in the second case, are more authentic. They are therefore more persuasive, and their voices have greater credibility. As messengers go, even a "friend of a friend" sounds better than an organization.

That is why an outside messenger—a donor who fundraises for your organization—has the potential to cut through the communications clutter. It is one thing for your charity to say you urgently need funds. It is quite another for a person to tell another person why she personally feels a sense of urgency about your cause and believes in your work, and then to ask for help on those grounds. When your organization's need is filtered through one person's experience, it is easier to understand and far more compelling. Seth Godin calls this "Flipping the Funnel.[2]" That is because instead of trying to funnel messages into people's minds, we are flipping that paradigm and handing our supporters a megaphone. Let your supporters hold your megaphone for you, and your message will be amplified many times.

For example, the Transverse Myelitis Association says it "facilitates support and networking opportunities amongst families; provides educational information; functions as a clearinghouse for articles and research literature; and investigates, advocates for and supports research and innovative treatment efforts" for a "rare neurological disorder that is part of a spectrum of neuroimmunologic diseases of the central nervous system." Whew.

A person who had transverse myelitis used a virtual charity badge that can be added on any website to fundraise for the cause last year. The person, named "James," featured his picture and this message: "I became a ventilator-dependent quadriplegic, paralyzed from the neck down, due to transverse myelitis, a rare neurological disorder that affects the central nervous system. I am trying to help raise funds for education and research." This story is authentic and persuasive in general and especially to James's friends and family.

People-to-People Fundraising Is Based in Story

As James's appeal demonstrates, story is at the heart of personal fundraising and its effectiveness. When people hear a story, they are transported with the storyteller outside the present moment, to another time and place, creating a shared experience. There is no more powerful form of communication.

People do not remember how many houses were destroyed by Hurricane Katrina. We remember stories of people stuck in the Superdome, women screaming from their roofs, or an elderly man leaving his pets behind. Those stories were what made us give, and together, those stories are the filter through which we experienced and remember the disaster.

Andy Goodman, a communications consultant specializing in the art of storytelling, says, "Stories define a person, a company, a movement, a culture, or a nation. You as an individual are the sum of the stories that you tell about yourself."[3] A nonprofit, of course, is also a sum of stories, including the stories told by its staff, its donors, and its beneficiaries.

Bill's American Cancer Society story was the story of his mother. James's Transverse Myelitis Association story was the story of his own disease.

Andy said in *Robin Hood Marketing* that his first job was writing for the television show *Dinosaurs*.

> *I'll never forget sitting down with Michael Jacobs, the executive producer of the show, who said to me, "It's great if you're funny and can write jokes, but there are a million guys who can write jokes. Our show is 22 stories a year. Breaking a story, now that's tough. If you can break stories, you can make it." That advice always rang in my ears. Robert McKee, famed for his scriptwriting course, bases his teaching on the theory that it's all about the story. If you don't have a good story, you've got nothing.*[4]

And if you have a good story, you have everything. That is why as nonprofits, we should listen to the stories our supporters tell, and we should give them the freedom and tools to share those stories broadly. Our work can be broad and complex, and that can make it hard to communicate compellingly. Donors tend to talk about our work through their own stories, making it specific and simple. That is a great gift to us.

Bill and Katya both sit down with their children every year around Christmas and give them money to donate to any charity they want. In talking about the work of different charities, we find ourselves telling stories about how certain charities came to be, whom they help, and what happens as a result. We find ourselves saying far more compelling things than we have said for days in the office. That is the beauty of talking to another human being; we naturally start relating in stories instead of the dull numbers and statistics of memos or brochures. We grow up hearing stories, and we never grow out of telling stories—or wanting to hear them.

People-to-People Fundraising Translates Impulse into Action Online

Impulse is a good thing. The word "impulsive" is often used to describe someone flighty, but we are talking about a more profound and admirable concept here. Impulse is motivation, and fundraising is all about motivating people. We want people to feel an impulse to help. Impulse is a uniquely human reaction to a need, a spark of interest and concern. We need to create it and then have a way for people to act on impulse before that spark fades.

There is no better place to make that fast connection between interest and action than online. Online giving (and advocacy) is especially impulsive in nature. Take, for example, the outpouring of online donations at times of disaster. It shares some interesting characteristics with people-to-people fundraising.

Online giving is growing exponentially per year, from just over half a billion in 2000 to more than $4.5 billion in 2005, though it still represents a relatively small percentage of total charitable giving.[5] The notable exception is giving in response to humanitarian crises, when the Internet is becoming donors' avenue of choice. The *Chronicle of Philanthropy* has noted that Internet donations for tsunami relief accounted for more than one-third of the total raised—more than twice the proportion of online gifts in the aftermath of the September 11, 2001, terrorist attacks[6]. After Hurricane Katrina, half of relief giving was online, representing the largest outpouring of donations online in history.

The study "Impulse on the Internet"[7] found that giving through the Network for Good portal followed this pattern:

- **Tsunami.** Web traffic 10 times normal volume, donations 6 times normal volume
- **Katrina.** Web traffic 75 times normal volume, donations 20 times normal volume
- **Earthquake.** Web traffic double normal volume, donations double normal volume

Disaster giving is impulse giving. People are shocked by the disturbing words and pictures that emerge from humanitarian disasters, and they want to help in that moment. By enabling people to react immediately—when they feel moved by the unfolding story—online giving likely increases the rates at which feeling is converted to charitable action.

For all the reasons we have discussed in these pages—relationship, authenticity, story—people-to-people fundraising generates a similar sense of immediacy and urgency. In disaster, people feel an impulse to help because of the scale of need. With people-to-people fundraising, people feel an impulse to help because of they share a relationship or experience or story with the person asking for help.

That impulse is ideally matched to online outreach. When we hear the news of a disaster on the radio in our car or a friend tells us a heart-rending story, we feel an immediate impulse to help. But then something happens. Life and its mundane details get in the way and distract us. The dry cleaner may be closing or the kids are fighting or the phone is ringing. We attend to those details and by the time we are in a time or place when we can act, the moment of impulse has passed.

Online, there is no lag between the desire to act and the opportunity to act, resulting in more gifts. You see a message, you feel motivated to act, and you can immediately help with a few clicks of a mouse.

In marketing, we call this an "open-minded moment." The reason we do not see many ads for H&R Block tax-preparation services in October has to do with open-minded moments. Open-minded moments occur when we are thinking about an action, want to take it, and are able to take it.

Think of the human mind as a camera. Open-minded moments are those fleeting seconds when our mental shutter pops open in response to something compelling (like a friend asking for help). The aperture suddenly broadens to let in light, and we focus momentarily on an image or idea or word from that friend. If we are online, we might see a "donate" button in that split second. That is a good thing, because there is a chance we may act before our impulse, and our moment of selective attention, passes. And, unlike most impulse purchases, there is no buyer's remorse with donations.

We have identified four principles that influence giving: relationship, authenticity, story, and ability to act on impulse. So how do they work together?

Imagine yourself at a cocktail party. A stranger approaches you, introduces himself, and says, "Hi, let me tell you all about myself and why you should donate to the charity I work for." This sounds unappealing, but it is exactly what nonprofits are doing when they send an untargeted mass letter or e-mail. It is a form of preaching at people without any interest in them, and that approach simply will not work to win friends and influence people. There is no relationship, no appealing messenger, no story worth hearing, and so no impulse to act.

Now imagine you have fled that awful stranger at the cocktail party, and a second person approaches you—someone you know through a mutual friend. You have a conversation. He tells you about running a marathon in memory of his mother, and you offer to help. He has a pledge form with him, and you hand him a check. This example, of course, is person-to-person fundraising in action.

You did not flee the second person because you knew him, however indirectly. You listened to him because you valued what he had to say. You were moved to help because of his story. You were able to help because he gave you a way to help, right away. That is exactly what happens with effective people-to-people fundraising online, but in fact it is even better online than it is at the cocktail party. For one thing, even no one we know carries around pledge forms at cocktail parties—laptops and mobile devices maybe. Again, online fundraising combines rich, compelling media; relevant content and background information; and an easy safe and convenient way to take action. For another thing, media such as e-mail diminish the social awkwardness of "the ask." Except for development professionals, no one is particularly fond of asking for money face to face. E-mail provides a nice veil for both the fundraiser and the donor. It is easier to ask, it is easier to say no, and most important, it is easier to say yes.

PUTTING PERSONAL FUNDRAISING TO WORK FOR YOU

Now that we have deconstructed why people-to-people fundraising is so appealing, let us turn to how to do it effectively. How do you capitalize on the psychological principles we have highlighted? How do you interest your supporters in raising funds for you? How do you give them the tools to do that well?

Five laws of marketing will help you do the job. The first three are part of the marketing trifecta of prompting people to take action—make it easy, make it fun, and make it popular—and the fourth focuses on rewarding donors. The fifth is: Do not forget to directly cultivate the broadening circle that your efforts will create.

1. Make it easy.
2. Make it fun.
3. Make it popular.
4. Reward your supporters.
5. Cultivate your growing circle.

Each of these laws builds on the psychological strength of people-to-people fundraising. Together they seek to capitalize on the power of relationships, personal messengers, story, and impulse—and to turn those factors into a donation.

Make It Easy

As marketing guru Seth Godin likes to say, people are lazy and in a hurry. Always, all the time. No exceptions.

The first and most important law of people-to-people fundraising takes into account this immutable fact. Whatever we ask people to do, it needs to be very, very easy. We cannot emphasize this law enough. Just because someone may be devoted to our cause or devoted to a friend or family member does not mean he or she is willing to invest huge amounts of time and energy to take action.

In response to the question in our workshops about why people take action, we said the most common answer is "because someone I know asked me." The second most common response is "because it was easy." People describe signing online petitions, donating online, and other actions that took just moments. When asked if they would have done the same thing if it had taken 15 minutes, they look doubtful.

In a survey, Network for Good recently asked our online donors a very important question: "Why do you donate online?" The most common answer—"It's easier than writing a check"—shows that convenience can be as important a consideration as the cause itself.

"Easy" is also the reason behind the rapid growth of online advocacy. A 2005 Craver, Mathews, Smith and Prime Group study found that one-third of surveyed individuals had used the Internet in the past 12 months to urge a friend or public official to take action on an issue.[8] We think that is because it is so very easy to do online—a matter of forwarding an e-mail or URL.

Keep in mind that statistic, because advocacy is not only popular, it is the road to donations. Do not eschew advocacy programs in place of fundraising. Advocacy efforts are particularly powerful as a foot-in-door technique that creates a "momentum of compliance." If people have signed a petition for a friend, they are far likely to give money later.

The importance of convenience means you need to keep things simple on two levels. First, you must make it easy for people to do personal fundraising. Second, you must make it easy for that person's friends and family to support the fundraiser. Fortunately, this book is focused on online fundraising, and making things simple and easy is a good match for the Internet. Asking a supporter to forward an e-mail takes only seconds. Asking someone to donate online takes just minutes. That is good for people who are lazy and in a hurry.

There are other considerations besides time, though, when thinking about how to make things easy. You want it to be comfortable for donors to ask for help. Again, by creating online programs, you are giving your supporter an e-mail or other electronic tool to hide behind instead of asking someone for help in person.

You also want to make it easy for people to fundraise where they already interact with their personal circles online. Why make them build a fundraising page on your Web site when there are widgets and e-mail tools that allow them to add a fundraising appeal to the Web pages, blogs, online communities, or e-mails they already use to communicate with friends and family?

The Sharing Foundation raised nearly $50,000 with over 700 donations in less than a month by making things easy. The founder, a retired doctor in her 70s, went around her retirement community with her laptop getting her neighbors to donate through a personal fundraising badge. A Cambodian monk got everyone in his congregation donating using the badges online at church. Beth Kanter, a blogger on nonprofit technology from Sharing Foundation, recruited people in her yoga class. Board members took their laptops parties and got people to donate.

Last, remember to keep things easy with a clear call to action for both your supporters and the friends and family they will cultivate for you. Make sure your call to action is:

- **Specific.** Ask for one concrete action. Telling people to click on a button to donate now is better than asking them to participate in a fundraising campaign—or worse, presenting them with a menu of options. Asking a supporter to forward an e-mail is superior to urging them to recruit friends and family. Specific actions are easier to do and harder to decline.
- **Feasible.** For most people, if the action does not seem doable, they will not do it. "Help our cause save the earth" does not sound like something any one person can do easily. Make the action you are requesting small and easy. It is a step toward momentum of compliance.
- **Filmable.** A good test of whether your call to action is simple and specific enough is to ask if it would be possible to film the audience taking the action you desire. If you do not have a simple visual, your audience will not. People cannot picture themselves as being against a legislative bill but then can see themselves writing to a member of Congress via an e-mail form.
- **First priority.** Make sure what you are asking for is an action that, if people did it, would significantly and immediately advance your marketing goals and your mission. If your call to action will only "raise awareness," take it one step further. We want people to *do* something that will truly make a difference for your organization.

Then, if you think your call to action is easy, confirm that assumption with some testing. Do not assume anything. Ask some loyal donors to try out your program and see what reaction they get. If you do not have time for that, at least show your tools and language to friends or family members who will have fresh eyes. Those fresh eyes inevitably catch elements you may never have thought would be confusing.

Here are some recommended approaches that make it easy for your supporters to help you:

- **"Forward this e-mail to a friend" calls to action.** Send them a nifty e-mail and ask your supporters to forward it to five friends. Make it an e-mail that just asks for a simple action, like signing a petition or joining a community so you can get the e-mail addresses of those five friends and cultivate them as donors.
- **Share photos.** Send your supporters cool pictures or put them on www.flickr.com and ask people to share the good work you are doing. Pictures are so compelling.

- **Offer easy-to-build personal fundraising pages and widgets.** Ask your supporters to hold events for you, such as dinner party fundraisers or races, and make it easy for them to recruit people with tools like www.chipin.com or www.firstgiving.com.
- **Personal fundraising badges.** If your supporters are active bloggers or have Web pages, ask them to link to you or fundraise for you in those locations. It is where their personal circles already visit. Give them cool tools to do it.

The rise of personal fundraising badges and widgets helps make it easy for your organization and donors to take action. There were a proliferation of badges online at the time of this writing, including www.chipin.com and www.wordofblog.net. Network for Good and SixDegrees.org also have charity badges. Word of Blog, ChipIn, and Network for Good have seen rapid adaptation of the badges—thousands are created per month—in large part because it is a simple process (see Exhibit 5.1).

We should reinforce how making it easy, the first law of marketing, is so important when considering the first social principle: It is a two-way relationship. It is more important than ever to make the first action easy in person-to-person fundraising because donors know they are entering into a relationship. They are actually entering into two: the relationship with the fundraiser and the relationship with the nonprofit they choose to support.

Few things are more daunting than entering into a relationship. The online "relationship" industry gets this. ItsJustLunch.com has based its entire market

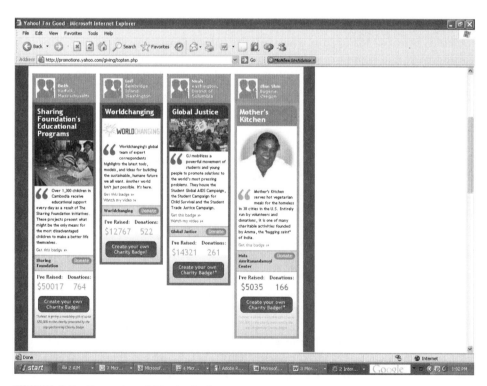

EXHIBIT 5.1 Examples of Charity Badges

differentiation on the commonly accepted notion that it is easier and less is committed by either party to have a first date over lunch date versus a first date over dinner. In fact, ItsJustLunch leads with making it easy and follows up with our second law of marketing: "Dating & Match Making Services for Busy Professional Singles. It's Just Lunch is a fun proactive approach to your personal life ... after all its just lunch."

Make It Fun

Just as people do not like to do things that are complicated, they are not attracted to things that are tedious or depressing. Make your people-to-people fundraising initiatives fun for the personal fundraisers and fun for the people they are asking for help.

Fun does not always come naturally to our sector. We are used to dealing with serious social problems and sad stories of need, and it is natural to communicate those woes. But it should not be a woeful process to act in support of your organization. It should be uplifting. Network for Good has the slogan, "Do good, feel good," to capture the good feeling people should get from helping a charity. Leverage online tools and events to create attractive, appealing positive messages and to differentiate your cause from the doom-and-gloom, wagging-finger messages that proliferate in the fundraising world.

UNICEF had fun with its "trick or treat online" page. Instead of hauling around that orange box on Halloween, kids could create a trick-or-treat page where their friends and family could contribute to UNICEF's programs. The top fundraiser was a third-grade class from Providence, Rhode Island, that was studying about UNICEF's work in school.

Those students had a great personal circle of parents, friends, and teachers that they asked to support their cause. For their supporters, it was a fun way to help: no need to buy Halloween candy or scramble for change at their front door. All these people had to do was click to give (see Exhibit 5.2). It was easy, fun, and rewarding. As Alia McKee, who worked on the campaign, says, "You're never too old to trick-or-treat for UNICEF!"

Another fun example is CARE's I Am Powerful campaign, which seeks to create a community of engaged, passionate donors who care about combating poverty among women. We would like to pause for a moment to consider just how hard it seems to make the topic of "women and poverty" fun. Thank goodness we were not charged with that task. CARE achieved it by focusing on the positive: the idea of being powerful by helping a woman across the world to be powerful. The person-to-person approach was well positioned.

Then CARE created a fun symbol of the act of being powerful for another person. CARE asks people who want to help other women be powerful to input their e-mail address and join a "Power Circle" online. When they do, their name and any personal message they include appears in an animated, moving circle on CARE's Web site. CARE then contacts the people in the circle with e-mails detailing progress in real women's lives around the world and asks for your time on advocacy efforts and donations. This is following the "momentum of compliance" method from our second social principle with an easy first step of engagement, and it is very effective.

The personal fundraising components are especially interesting. CARE sends donors a "power quiz"—a fun e-mail with a variety of questions to create a

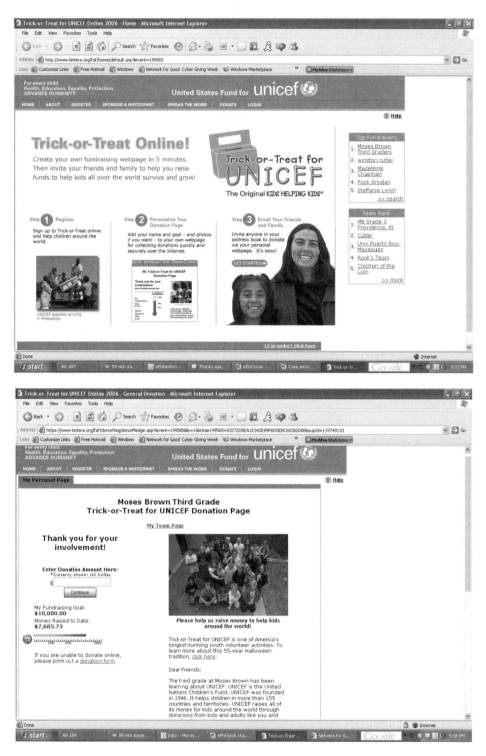

EXHIBIT 5.2 Putting "Fun" in Online Fundraising

philanthropic personality profile. It is also a way for CARE to get people in the mind-set of activists and donors as well as a way to collect research on their audience.

After a series of such questions, quiz-takers get their philanthropic profile type (Bill and Katya happen to have the "power of compassion") with customized ways they can help CARE's work. The personal fundraising component is fun: You are asked to "pass our power quiz on to your friends" so they can discover their power in the fight against poverty. An easy e-mail form has fields for up to six e-mail addresses, so your friends can take the quiz. They then can also get engaged in thinking about empowering women as well as provide useful data to CARE and build its database of potential donors!

CARE staff said in 2006 that the "I am powerful" approach has increased their acquisition rates by 30 percent after less than a year. Our favorite story showing the effectiveness of the campaign was a woman whose wedding was canceled at the last moment. The would-be bride decided to go ahead and have a party for friends and family anyway, but instead of gifts, she asked for contributions to CARE.

Why, the *New York Times* asked this personal fundraiser extraordinaire, did she choose CARE? The would-be bride said she selected CARE after seeing the message "I am powerful." The idea of supporting strong women, she says, was particularly appealing to her as she was declaring her independence from the man she planned to marry (see Exhibit 5.3).

Here are some recommended approaches to make it fun for your supporters to help you:

- **Let them share personal information.** It is fun for people to express themselves, as in the charity badge, the trick-or-treat program (which let you explain why you personally are involved), and the CARE Power Circle, which allows you to put your name on the CARE Web site and enclose a personal message.
- **Use humor.** There is a reason those marginally funny jokes on e-mail get forwarded to you by friends and family. We like to share amusing stories and doing fun things. Some nonprofits hold imaginary black-tie dinners—no rubber chicken, just donations.
- **Give them instant gratification.** Things are fun when we get instant payback. All the examples cited here allowed people to share personal information, be amused, and see the difference they were making immediately. Use technology creatively so people see visible, tangible (and fun) results quickly.
- **Let them use photos and videos.** With the advent of YouTube, Flickr, and other rich media Web sites, it has never been easier to add more personal and visually engaging rich content through a simple hyperlink.

Make It Popular

The last part of the marketing trifecta is "Make it popular." What we mean by that is we need to create "social proof" around our call to action. Social proof is the powerful idea that if we think everyone else is acting in a certain way, we are likely to act that way too. People are conformists by nature, and we take cues about how to think and what to do from those around us.

In *Robin Hood Marketing*, Katya talked about social norms fueling entire industries: "Would the fashion world be able to motivate us to buy a narrower tie or a longer skirt this year if we didn't care what people think?"[9]

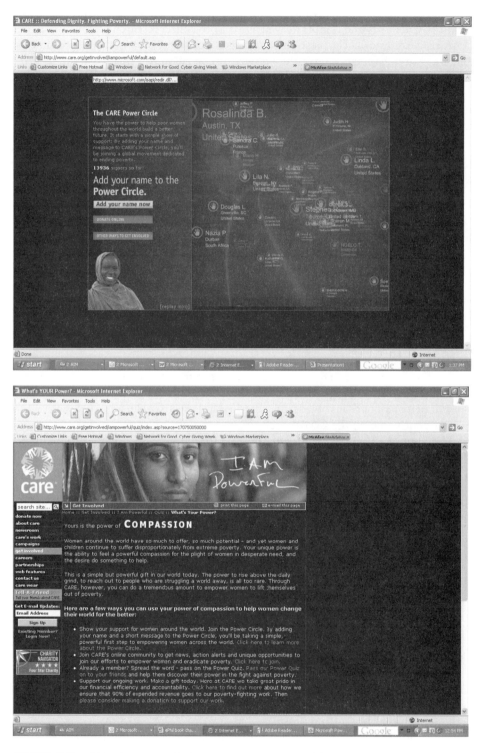

EXHIBIT 5.3   Philanthropic Profit–Type Quiz: I Am Powerful

At Network for Good, we have sought to use the principle of social norms to increase donations through our Web site. After simplifying our home page and putting social proof on the page, we have seen our conversion rates increase by 30 percent. The social proof? We state that more than 325,000 people have given more than $112 million through our Web site to show new users just how popular we are.

In December 2006, when our traffic increases, we feature a real-time ticker of total donations so people can see just how many other people are taking action (see Exhibit 5.4). In December 2006 and 2005, we partnered with Yahoo! on a "cybergiving week" to promote the idea that just as retail sales has black Friday, charities have "cybergiving week"—that end-of-year spike in online giving. The psychological subtext? Everyone is doing it, so you should too!

Of course, the very idea of personal fundraising capitalizes on the concept of social proof. When people send out an e-mail to friends and family asking them to help, they are essentially engaging in peer pressure. Take that a step further and be sure that there is a mechanism for showing the personal fundraiser and the members of his or her circle that more and more people are taking action. You want your supporters to feel they are part of a successful movement, not a lone voice in the wilderness. This is why Network for Good included a real-time donations count and ticker on our badge. It is also why fundraising thermometers and scrolling lists of other supporters are so popular. They send the message "Other people are doing it, and we are part of something larger."

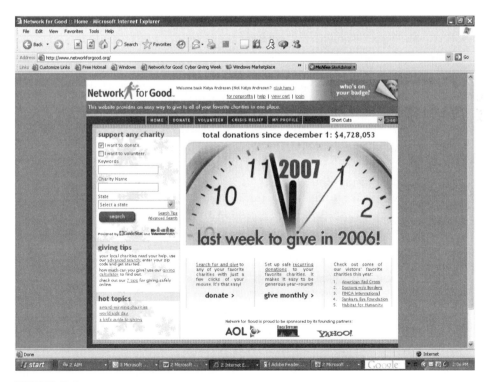

EXHIBIT 5.4 Real-time Donation Tracker

Here are some ways you can generate social proof:

- **Use fundraising tickers.** Show how many people are giving, in real time.
- **Count your community.** Show how many people have taken action to create a sense of a growing community of like-minded people.
- **Use testimonials.** Quotes from people talking about why they are a fundraiser or a donor are powerful because of the principle of the authentic messenger we discussed earlier in this chapter.
- **Use "social proof" wording.** In calls to action, choose wording that demonstrates that others are already participating: for example, "join millions of other generous Americans" or "hundreds of other concerned members in your community."

Reward Your Supporters

Now that you have made it easy, fun, and popular to act, you will be close to success in creating fundraisers to support your cause and helping them to generate donations. All that you need now is a carrot—a reward or incentive—that will ensure that people actually do want you want them to do.

A good reward has four qualities: It is immediate, personal, credible, and reflective of audience values.

- **Immediate.** The reward should be available to the audience right away, because it is human nature to seek instant satisfaction over distant gratification. What does the fundraiser get in exchange for acting immediately? The donor?
- **Personal.** Audience members, whether they are fundraisers or donors, need to believe the reward will make life better for them personally. How can you speak to the individual merits of taking action?
- **Credible.** Make sure the action is feasible and the reward that you offer is possible.
- **Based on audience values.** Since it is impossible to change what people value, connect the call to action to the audience's existing values. By plugging into their mind-sets, you will get their attention and inspire action.

So what does this mean in practice?

McKee worked on a student-focused campaign for Amnesty International that offered an iPod to the student who recruited the most friends to the cause (see Exhibit 5.5). That is immediate, personal, credible, and based in the values of a college student.

She also cites the example of www.guluwalk.com, which raises awareness of the plight of Ugandan night walkers (children who go miles to sleep in safety). That campaign enabled people to get an assigned icon on their fundraising page at http://guluwalk.com/main/. The reward was less commercial than the iPod, but equally effective—a visible, tangible place for your name and icon in a growing community doing good.

Network for Good jump-started its charity badge campaign with a several rewards. For personal fundraisers zealous about their charity, they could receive up to $50,000 for their charity and billing on the Yahoo! Web site as well as on a

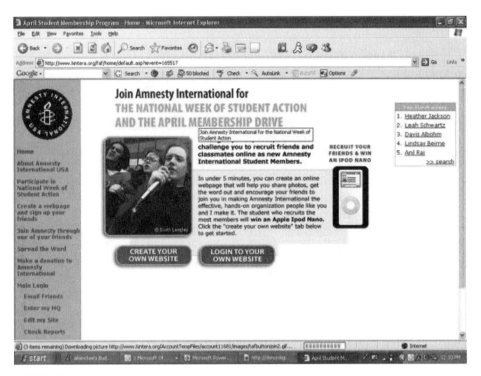

EXHIBIT 5.5   Reward Your Sponsors for Their Support

billboard in Times Square. For the people supporting the person with a badge, they made their friend happy and got to see their action add to their friend's total.

Cultivate Your Growing Circle

Now that we have covered the rules for engaging fundraisers and their donors, we would like to focus on what to do once you succeed, because this is where so many nonprofits fail. They get people excited and involved, have success, and then they do not continue to cultivate the fundraisers and donors. You are creating an ever-widening circle of supporters when you engage in people-to-people fundraising. Do not forget to tend to it!

Rovner and McKee, both of Sea Change Strategies, recommend that you first focus on the personal fundraisers. "Identify the uber-activists who were the voice of your campaign. Find them, thank them, and make them part of your overarching strategy going forward," says McKee. "Make them feel they are part of your organization. Ask them for input and involve them in future people-to-people campaigns from the start. Too often, nonprofits ask, 'Oh, what do we do with those people?' rather than treating them as an extension of the organization."

Then focus on the donors that those uber-activists recruited for you. Seek to get them involved over time, for example, with recurring donations or by asking them to support the fundraiser in future efforts. Keep in mind that it is that relationship with the fundraiser, rather than your organization, that was (and may continue to be) the reason for their support.

Here are some ways to cultivate your growing circle over time:

- **Thank your fundraisers and your donors, several times.** Thank them as part of the sign-up process for fundraising and the online donation flow. Thank them again when you provide information or a receipt. Thank them again after six months, with stories about what their contribution did.
- **Give your fundraisers ways to thank their own donors.** Give them an easy way to send a personal thank-you.
- **Inform donors.** Send donors who gave to the fundraiser some information that links the fundraiser and their work with what the donor supported.
- **Report and reward fundraisers.** Send your fundraisers a report on the impact they have had and reward them with special recognition or great stories about the difference they made.
- **Ask your fundraisers for their input.** How often do they want to hear from you? What was their experience in helping your organization? What ideas do they have? Keep the conversation going, because you want a relationship with them over time. They are the most important supporters you have.

If you think these points are overly obvious, that is good. But you may be in the minority. We believe that most donors stop giving to charity because of dissatisfaction with how they were treated by the charity rather than personal constraints such as financial problems. The poor service? Too much mail, no thank-you acknowledgments, and little information on how their money was spent.

We cannot think of a better illustration of the importance of the advice we have given here than the story that opened this chapter. Remember our friend with the forgotten donation? Well, he had another thing to say: "How pathetic that I didn't recognize the organization! I'm not the pathetic one, by the way—the charity is. Why didn't they reach out to me? Why didn't they thank me and leverage my relationship to one of their supporters? What a wasted opportunity."

Harsh but true. It is a wasted opportunity!

If you apply the rules in these pages, you will succeed, with great opportunities to create an ever-expanding donor base. Just be sure you are not forgotten after the first gift. Fundraising is not a one-time effort. It is a never-ending process, just like any relationship. We sincerely wish you—and your supporters—the best of luck in cultivating that relationship, for years to come.

ABOUT THE AUTHORS

Katya Andresen is vice president of marketing of Network for Good and author of *Robin Hood Marketing: Stealing Corporate Savvy to Sell Just Causes.*

Bill Strathmann is chief executive officer of Network for Good and is responsible for leading the organization, developing its strategy, securing its future through fundraising and earned income, and managing its board and external partnerships. Formerly with BearingPoint, Bill provided strategic planning and business improvement consulting to corporations and nonprofit organizations across the nation. From 1995 to 2002, Bill was with Andersen Business Consulting, where he developed and led a consulting practice serving national nonprofits including the Nature Conservancy, National Geographic Society, National Association of Home Builders, and the United Way. Most recently, Bill managed corporate mergers, such as The Sports Authority's acquisition by then Gart Sports and the acquisition of NCNG from Progress Energy by Piedmont Natural Gas. Bill serves on the board of Network for Good, The Anacostia Watershed Society, and The Camp Shohola Scholarship Fund. Throughout his career, Bill has spoken and written on topics including strategic planning, Internet strategy, performance management, mergers and acquisitions, knowledge management, and socially responsible business. Bill has a bachelor's degree in philosophy from Haverford College and a master's degree in business administration from the Darden School at the University of Virginia.

NOTES

1. R. B. Cialdini, *Influence: Science and Practice* (Boston: Allyn & Bacon, 2001)
2. Source is an e-book written by Seth Godin, and self-published: http://sethgodin. typepad.com/seths_blog/files/flippingfunnelPRO.pdf
3. K Andresen, *Robin Hood Marketing: Stealing Corporate Savvy to Sell Just Causes* (Jossey-Bass, 2006) Page 181
4. K Andresen, *Robin Hood Marketing: Stealing Corporate Savvy to Sell Just Causes* (Jossey-Bass, 2006) Page 181
5. Source: ePhilanthropy Foundation at www.ephilanthropy.org
6. Chronicle of Philanthropy, June 15, 2006. Available online at http://www.philan-thropy.com/premium/articles/v18/i17/17001901.htm
7. Study by Network for Good, 2006, available at www.networkforgood.org
8. Source: http://www.cravermathewssmith.com/services.php?id = 61
9. K Andresen, *Robin Hood Marketing: Stealing Corporate Savvy to Sell Just Causes* (Jossey-Bass, 2006) Page 146

CHAPTER 6

Online Tools to Manage Special Events, "-Athons," and Auctions

Jon Carson
cMarket

MANAGING EVENTS THE "OLD WAY"

Nonprofit organizations have turned increasingly to special events to raise more funds. Long gone are the days in which the annual dinner was a boring event whose major donors sponsored the obligatory table and patted themselves on the back for a job well done. In the 1990s, these events expanded to multidimensional "galas" with auctions (silent and live), journals, raffles, live entertainment, and other activities. In fact, it is not uncommon for large organizations to raise in excess of $1 million from a single gala event. Although organizations initially used Excel and Word to manage ticket sales and guest lists for these events, they now need event-focused software to manage the complexity of the expanded activities.

In the past, to organize a team for an "-athon," the captain would typically circulate a sign-up sheet and entice friends and family to sponsor or participate. The sponsorship was usually based on some measure of performance, such as a $1 for each mile walked. The participant would collect payment after the event, based on the final result. Unfortunately, the collection process was easier said than done. Collecting pledges was often time consuming and could not be completed until after the event. As a result, organizations usually received the money well after the event took place and then had to manually process the donations, many of which were in small bills and coins. Reconciling payment forms with bank deposits, tracking who had responded and who had not, became a labor-intensive part of the event management process that reduced the event's net profit. Although organizations may have been able to obtain some pledges in advance, there was little other financial information available prior to the event that would indicate its success, and audit control was basically nonexistent. More often than not, the donors' information was never entered into the organization's donation management system, thereby forsaking future opportunities to prospect potential donors.

HOSTING EVENTS THE "OLD WAY"

Fundraising events are critical to charitable organizations. They perform many obvious and some not-so-obvious functions. Of course, they help provide the revenue necessary to fund the organization's activities. But they also create a sense of community and shared interest among the supporters of a group. They provide a forum for communication, where key messages can be stressed and where ongoing education is delivered. Finally, fundraising events give members the opportunity to express their support in a variety of tangible ways. For example, they can help to organize and promote an event, make a donation, and, in the case of sweepstakes, auctions, and sales, they can purchase goods and services from the charity.

Traditional "in-room" or "live" events include galas, balls, dinners, silent and live auctions, and any number of sports, entertainment, and other activities. These events are invariably one-day or one-evening affairs that present wonderful opportunities for personal contact and communication. However, such live events are limited in their scope in several very important ways. Specifically, their duration is necessarily brief, and they occur in one location. These two factors naturally limit the number of people who can participate. Such constraints that impact attendance inevitably reduce the social, communication, and revenue potential of an event.

ROLE OF THE INTERNET IN EVENTS MANAGEMENT

Toward the latter part of the 1990s, the reach of event management software expanded to the Internet. Registration, which was traditionally a back-office function, now became available on the Web. Instead of receiving registration forms by mail and having staff spend inordinate amounts of time entering names, addresses, and payment information, the Web provided a self-service platform where donors could register and pay online.

The management of galas was transformed by the use of the Internet, as was the management of participatory activities, including bike-athons, walk-athons, and many other "-athons." In the "old days," organizing teams, raising, and collecting money was an administrative nightmare.

The Internet has truly transformed the ways in which events are organized. In the pre-Internet era, solicitation was largely linear. Development or events staff would recruit participants, and those participants would then contact potential sponsors in person, one by one, and ask each one to sign a paper pledge form. By using the Internet to manage an "-athon," potential sponsors can be directed to a registration Web site, thus allowing all contacts to register simultaneously, at a time convenient for them. By empowering people to define their role in an event, organizations have facilitated an open environment in which anyone—not just existing constituents—can participate.

This viral aspect of participation, in which friends invite friends who then invite their friends to participate, can be termed "peer fundraising." It not only broadens support for an event, but it also fosters teambuilding. In the days before the Internet, sponsors were unaware of who else was sponsoring a participant. Some online event sites allow visitors to view team members and donation amounts, both of which may encourage an individual to match or even exceed the level of support provided by other sponsors.

PROVIDERS

A number of firms provide online event and auction management services. Deciding which one is right for you can be a daunting task. To start, it is important to identify the core strengths of each vendor and determine if those strengths relate to your requirements. Although later we go into greater detail in how to define your requirements, you will need to identify a subset of vendors that could be a possible fit. How many vendors should be included within this subset? There is no magic number, although you should probably aim for between two and six vendors.

For online event registration and management, the three leading providers are Convio (www.convio.com), Kintera (www.kintera.com), and GetActive (www.getactive.com). Although all of these vendors offer other online services, such as Content Management Systems (CMS) tools, e-commerce, advocacy, and e-mail management, they also have robust event management platforms. Convio's TeamRaiser™ allows an organization to build a framework to manage an event. Once that aspect of the event is configured, volunteers can use the system's tools to create related Web pages, e-mail communications to mobilize friends and family, and online donation pages with reports for measuring progress. TeamRaiser also offers optional event management tools for posting a calendar to the organization's Web site that displays event listings and allows constituents to register or purchase event tickets online.

With Kintera's "Thon" product, organizations can launch an online event site complete with Kintera's Friends Asking Friends® e-mail capabilities, configurable individual and team pages, donor and participant recognition, donation support, pledging, and comprehensive reporting and bookkeeping services. Event participants can use intuitive front-end tools to create, manage, and monitor a personal fundraising page as well as to e-mail personalized solicitations to friends and family inviting them back to make a donation or become a participant. Kintera also has an Honor Roll™ feature that recognizes online donors and participants by presenting their names and respective contributions in a scrolling window.

Kintera claims to offer 150 separate options, which can be activated through a wizard-driven interface, to accommodate many different types of events. Like many other vendors, Kintera's Web sites can be customized to reflect the look and feel of the organization's own Web site.

GetActive, although known more for its strengths in online advocacy and outreach, also offers robust events management functionality through a partnership with Artez Interactive, one of the pioneer firms in online team fundraising. GetActive's events module includes event calendars, registration pages, goal tracking, ticket purchasing, personalized invitations, and reporting. The system supports multiple types of events, and can be adapted to manage workplace and community "-athon" campaigns specifically designed to help rally peer groups around shared causes. GetActive's online features support individual and team peer events through both gift and pledge-based online fundraising tools.

Products and services available to organizations from these providers and others are listed in the next table.

Organization Name	Description	Web Site URL
Active Networks	An online community where participants can discover, learn about, share, and register in activities they are interested in.	www.active.com
AuctionPay	Offers a complete event fundraising solution that includes event management software, an online registration and donation service, and on-site payment processing the day of the event.	www.auctionpay.com
Convio	Provides online Constituent Relationship Management (eCRM) solutions for nonprofit organizations. Convio recently acquired GetActive, a provider of online communication tools for membership organizations	www.convio.com
First Giving	Helps individuals build Web sites and promotions for fundraising efforts that support nonprofit organizations.	www.firstgiving.com
Kintera	Social constituent relationship management (CRM) system enables organizations to quickly and easily reach more people, raise more money, and run more efficiently.	www.kinterainc.com

ONLINE PRODUCTS THAT HOST AND MANAGE EVENTS

Online applications can be used to manage and promote charitable events to yield great results. However, the Internet is not limited to a supporting role. Charitable events of all types, especially auctions, can be extended to the Internet, making them universally available, 24 hours a day, seven days a week. A Web event can stand on its own or can enhance and promote an upcoming live event. Online events bring features and functions to the planning and execution of a fundraising event that simply cannot be duplicated at a live event or through traditional means of promotion and communication.

On the sponsorship front, every charitable organization values the contributions made to it by businesses. The generosity of community-conscious commercial enterprises is important to virtually every nonprofit. However, the trend in corporate financial support is toward sponsorship rather than giving, such that businesses are interested in helping nonprofits, but also wish to be recognized by the membership at large for their help.

Online events, and e-mails promoting those events, make it possible for organizations to include logos and other messages in their Internet communications. These clearly announce the support of a business and can be "clickable" so that bidders are directed to the business's Web site. This clear communication offers sponsors a demonstrable benefit and rewards long-term supporters and attracts new ones. Messaging is clear, spread over weeks rather than the hours of a live event, and clearly associates the commercial brand with the cause.

A classic example of extending an event into the Internet is the online auction. Pioneered by eBay, Internet auctions are a familiar and extraordinarily popular way of offering goods and services for sale. Because auctions (both silent and in-room) are a traditional part of charitable fundraising, their online counterparts are a natural addition to any organization's fundraising plans. People understand and enjoy this means of making purchases.

Many online auctions are hosted in conjunction with a live event. This strategy has a number of advantages such as an online auction that attracts participation outside the geographical and temporal limits of an event. People who cannot attend, or prefer not to attend, an in-room fundraising event can often participate in one that is offered online. Studies have shown that a significant portion of the bidders in charitable online auctions prefer the anonymity and convenience of bidding online. As a result, not only are practical limits avoided, but psychological ones are as well.

Certain types of organizations benefit greatly from online events. Alumni associations are an excellent example of a group with dispersed members. Online auctions can engage and include all individuals in these groups, regardless of their whereabouts.

An online auction that precedes a live event supplements even the most effective promotional strategies that Web sites and e-mail offer. Posting items online encourages bidding enthusiasm for items and drives activity online. It also promotes attendance at the upcoming live auction. Online auction strategies that offer a mix of bidding opportunities can maximize this effect. For instance, some items may be available only online, whereas others are simply described on the online auction Web site and put up for bid at the live event. Online auctions can combine these different approaches by accepting bids online, but keeping the item open for bids at the live event.

The impact of online postings prior to a live event is considerable. Good online auction software will permit bidders to also become donors, contributing items that they wish to see auctioned off. They can submit these items online, make cash donations directly through the auction Web site, buy tickets to live events, and even offer to pay for all or a portion of an item's cost when it has not been fully donated to the charitable auction. All of these opportunities to become more deeply involved in an organization contribute to the loyalty and commitment of the membership.

The ease with which a bidder can "forward to a friend" information about an interesting item is a boon to the viral effects of promoting events online. The contagious nature of auction fever and the playful but competitive spirit of charitable giving is very real. Bidders often report terrific enthusiasm for unusual items discovered online.

Online auctions are also fun. They create a sense of friendly competition and community that is infectious. In its 2006 Charitable Online Auction Bidder Analysis, cMarket carefully studied the motivations and preferences of charitable auction online bidders.[1] It was found that, in the broadest sense, bidder focus can be characterized in three ways: by

1. Their impulse to give
2. Their interest in receiving something in return
3. The personal experience they enjoy online

Sixty-seven percent of all cMarket survey respondents cited lending support to the causes that are important as "a" primary motivator in bidding during an online auction. In a similar query regarding "the" primary reason for bidding online, 59 percent cited "donating to a worthy cause." These responses clearly demonstrate that generosity and involvement in a cause is first and foremost in the minds of bidders.

Another frequent response to a question about motivation was "an" interest in purchasing great products and services at the auction (50 percent). This response came from several segments of the surveyed population. Again, in a query asking for "the" primary motivator in bidding online at a charitable auction, 27 percent cited "looking for a deal." Clearly the "shopping" element of the experience is important.

Finally, a consistently sizable number of respondents described their experience online and their reactions to that experience as important. This result suggests that the fact that the auction occurs online is, in and of itself, significant. It appears that because online auctions offer a wide variety of personal experiences, they appeal to a diverse psychographic group. Among respondents asked for "the" primary reason for bidding at an online charitable auction, 11 percent cited "having fun" and "entertainment."

Clearly, there is an underlying pleasure and satisfaction to the online auction experience. Additionally, the convenience and control that bidders enjoy add to the value they derive from making charitable contributions at online auctions. It is an important and involving part of the experience, and encourages participation both in the auction and in the organization that hosts it.

To recap, online charitable auctions appeal to a variety of donors and potential donors of charitable causes. They offer a wide range of experiences and satisfy a number of motivations among charitable contributors. In fact, the dimensions of their appeal are remarkable. Very different preferences and motivations move bidders toward goals that are critical to charitable organizations: raising funds, attracting new supporters and members, and building community. Online charitable auctions extend their appeal to an audience that very few others could satisfy with a single approach.

The geographic limitations of live events and their finite time constraints are largely alleviated by online auctions, which allow extended fundraising and national (even international) appeal. Online functions also provide the personal control and freedom to manage the donor's involvement in ways that a live event cannot. Twenty-four-hour, seven-day-a-week availability along with some degree of anonymity provides bidders with a level of freedom that they could not enjoy at a live event. As a result, an online event can attract new supporters by eliminating geographic and time constraints, and by also adding participants from a broader range of demographic and psychographic profiles.

Online events also build a sense of community and loyalty. The connections that bidders develop with the auction and its participants, its cause and the cause's message, are undeniable. The extended exposure and involvement of bidders expands an organization's reach and engages members in ways that live events cannot.

Fundraising is also a key element to the importance of online auctions in any organization. These online events foster unique means of fundraising, through the sale and donation of items and the solicitation of sponsorships, in meaningful ways. They promise the fun of bargain hunting and the excitement of competitive bidding. They are clearly an entertaining way to give. Thus, online auctions should become a strategic element in an organization's membership and fundraising plans. An online auction can expand the appeal of a live event as well as contribute considerably on its own. Most important, an online auction will appeal to motivators and preferences across a wide range of current and potential members, attracting interest from new and valued supporters.

PROCESS REQUIREMENTS

How would you go about managing your events online? The first thing you would need to do is to define your requirements. Although you are most likely capable of identifying most of your event management needs, it is always best to get input from other groups within your organization. Creating cross-functional groups will help you get the buy-in and support from others, both of which are critical because all of you need to be on the same page to make this work. Broad participation in the project also ensures that all of the institution's needs are addressed, from marketing, to development, to programs.

You and your group would then review all events and segment them into their various components. For example, a gala might consist of a dinner, an auction, a journal, and a raffle. Boil down each of these components to specific requirements. For example, an auction might have specific requirements, such as "Create an online bid sheet" or "Track and manage all donated items." Do not be afraid to drill down even further and get very specific, such as: "Store name, address, phone number, and e-mail address for all in-kind donors."

Once you have created this listing, you can put the requirements, grouped by function, into a grid similar to the next table.

Requirement	Y/N/M	Comment
1.1 TEAM BUILDING		
1.1.1 Allow anyone online to create a new team or join an existing team.		
1.1.2 Allow each sponsor to prevent his or her amount from displaying online.		

As indicated, each requirement can be numbered for easier reference. Then, for each vendor that is being considered, you can create a column that records whether the vendor's product can meet that requirement ("Y"), cannot meet that requirement ("N"), or can possibly meet the requirement if the software is modified ("M"). Last, a column can be used to record any comments that will help you decide which software elements might be best used to manage the relationship with each vendor.

Once you have created this grid, you will need to decide how to go about evaluating the various online service providers. We recommend one of three approaches. In the first approach, you could consider issuing a formal request for proposal (RFP) in which you would send a formal document to each vendor. Included in the RFP would be an overview of your organization, a brief narrative of the various events that you hope to manage online, a checklist of requirements and requests for such items as a listing of the available reports, a statement describing their technical support options, and, perhaps, samples of the vendor's training manual. Most important, you would also provide a deadline for vendors to respond with the materials requested.

An RFP is helpful if you are a large organization with complicated requirements. If you are a smaller organization without complex requirements, it might be difficult to justify the time that you would invest in preparing the RFP. Similarly, vendors may not take the time to respond if the total amount of the deal is not large enough. Therefore, if you feel you do not warrant a full-blown RFP, as a second option, you might consider sending a request for information (RFI) to the vendors. The RFI is simply a request for a basic amount of information on services and prices offered. Many times a vendor can respond to an RFI by sending standard marketing literature supplemented with custom pricing.

The third option is to bypass the RFP and RFI and head straight into vendor demonstrations. Prepare a use-case scenario that each vendor must follow. The scenarios should contain a broad cross-section of functionality that you require. Use names, events, and scenarios that are realistic to will help you visualize how you could actually use the system in managing your events. Remember, it is important to evaluate each solution in terms of currently defined requirements, although you should also keep in mind your future needs. Most of all, do not be swayed by exciting features that do not address your business requirements.

Once you have settled on a system that meets your operational and budget requirements, do not forget to do your due diligence. Check out the vendor's references. What problems have other organizations had, and how did the vendor respond? How is the technical support? Have clients been successful in using their product?

As you finalize your decision, make sure you give some thought to how you will protect and safeguard your organization's data. With any firm that houses your data, you must be sure that the data are secure. You need to ask such questions as whether the vendor properly stores credit card data and processes your credit card payments. Does it comply with the credit card industry's guidelines and regulations, such as Payment Card Industry (PCI) and Cardholder Information Security Program (CISP) compliance?

Before you sign on the dotted line, make sure that there are ownership and privacy statements concerning your data. Ensure that your organization owns all of the data that the vendor collects on your behalf. Should you decide to switch vendors at some point, you want to have full access to the data in a standard database format.

And now for the worst-case scenario: What happens to you and your data if the vendor goes out of business? Can you get the software so you can continue to run it in the short term until you find another vendor? To protect your organization, see if the vendor can place a copy of the source code in escrow and give you a perpetual license to run the software.

As a final caveat, be aware of contractual red flags. Do not pay more up front than you have to. Do not agree to payment and delivery schedules that appear to be unreasonable. Give yourself an out, and do not sign any long-term commitments.

You have done it! You are moving your events online. It is time to plan for the implementation. Hold your breath: The fun has only just begun!

ABOUT THE AUTHOR

Jon Carson is the chief executive officer of cMarket, the leading online auction platform for nonprofit fundraising. He is a nationally recognized entrepreneur with a passion for mission-based social entrepreneurship. Other than brief stints at Boeing and McKinsey & Company, he has always worked on new ventures. He has founded and profitably sold three companies in which no investor has ever lost money. Cumulatively, Jon has returned in excess of $175 million to investors, cash on cash. He is a graduate of Babson College and the Yale School of Management.

NOTE

1. Source: http://www.cmarket.com/docs/cMarket_bidder_study.pdf

Relationships Take Two: Donor-Centered Stewardship

Jon Thorsen
Kintera

David Lawson
Kintera

Stewardship is a critical element of the development process. Few would argue that providing adequate and appropriate attention to our key supporters needs to be a priority. This may, in fact, be the primary area where the people-to-people approach can make a significant—and lasting—difference in developing the donor relationship. Yet for too long we have established systems, processes, and even staffing models that either remove the emphasis from stewardship or approach it from the wrong perspective.

BUT ENOUGH ABOUT ME . . .

Every development professional needs to attend to the priorities—particularly the funding priorities of her or his organization. Securing support for the most pressing needs is a central component of our work. Traditionally, this has led to models that address the solicitation cycle as a three-stage process: identification, cultivation, and solicitation.

For most gift officers, this is a logical model, since the desired end of their work is making the successful solicitation and securing the gift. There is, after all, a bottom line to development work, and the most common measure of progress—individually and for the development group as a whole—is expressed in terms of a dollar goal. Did we reach our target amount? Did we make the required number of visits, send out the adequate number of proposals, bring in the necessary number of dollars?

Systems that approach the solicitation cycle as a series of moves designed to position donors where we would like them to be are a logical outgrowth of this model. If a certain number of dollars needs to be raised for certain projects, then we need to move a certain group of donors to support those projects at certain levels. But the emphasis of this approach is decidedly one-sided, evaluating our dollar goal, our programmatic needs, our modes and methods of interaction with potential supporters. At a very real level, this model depersonalizes the interchange, on both sides. Donors become the means to an end; gift officers become interchangeable.

It is easy to see how stewardship can be overlooked in such a model. When we incent gift officers primarily—or solely—according to the number of dollars they raise, then the gift becomes the end of the process for them. But for the donor, the gift is the start of their relationship with the organization, or at least the start of a new type of relationship.

The most effective systems recognize both the need for internal efficiency and the focus on external relationships. The "people-to-people" approach becomes paramount, as we learn to place the donor's interests and philanthropic goals above the (often limited range of) organizational needs. Paul Pribbenow, an academic, explains:

> *Moves management is a process that has two broad purposes. First, it is designed to honor the relationship a donor has with an institution or organization by ensuring that the institution recognizes and documents the "history" of the relationship. Second, the program encourages strategic thinking on behalf of the institution to further donor relationships and appropriate cultivation processes.*[1]

Effective stewardship should be a natural outcome of a responsible moves management—or relationship management—approach. It requires a thoughtful and intentional focus on the donor relationship and a full-scale shift of perspective. Considering the donor's interests and aspirations above those of the organization can be challenging, but there is no doubt that it can prove effective in securing long-term investment in the organizational mission.

It is also clear that our supporters are expecting this level of attention—because they are receiving it elsewhere. And experience raises expectations.

CAN YOU HEAR ME NOW?

Do we want to know what donors want, or do we really want them to want what we need? We start the process by reviewing what the donor has given to in the past and what other prior activities might indicate current interests. This approach works all right if the current needs match up well to past involvement, but when they do not, this method begins to break down.

Surveys are utilized to try to gauge current interests, but these surveys are normally designed more to gather facts than feelings. Yet it is often feelings that influence a person to give at higher levels. Companies like Southwest Airlines actually measure customer happiness; it is no surprise that Southwest is almost always rated the most-liked airline.

Donors are just like the rest of us. What we crave is the ability to tell people with whom we are communicating exactly what *we* are interested in. We do not want to be tied to what we did in the past, and most assuredly we do not want someone else telling us what we should be doing with our money. Today's people-to-people fundraising approach requires respectful two-way communication of thoughts, ideas, opinions—and yes, feelings.

Until the Internet, we had to wait patiently for businesses to contact us with surveys or, on rare occasions, to talk with us directly. This was looked on as an intrusion into our limited time, so we limited our participation.

Then Web sites started posing such questions as "What kind of books do you read?" and in an instant we were provided with exactly what we were looking for. At the same time, shopping cards appeared that tracked our purchases and then provided us with coupons for merchandise we actually wanted.

What fundraisers need to focus on is creating real-time two-way communication that empowers donors to provide invaluable data on an ongoing basis. Some of this results from face-to-face interaction with our supporters, but we can do it on a much broader basis by tracking what information people view on our Web sites, assessing what stories engage them, asking their opinions using online surveys, and giving them options for what material they would like to receive from us, in what form. By listening when people tell us what is important to them, we not only intuit what they *do not* want more data about, we personalize our approach by respecting their priorities.

One note of caution: Do not ask questions if you are not willing to respond, in real time, with the answers. The only thing more frustrating than not being heard is being heard but not understood. As Kathleen D. Vohs, Nicole L. Mead, and Miranda R. Goode, academics and co-authors of The Psychological Consequences of Money (2006, Science, 314 [5802] 1154–1156), explain: "The mere presence of money changes people. The effect can be negative, it can be positive. Exposure to money, or the concept of money, elevates a sense of self-sufficiency, and can make people less social."[2]

MONEY CHANGES EVERYTHING

Remember the last time you said about a new restaurant "Let's try it for lunch before we go there for dinner?" When we do this, what we are saying is "I am willing to pay a little to find out if I want to pay a lot."

That is exactly what donors are doing when they make small donations. They are making a small gift to find out if they want to make a larger commitment. Unfortunately, unlike a restaurant that knows what the diner is doing and serves high-quality food and provides excellent service at lunch, nonprofits too often provide the worst service to small donors and serve a tasteless soup of generic messages.

The best-case scenario for nonprofits that fail to understand the importance of delivering a great experience to small donors is for the donor to continue to giving at the lower level. Back to our restaurant example, these donors see your organization as "fast charity" that provides some value but does not deserve a bigger commitment. Of course, the other choice is to stop giving altogether.

Now that we have you hungry, let's examine what is going on inside the donor's mind when a donation is made. Depending on the donor's financial circumstances, and his or her personal feelings about money, expectations are set about what a nonprofit should do when a certain amount of money is given.

For some wealthy individuals, there may not be a high level of expectation even when a five-figure gift is made, while others expect a high level of interaction even with a small donation. You have to listen to your donors carefully, because too much or too little interaction can end the relationship. If you rush a donor to the next level before he or she is ready, you could short-circuit the entire relationship. However, if you do not provide the next level of service in time, the relationship ends anyway.

A common mistake is to think that what worked at one level of giving will work at another. That is like serving lunch portions at dinner. When the transition is made from a low-commitment donation to a high-commitment one, you need a plan for how you are going to transition the relationship.

Most organizations have this plan for dramatic increases in giving, but the move may be more subtle, with a donor going from $50 to $500, advocating for your cause, requesting information about your planned giving program, attending an event, becoming a volunteer, or registering to participate in your online community. Keep in mind that the most valuable asset we all possess is not the money in our bank accounts but rather our time. The richer we are, the higher the dollar value that time represents.

Going back to the restaurant example: Be sure that you provide a great experience at all levels of giving and involvement. Provide donors with multiple ways to communicate their current interests and needs. Be sure to act on this information promptly. There are a lot of choices to make a difference. If you are not careful, you could find your donors giving at another establishment all too soon.

SHOW ME (MORE THAN) THE MONEY

Regardless of the size of gift they make, donors want to know what their donations accomplish. Fiscal accountability among nonprofits is an issue that has gained prominence in recent years as donors demand more responsible stewardship of the dollars they contribute.

The Internet makes it easier for us to report back to donors in a quick, informative, and dynamic manner. For example, a disaster relief organization can post a stewardship report online and provide a link to that page in the acknowledgments it generates for online donors. The URL can also be listed in hard-copy acknowledgments sent to offline donors.

This report would contain the latest information of the organization's response to the disaster and how the money it has collected has been used in that response. Similar models can be used by other types of organizations. Arts groups can post photos of works acquired or play clips of recent concerts, plays, or recitals.

As the level of gift grows, the personalization and complexity of online stewardship reporting can increase as well. Expectations rise with the ask amount, and our response needs to change accordingly. Sending a streaming video of a popular lecture by a professor who occupies an endowed chair to the donors who created that endowment will be more meaningful than a number of thank-you notes from the development officer or president.

Utilizing a site that requires supporters to log in, we can provide information that is both more sensitive and more personal. Imagine showing our supporters, in a single space, the sum of their contributions: the gifts they have made, the volunteer hours they have contributed, the other members of the community with whom they have interacted on boards and committees, the advocacy actions they have taken on our behalf. Then imagine tying those contributions to outcomes: for each gift listed, a link to something it made possible; for each volunteer activity, a link to the result of that effort; for each advocacy action taken, the organizational activity it advanced.

Creating a more tangible connection between donors and what their contributions produce creates not only a sense of accountability, but a connection that enhances their relationship to the organization. More important, donors feel invested in the mission of the charities they support when they see the manifestation of that mission.

Too often in development, we confuse the ends with the means. Just as the gift is not the end of the relationship with the donor, the number of dollars raised is not the end of the work we do. The money is the means to enacting the mission.

Creating that clear and visceral link between the donor and the mission is at the core of successful stewardship. That is the link that can continue to develop long after the development officer who landed the gift had moved to another organization, the campaign during which the gift was made has ended, and the funding priorities of the organization have shifted. The faces will change and the projects will evolve, but the mission will endure.

Attending to relationships with donors is not only an obligation, it is a sound business practice that requires continuous attention. Advancing the relationship between supporters and the organization is really our goal: Relationships are what we should be developing in "development."

Perhaps the least unique thing any nonprofit does is ask for money. Our real opportunity to distinguish ourselves—and the mission we are advancing—is between the times we solicit. Donors want to feel that they are making a difference, both in the general emotional sense, and also—and more increasingly—in a demonstrable, tangible manner.

Delivering on donor needs and expectations provides us with the credibility necessary to seek increased levels of commitment from them. We can relate to this on a personal level. We are far more likely to develop a serious relationship with someone who clearly understands and appreciates our needs. This does not require that person to sublimate his or her own needs; relationships are a two-way street. But if we show the appropriate level of sensitivity and appreciation, things are likely to develop in a positive manner.

Contributing to a cause is, as we have discussed, an emotional decision, perhaps even more than we have suspected. As Holly Hall, an academic, explains: "The warm glow that many donors get from giving to charity involves the same brain mechanisms that evoke pleasurable sensations after sex, eating good food, and using heroin or other drugs, a new study has found."[3]

The band Roxy Music told us that "Love is the Drug," but perhaps they should have taken a close look at philanthropy before making that determination. Developing continuous relationships with people who obtain enjoyment from contributing to our missions is not only an obligation; it is a privilege.

RELATIONSHIP OR RELATIONSHIPS?

Personal relationships are initially managed by one person. That person might be in a particular part of the organization, such as a school at a university or a chapter of an organization. The person might also be responsible for a certain level of donation.

Often at the moment a relationship starts to deepen, the person who began working with the donor is replaced by someone higher up in the organization. The irony is that we do this because the donor is so important, but in fact what donors want is a single point of contact. They are seeking personalized attention, which is of course best embodied by a single body with whom to interact. Person-to-person fundraising relies on the most immediate, focused, and specialized attention, and that is what our supporters—particularly our most loyal and generous supporters—deserve.

Instead, many organizations will assign multiple points of contact for different areas of interest and/or levels of giving. In a major university, this can create the phenomenon of the annual fund, campaign, school, alumni association, and athletics coming at the donor throughout the year. Suddenly instead of a single person, the donor has multiple contacts, and the result is a fractured relationship with the organization.

Once you have established a multiple-contact relationship, you have the problem of communicating the donor's interests and feelings within the organization. The donor sees the organization as one entity and expects that if he or she tells one area something, that information is communicated to all other areas.

Donors are increasingly demanding a single point of contact and communication within the organization about their involvement and needs. Succeeding in this environment demands that organizations end the silo model where donors are seen as the possession of a department rather than an asset for the entire organization.

Ask yourself if you can identify all of the communications, offline and online, that were sent to any one donor last year. Too often organizations cannot answer this question. This leads to overcommunication and irrelevant communication. It should be no wonder that donors do not respond to what you feel they should because they are being overwhelmed with communications that are not what they want.

To achieve more meaningful interaction, you should be able to coordinate your messages so donors have a clear idea of how each area of your organization interacts with the others. The goal is for donors to feel they have one primary point of contact who can quickly bring other individuals into the relationship to address specific needs, as appropriate to each donor's wishes. Joe Pilotta, a former professor, explains:

> *Engagement has both a process and a product component. The process component relates to the conjoining of sensory modalities between the consumer and the technology. The product is the influence generated from the engagement, which can be general or acutely directed.*[4]

The ultimate goal is for donors to have a relationship with the organization, so that even if an individual leaves, the affinity for that organization does not disappear as well. Again, this relationship involves connecting the cause to the commitment—and stewardship is the critical link.

THE MEDIUM *AND* THE MESSAGE

The stereotype of technology is that it leads to an impersonal world filled with robotic actions and interactions. Technology is seen as a barrier to personal contact rather than a means of advancing relationships. In fact, proper use of technology can—and should—be part of a strategy for personalized communication with our supporters, regardless of where they may be located. Results of a Pew Internet and American Life Project indicate that:

> [t]he internet and e-mail play an important role in maintaining these dispersed social networks. Rather than conflicting with people's community ties, we find that the internet fits seamlessly with in-person and phone encounters. With the help of the internet, people are able to maintain active contact with sizable social networks, even though many of the people in those networks do not live nearby.[5]

Technology is enabling user-controlled actions leading to an unprecedented level of very personalized interactions. For nonprofits, this link provides an incredible opportunity to provide donors with a rewarding experience that makes giving the best thing our supporters can do with their money and time.

Early attempts to use technology to deliver a nonprofit's message were not much more than brochureware filled with generic images and messages aimed at no one in particular. They had little or no impact, and led many fundraisers to think that this proved technology was not going to work with donors.

Similarly, just posting a Web site has limited effect. Some see establishing a Web presence as a means of sending multiple public services announcements. In fact, it is like setting up a billboard on a cul-de-sac: It may garner a lot of attention, but only among those who drive to the location. It is our responsibility not only to encourage others to steer toward our sites, but also to make sure they come away feeling the visit was worth the trip.

Today what we are seeing is technology combined with segmentation to deliver custom communication. Bringing these three elements together creates the medium for your message.

For segmentation to work, you need to break down your organization into its logical pieces, understanding that the logic is applied from the donor perspective. For a university, this could simply mean presenting the various departments in which an individual may have an interest. For some organizations, it could be dividing content by the constituencies they serve. Consider how your supporters will look for information, and make it easy for them to find it through effective segmentation.

Once you have the segments, the next step is creating the right messages. The number-one thing people want to know from those who contact them is "Who are you?" Clearly stating your organizational mission on your Web site's home page—the most valuable virtual real estate you possess—is therefore vital.

The next question is "Why should I care?" Again, making it clear to interested parties what contributions your organization makes—particularly unique contributions—helps to distinguish your cause and encourage these parties to support it.

Finally, anticipate the question "Can I trust you?" Donors have an ever-increasing range of options for directing their charitable dollar. Emerging from the crowd is important; inspiring confidence is even more crucial. Make it easy for visitors to your site to understand how you fulfill your mission, responsibly and effectively. For donors, customize the content according to the interests they have demonstrated.

Understand, too, that people process information in very different ways and use multiple techniques to engage them. Communication is much more than words; it involves images and sounds as well. As we move into a world of personal technology, people expect to receive multilevel communications customized to their unique needs. The Class of '69 wants to read about their time at the university, complete with images of the campus when they were there and such sounds as the voice of a favorite professor. A donor to a museum expects to not only see the art, but also learn about the artists and hear from them when possible.

Another challenge this new world creates is the need for change. What worked so well yesterday can quickly stop working today. Thus, you have to build change into your communication plan. This is a good time to think like Disney. It is no coincidence that every time you visit Disney World there is construction going on. They want you to enjoy what they have but also be intrigued about what is coming so you will come back. They also knew when "Tomorrowland" had become "yesterday," and responded with significant changes.

We all know that a nonprofit's mission is never complete. There will always be people to educate, heal, feed, inspire, and otherwise help. This is why it is so important to maintain relationships. Nonprofits need donors to continue to support them, and at even greater levels. For a relationship to grow and flourish, it needs to evolve as both the individual and organization change.

When discussing people-to-people fundraising, it may seem counterintuitive to emphasize technology, which for many years added a layer of complexity and removal to personal relationships. But the promise of today's technology is to provide a platform for interactive two-way communication where the donor and the nonprofit form a lasting relationship based on mutual respect, understanding, and trust. Truly effective stewardship contributes to, and benefits from, this approach.

ABOUT THE AUTHORS

David Lawson is vice president for market strategy at Kintera, Incorporated, a leading provider of software as a service to the nonprofit market. David is the cofounder of the *WOW! Institute* and founder of *Prospect Information Network* (PIN). He is a frequent presenter at local and national conferences of the Association of Professional Researchers for Advancement, the Association of Fundraising Professionals, and the Council for Advancement and Support of Education.

Jon Thorsen is vice president of strategic solutions at Kintera, Incorporated, where he works with clients to develop coordinated online strategies. Jon is a former president of the Association of Professional Researchers for Advancement and received APRA's Distinguished Service Award in 1999. He is a frequent presenter at meetings of professional associations in the fundraising field and serves on the board of directors of the National Schizophrenia Foundation.

NOTES

1. Paul Pribbenow, "Moves Management," *Common Work* newsletter, Johnson, Grossnickle and Associates (February 2005).
2. Kathleen D. Vohs, Nicole L. Mead, and Miranda R. Goode, "The Psychological Consequences of Money," *Science* (November 2006).
3. Holly Hall, "Sex, Drugs, and ... Charity? Brain Study Finds New Links," *Chronicle of Philanthropy*, December 7, 2006.
4. Joe Pilotta, "Who Cares About Engagement?" *Consumer Acquisition* newsletter, BIGresearch, August 15, 2005.
5. Jeffrey Boase, John B. Horrigan, Barry Wellman and Lee Rainie, "The Strength of Internet Ties," Pew Internet and American Life Project, January 25, 2006.

CHAPTER 8

How Individual Supporters Use Online Fundraising Pages to Make a Difference

Mark Sutton
Firstgiving, Inc.

W hen you consider what an organization's supporters can do to help, the three main things that come to mind are contributing (wealth or assets), volunteering, and reaching out to others on behalf of the organization. Involving supporters to reach out to family, friends, and beyond is one of the most proven methods of raising funds.

As it has with so many other things in our lives, the Internet has revolutionized the way an organization's supporters can reach out to "their" communities to garner support. In addition, it has enabled individuals to support organizations they care about in a way that was simply not possible in the past. The evolution and adoption of Web 2.0 and online social networking promise to take the prevalence and success of person-to-person fundraising to new heights in the years to come.

Initially made popular by larger organizations with pledge-based fundraising events, online fundraising pages are now being used by organizations of all sizes to engage their supporters to raise funds, whether they are participating in a walk-athon or raising funds because they would rather help an important cause than receive birthday gifts.

Online fundraising pages have become an essential part of *every* organization's online strategy.

WHAT IS AN ONLINE FUNDRAISING PAGE?

An online fundraising page is the marriage of passion, community, and technology (see Exhibit 8.1). An online fundraising page is a Web page that is created by any individual and used to ask for and accept donations online via credit card or other means for an organization. It is essentially the online version of the old pledge form that fundraisers used to carry around to record pledges from family and friends. The best form of support makes the process of creating an online fundraising page fast and easy for anyone, regardless of their technical knowledge or experience with the Internet.

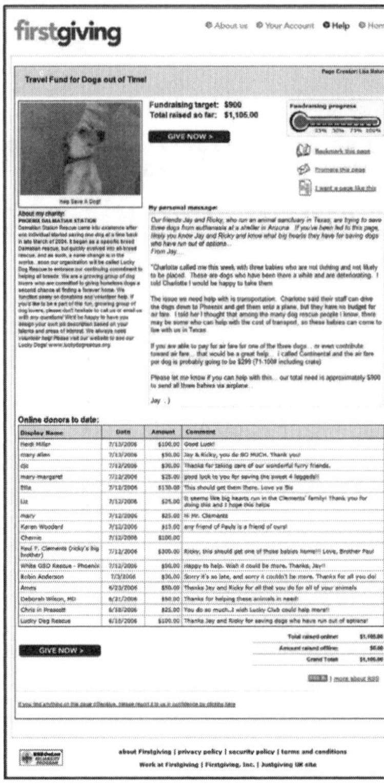

EXHIBIT 8.1 Example of an Online Fundraising Page

The power of an online fundraising page lies in its ability to put a personal face on your organization. In fact, it can put many personal faces on your organization.

An online fundraising page enables your supporters to personalize their appeal by letting them:

- Post personal pictures and images
- Write a personal message about what they are doing to support your organization, why they are doing it, and why they need the help of their family, friends, and colleagues
- State their fundraising target
- Recognize others who are part of their fundraising effort, such as teammates and people they are fundraising in honor of or in memory of
- Display a list of their donors and donors' supportive comments
- Collect funds for your organization

Online fundraising pages enable your organization to harness the passion of individuals to support your organization by making it easy for them to help beyond the size of the check they could write on their own.

The page is asking your supporters to do something other than donate or volunteer (see Exhibit 8.2).

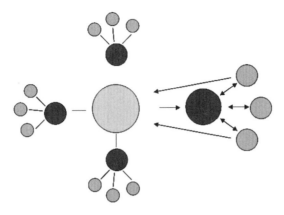

EXHIBIT 8.2 Funds that Fundraisers Can Bring to the Organization in Relation to the Money They Can Donate

LEVERAGE AN INDIVIDUAL SUPPORTER'S SOCIAL NETWORK

The Internet dramatically expands an individual's community and the number of people with whom he or she is able to be connected with.

How many supporters does an organization have in its database? Hundreds? Thousands? Tens of thousands? Whatever is the number, it pales in comparison to the number of the people that you have access to through your supporters' social networks (see Exhibit 8.3).

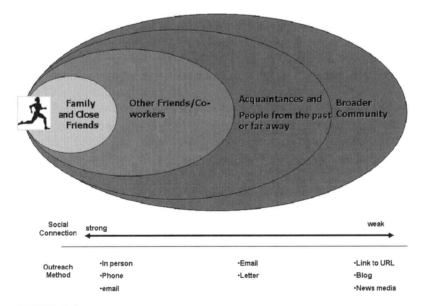

EXHIBIT 8.3 Social Network Diagram
Source: First Giving

British anthropologist Robin Dunbar suggests that an individual's capacity for a social network is roughly 150 people. This number grows substantially when you include people with whom individuals have a weaker relationship, such as those who go to the same church or school, vendors or business partners, people who live in the same town, and so on.

The dynamics of, and developments around, social networking have had a significant impact on how people-to-people fundraising works. The pervasive emergence of online tools, including blogs and social networking sites, has enabled more and more people to tap into the weaker social relationships (to the right side of Exhibit 8.3). In fact, over the past several years, with the growth of social networks and blogs, the broader community very often does not necessarily even rely on personal relationships at all. Instead, it leverages common interests, values, or passions to unite individuals who do not personally know one another and will most likely never meet or form a personal relationship.

By using online fundraising pages, your volunteer fundraisers can raise more money, more easily, for your organization, with greater ease.

LEVERAGE THE PERSONAL CONNECTION

Your supporters' use of online fundraising pages puts a personal face on your cause because an appeal is made on your behalf at a personal and possibly emotional level. Leveraging you supporters' personal relationships, at all levels of strength, is a proven and powerful method for raising funds and engaging others. Donors are compelled to support their friend's efforts in a show of personal loyalty even in cases where they are not familiar with the organization prior to the solicitation. In fact, the lack of familiarity with the organization appears to have little bearing on an individual's decision to make a donation.

The personal connection your supporters have with their networks is so powerful that donors genuinely appreciate being asked to contribute to the point of thanking you for the chance to be included in your fundraising efforts, such as in the following responses:

> *"Thanks for letting us be part of your success, Victor!"*
> *"Thanks for doing it for the kids."*
> *"Thanks for requesting my support."*

How often do organizations get new donors to thank them for the opportunity to make a contribution?

IT'S ALL ABOUT THE ASK

As development professionals know, the way to get the donation is to make an effective ask. The trouble has been that although development professionals are skilled in making the ask, there is no guarantee that your supporters share this ability. In fact, it is probably safe to assume that they do not.

Making the ask is a daunting task for most fundraisers. I speak from both personal experience and from conversations with many fundraisers. Years ago, having been talked into doing a 100-mile charity bike ride by a friend where I had to raise funds (without the benefit of an online fundraising page), I was so apprehensive about the fundraising aspect of the event that I put off making my asks until the week before the ride. I proceeded to ask my direct family and a handful of work colleagues. Needing to get pledges quickly, I simply asked each person for $25. To my relief, each person very gladly gave me the $25 I had asked for, and I raised a total of $225. Decent results, but I realized afterward that I probably should have asked more people for money and that I had not asked each for enough.

I did the same ride the following year. However, this time, I was equipped with an online fundraising page. To my surprise, I raised over $1,200 from 27 people, almost half of whom were from out of state (and would not have been asked without this fundraising page), including 2 from outside the country. The largest donation amount was $200, an amount that I would not have been comfortable asking for face to face. This dramatic difference in results is the norm with online fundraising pages.

I have come to appreciate that my apprehension around making the ask is normal. Putting oneself in the role of fundraiser is a significant commitment. It takes passion, confidence, and guts.

I recall talking to a group of first-time marathoners who had to fundraise as part of their run. One of the runners commented, "I'm not worried about doing the run, it's the thought of raising $2,500 that has me freaked out." This is a pretty common sentiment.

Enabling your supporters to raise funds online will make their lives easier and will ease the uncomfortable aspects of fundraising (i.e., making those asks). This will help you to recruit more supporters to step up and fundraise for your cause.

More Asks

For the average online fundraising page, approximately 33 percent of e-mail asks are answered with a donation. As expected, this conversion ratio declines as the funds raised increases because more asks are made to individuals with weaker connections to the fundraiser. For example, individuals who raise approximately $1,000 (about twice the average) see an ask/donation ratio of between 20 and 25 percent.

Clearly, the success of fundraising efforts really is a function of how many people supporters are reaching out to for assistance and asking for help. With online fundraising pages, supporters are able to reach farther geographically than if they did not fundraise online. Data suggest that approximately 35 percent of donations will come from outside the state where the fundraiser is located.

Online, the ask can be made in a wide variety of ways to best suit your supporters' personalities and comfort level with fundraising. Asks can include:

- **Initial ask** sent via e-mail or by posting a URL or widget for the page on a blog or Web site.
- **Reminder ask.** It is much easier to send another e-mail out to your list of people reminding them that they can help out by making a contribution than to pick up the phone to ask again. In some cases fundraisers simply send an update

on their fundraising progress or athletic training progress if they happen to be running a marathon.

- **Thank-you ask.** After the event or fundraising effort, it is easy to send a much-appreciated thank you to donors for their support along with a summary of your fundraising efforts. Some people who already donated will donate again, and those who did not but intended to will have another opportunity to do so.

CASE STUDY: A MAN ON A MISSION, THE POWER OF THE ASK

In just over a month, Aaron Lieberman has raised $14,000 for the Organization for Autism Research (OAR), an online fundraising page from Firstgiving. His remarkable success demonstrates the endless possibilities when you unite the passion of your supporters with the power of the Internet.

We spoke with Aaron about his online fundraising page (www.firstgiving .com/aaronlieberman), and our conversation gave us insight into the practices of a very savvy online fundraiser. The three keys to Aaron's success were readily apparent: organization, resourcefulness, and persistence. Aaron began putting together his list of people to ask months in advance. He recognized that he would need to e-mail his link to a large number of people in order to raise $10,000; the next step was figuring out how to reach as many people as possible.

Like so many of us, Aaron uses e-mail to keep up with friends, family, colleagues, and clients. When he took the time to gather all of these e-mail addresses, he realized he knew hundreds of people whom he could solicit for a donation to his online fundraising page. Aaron's busy work schedule would have made writing and mailing this many letters all but impossible. By sending his asks out via e-mail, he saved time and money while instantly reaching out to people all over the country.

Aaron raised $10,000 one e-mail at a time. He received 100 individual donations, the largest of which was $500, and most of which were between $25 and $100. The time Aaron took to collect and update his e-mail contacts this year made all the difference, and has made him one of Firstgiving's most accomplished fundraisers this year. Some of his tips for you:

- Plan ahead! Lieberman began his e-mail ask list months in advance.
- Add a link to your online fundraising page to all the e-mails you send out, whatever the overall subject.
- Think big by thinking small: Aaron realized his $10,000 goal could be reached if 500 people gave $20. Thinking this way reminds you that your goals are attainable.
- Remember that you are asking people to support your efforts for a great cause, so do not be shy to ask everyone you know!

Case study written by Dana Hagenbuch.

EXHIBIT 8.4 Ask Screen

Better-Quality Asks

Development professionals recognize the importance of the strategy around the ask. You identify what you believe the individual should be able to give and then proceed to ask for (at least) that amount. It takes skill, experience, and confidence to do this well. It is difficult to expect that *all* individual fundraisers possess the ability to make an effective ask.

An online fundraising page does not require the fundraiser to make targeted asks. Instead, a range of asks is available for donors to select from (see Exhibit 8.4).

While providing a menu of choices may not be the best method for professionals, it is important to remember that your volunteer fundraisers are not professionals. The simplicity of this comfortable approach will be rewarding in that more people will make more and more effective asks.

FUNDRAISER BEST PRACTICES

Fundraisers should aim to have the first two to three donations to their page be substantial ($50 to $100 versus $10 to $25) because the signaling effect to other donors who visit the page will cause them to donate at a higher level.

One strategy for doing this is for fundraisers to send their page to a small group within their network whom they believe will make these higher-level donations before broadly distributing their page to their entire community.

An analysis of nearly 100 fundraising pages shows that for pages where at least one of the first two donations is greater than $25, the average donation for the remaining donations is 73 percent higher than for pages where the first two donations are $25 or less (see Exhibit 8.5).

MATCHING GIFTS

Corporate matching gifts represent an attractive opportunity for most development offices. When a fundraiser uses an online fundraising page to solicit donations,

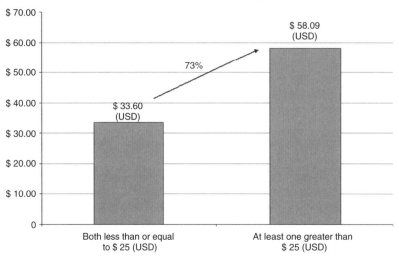

EXHIBIT 8.5 Donation Analysis

donors are asked whether their company will match the donation. This information is collected and reported back to you so you can follow up.

Data show that approximately 5 percent of all donations are eligible for a match. Assuming a $1 to $1 match, this translates into an increase in donations of more than six percent.

If the ask is made offline, the chances are great that the fundraiser will not think to ask about a corporate match, which means a lost opportunity for you both now and in the future.

TAPPING INTO THE BROADER COMMUNITY

On the Internet, this concept of weaker relationships has grown incredibly in the past few years with the explosive growth of blogs and social networking sites like such as MySpace, Facebook, and LinkedIn. These types of sites enable individuals who do not necessarily know one another, but who share common interests, beliefs, passions, friends, or acquaintances, to meet, interact, and maintain a connection over time.

The diagram in Exhibit 8.3 depicts the different types of relationships that all of us have. As you move farther to the right from close friends and family, the relationships become weaker. However, the Internet enables creative fundraisers to reach out and include acquaintances and the broader community in their fundraising activities. The broader community consists of individuals who share common interests or values, not necessarily a personal connection. This linkage has been increasingly the case over the past several years and will continue to develop rapidly in the years ahead.

The shared passion for a particular cause or charity can serve to strengthen the bond between individuals who share just a weak relationships or even no personal relationship at all. These types of situations are becoming increasingly common online and will emerge over the next several years as an essential way to leverage the Internet and people to raise funds for your cause.

These people are guerrilla marketers for your cause. They will post to their blog, e-mail friends, and reach potentially tens of thousands of like-minded individuals to support your cause.

Before the emergence of online communities, blogs, and social networks, individuals would tap in to the broader community by getting a story about their efforts posted in a local newspaper or mentioned at a community gathering. Although this approach did yield some additional donations, it lacked the potential for explosive fundraising potential.

BLOGS: AN IMPORTANT DEVELOPMENT IN FUNDRAISING

Blogs enable an individual or group of individuals to communicate their ideas, opinions, and perspectives to anyone who cares to "listen" or participate in the conversation. The people who listen are typically interested in what the blogger has to say and have a level of respect for that individual's opinion or ideas. At the very least, they share a common interest or passion. It is this dynamic that makes for a powerful fundraising opportunity.

The explosion of blogging activity worldwide has enabled some bloggers to completely modify social network dynamics to the extent they are able to increase donations for a cause from the blogger community Exhibit 8.6 is an example of the possible results of this effect can do in on some cases to the direct e-mail solicitation in Exhibit 8.3.

Following are three case studies of bloggers who used their blog as a platform for fundraising. There are subtle but significant differences between the two examples. In the first case study, the blogger runs an annual fundraising effort. In the second, the blogger reacted quickly to the 2004 tsunami to raise funds for relief efforts.

EXHIBIT 8.6 Social Networking Diagram

CASE STUDY: ANNUAL BLOG FUNDRAISING EFFORT

Three years ago, Pim Techamuanvivit, a well-known food blogger (chezpim .com) based in California, created an online fundraising campaign centered around a raffle of items from foodies to foodies. This community of food bloggers is a global one, using the Internet to share their passion for food, and, in Pim's case, for providing food to those less fortunate. In Pim's words on her fundraising page:

> To us Food Bloggers, food is a joy. On our blogs, we celebrate food as a delight and even an indulgence. Unfortunately, many others who share our world do not share that privilege. For them, food is a matter of survival. This "Menu for Hope" is our small way to help.

Pim launched her first appeal in 2003 with an online fundraising page (www.firstgiving.com/chezpim) simply asking for her readers' support of Doctors Without Borders, resulting in $910 raised. In 2004 she sent another appeal (www.firstgiving.com/meuforhopeunicef), this time raising $1,280 for tsunami relief through UNICEF.

In 2005, Pim tried something new, a raffle of items donated by her readers, supporters, and fellow bloggers (www.firstgiving.com/menuforhopeII), everything from restaurant meals to unusual edible items. She leveraged the community aspect and the flexibility of her online fundraising page by asking participants to make a $5 donation for each "raffle ticket" and to use the donor comment section of the site to indicate which prize they were entering to win. Hundreds of her supporters helped her raise over $17,000 in just a few weeks.

The year 2006 brought another raffle (www.firstgiving.com/menuforhope-III), this time supporting the UN Food Programme. In just 17 days, Pim has raised over $58,000 (as of 12/23/06), again, from a community that was almost entirely online. Many of her readers are bloggers themselves, and they are supporting her cause not only through donated raffle items and monetary donations to Pim's page, but also by posting about Menu for Hope III in their own blogs and inserting links to the raffle page. As of late December 2006, there are 719 blogs linking to Pim's fundraising page.

Pim's campaigns are a fantastic example of creativity, community, and technology coming together to great results.

Case study written by Laurel Ackerman.

Online fundraising pages can also be used effectively to act quickly in the wake of a natural disaster. It is simply a matter of having the right technology available to harness an individual's passion or desire to act. This next case study highlights an example of blogging in the weeks following the 2004 tsunami.

CASE STUDY: DISASTER RELIEF BLOG FUNDRAISING EFFORT

On December 26, 2004, after a tsunami of catastrophic proportions struck in Southeast Asia, people all over the globe asked the question "What can I do to help?" Edward Morrissey of Captains Quarters blog (www.captains-quartersblog.com/mt/) answered that question by declaring a Captain's Quarters "World Relief Day" and called on all of the readers of his blog to contribute their take-home pay for that day to World Vision, a well-known charity involved with the relief efforts. The personal message to readers of his blog from Edward's personal fundraising page (www.firstgiving.com/cq) follows.

> *CQ readers, fellow bloggers, and friends,*
>
> *We have before us one of the world's greatest natural disasters in terms of lost human life. Over 120,000 now (12/31) have perished, and unless we get immediate and effective assistance to the survivors, many more will die.*
>
> *Our friends around the world have given of themselves through their governments, and the US has also risen to the challenge. Our government has pledged $35 million to date, as well as ordering thousands of our military personnel and two US Navy task forces to the Indian Ocean region to provide assistance.*
>
> *However, many people question the ability of capitalist-based economies to show any generosity. Americans, and other Western people, have been judged by the amount of government assistance provided. We've been called "stingy." It's up to us to show that when people control their own resources, we can put it to the best use through our own decisions—and in fact, we can put it to better, more direct, and more effective use. At Captain's Quarters, we're declaring January 12th World Relief Day. I ask that CQ readers donate their take-home pay for January 12th to the tsunami relief effort. Obviously, we cannot hope to match the funds raised by governments—but we can show what a handful of determined private individuals can do to help. If you can't afford to donate all of your take-home pay for that day, please donate what you can. Let's show our friends in Asia that they can count on us to lift them out of danger and destruction, and show the power of the individual to change the world for the better. On behalf of the First Mate and I, I offer you our deepest gratitude.*

In the weeks after the tsunami, leading up to the declared "World Relief Day," roughly 300 people visited the page and made a donation. In all, over $35,000 was raised for World Vision for the relief efforts.

ONLINE COMMUNITIES

Online communities are also emerging at incredible rates. Similar to blogs or social networks, these communities are areas for individuals with common passions or interests to interact. The power of these communities was highlighted by an incredible charitable out pouring from fans of a popular BBC show whose host was injured in an accident.

CASE STUDY: ONLINE FUNDRAISING PAGE BY RICHARD HAMMOND FAN RAISES £190,000 IN SEVEN DAYS

FUNDRAISING POWER OF ONLINE COMMUNITIES

The fundraising page created by a Richard Hammond fan within hours of the BBC presenter's accident has become the best-performing page in Justgiving's history after fans donated nearly £190,000 in seven days.

The page at www.justgiving.com/phrichardhammond illustrates the fundraising potential of online communities and the benefits of the Internet for small charities.

On September 20, Alex Goss was one of several car enthusiasts discussing Richard Hammond's accident on www.pistonheads.com. Goss, a systems engineer from Bracknell, thought of creating a fundraising appeal on Justgiving for the Yorkshire Air Ambulance (YAA) charity, the organization that airlifted Mr. Hammond.

These fans posted a link to the fundraising page on the forum with a target of £340, the cost of a single YAA helicopter mission.

The response was immediate: Within three hours of the page being set up, donations had reached £2,475. Other online communities in the United Kingdom and beyond picked up the story, followed by broadcasters and newspapers.

Seven days later, the page has raised £190,000 including Gift Aid, the fastest response of any fundraising page in Justgiving's six-year history. The overall total, including offline donations, stands at £240,000 (see Exhibit 8.7).

GROUNDBREAKING APPEAL FOR THE YAA

The YAA raises approximately £1 million a year and relies entirely on donations to fund its life-saving work. Most of this income is raised locally, or from people with Yorkshire connections.

Alex Goss's appeal not only raised an unprecedented sum of money in record time for the YAA, but it also delivered a totally new audience for the charity.

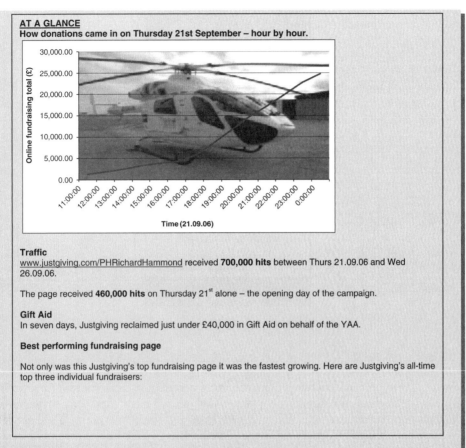

AT A GLANCE
How donations came in on Thursday 21st September – hour by hour.

Time (21.09.06)

Traffic
www.justgiving.com/PHRichardHammond received **700,000 hits** between Thurs 21.09.06 and Wed 26.09.06.

The page received **460,000 hits** on Thursday 21st alone – the opening day of the campaign.

Gift Aid
In seven days, Justgiving reclaimed just under £40,000 in Gift Aid on behalf of the YAA.

Best performing fundraising page

Not only was this Justgiving's top fundraising page it was the fastest growing. Here are Justgiving's all-time top three individual fundraisers:

EXHIBIT 8.7   Richard Hammond Fan Fundraising Page

"For the YAA to raise £240,000 in a week is extraordinary enough. But for us to raise 80 percent of this online is even more astonishing," says Martin Eedes, YAA's chief executive.

"Justgiving has enabled us to punch above our weight and reach out to a global audience," Eedes adds. "We are amazed by the power of this medium."

The page's online fundraising target now stands at £500,000 with donations still coming in. The success of the page will enable the YAA to bring forward its expansion plans with the purchase of a new helicopter to carry out 300 more emergency missions each year.

Case study by James Casey and Anne Marie Huby.

PERSONAL FUNDRAISING WIDGETS

As the continued adoption of new technology expands the broader community circle for all of us, new methods of reaching out to people in these communities will

EXHIBIT 8.8 Fundraising Widget

evolve. More personal methods for contacting potential donors will continue to be a primary method of reaching people with whom we have some sort of personal relationship (regardless of how strong or weak). In-person and phone asks, as well as asks that are sent via letters and e-mail, are an effective method of communicating with these people.

However, other less personal vehicles can be effective for reaching potential donors on blogs, communities, and social networks. The most basic (yet very effective) of these vehicles are simple HTML links to one's fundraising page (this is predominantly what Pim used). A more visually compelling form of link is the widget.

A widget is a snapshot of a fundraising page that is displayed by pasting a small piece of code in a blog or Web page (see Exhibit 8.8). It includes information from the fundraising page such as:

- Fundraiser's name
- Fundraising goal and progress
- Link to donate or to visit the fundraising page

Widgets will prove to be a helpful adjunct to other forms of solicitation for helping individuals and charities reach out to a broader online community.

FUNDRAISING CATALYSTS

What is the charity's role in making fundraising pages available to its support-ers? These pages are no longer available only to the largest organizations with commensurate budget, expertise, and pledge-based fundraising events. Here are a few ways that any organization can reap the benefits of online fundraising pages:

- Pledge-based fundraising events (walk-athons)
- Programs (missions and volunteer trips, etc.)
- Special appeals
- Grassroots/third-party programs

Pledge-Based Events

Special events, such as walk-athons, are where the personal fundraising page originally proved itself as a powerful tool. Traditionally available only to larger organizations, online personal fundraising pages are now accessible to any organization regardless of size, budget, or in-house technical expertise. Special events staff at organizations have seen how online fundraising has significantly contributed to grow the overall funds raised from events.

Aside from raising more money with online fundraising pages, charities also receive the funds raised online within weeks of the donation, as opposed to having to wait in some cases until the event day. Charities report that having access to funds sooner helps them to cover event costs and put funds into action more quickly. If the event is outdoors, the immediacy of online donations helps to mitigate the loss of donations should there be inclement weather on the day of the event that causes would-be participants to stay home.

Additionally, data indicate that online pages continue to receive donations even while the event is going on or after it has taken places. On average, 10 percent of all funds that are raised online come in either the day of the event or after. The majority of these funds are received in the weeks that follow the event, but some donations have been known to continue to trickle in months after. These are funds that more than likely would not have been realized through traditional offline fundraising, where donations are physically submitted on the day of the event.

Programs

Fundraising pages can be a very effective way to engage supporters to raise funds for your organization. By enabling passionate supporters to create pages that they can share with their network of family and friends, you help to turn supporters into active fundraisers on your behalf.

Examples of programs where charities have used online fundraising pages effectively include:

- **Disaster relief.** Fundraising pages offer supporters the ability to act immediately and make a difference after a natural or other disaster. In the days after the 2004 tsunami and Hurricane Katrina, many organizations sent e-mails to their supporters asking them to create fundraising pages in support of the relief efforts. Hundreds of pages were created and hundreds of thousands of dollars were raised as a result. This approach resulted in the creation of the www.firstgiving.com/cq blogger page, discussed earlier, that raised over $35,000.

- **Mission and volunteer trips.** Mission and volunteer trips often require that participants commit to paying a certain amount to cover the costs of their trip. In some cases, participants pay the cost themselves. In other cases, they are unable to do this; here having a simple tool available to help them raise the funds is useful. This fundraising page offers an example of how funds are being raised for mission and volunteer trips: www.firstgiving.com/matt_omo.
- **Board member appeals.** The board members of every organization are an important source of leadership and support (both financial and moral). Some board members are willing and able to contribute financially at significant levels. Other board members are not able to make contributions at substantial levels themselves, but still can have a significant financial impact by raising funds for your organization with an online fundraising page.
- **Alumni phone-athons.** Many private schools, including colleges and universities, run annual fund campaigns where alumni volunteer to phone old classmates to contribute to the program. Having done this myself, I know that these calls tend to be heavy on the "How have you been?" dialog and short on the "How much can you contribute?" dialog.

As an adjunct to alumni phone calls, schools can have their alumni volunteers create fundraising pages that are e-mailed out to their former classmates. The pages include a picture from the yearbook, a personal message from the alumni volunteer, and a list of who else has donated along with their comments.

This level of involvement fosters the community between former friends and classmates, and helps volunteers who are not comfortable to ask or catch classmates at dinnertime.

Special Appeals

Online fundraising pages enable organization staff to quickly and easily create pages for a special appeal, where the need comes up suddenly or unexpectedly. The page can be customized with pictures, text, and fundraising target specifically for that appeal.

In these situations, the charity itself usually is soliciting the donations for a specific appeal rather than asking for individuals to create their own pages, although individuals may also create their own pages.

The next case study offers an example of how one small organization has succeeded in using online personal fundraising pages for specialty appeals.

Grassroots and Third-Party Events

Personal fundraising pages created around an event produced exclusively by supporters themselves are perhaps the most powerful and fastest-growing use of online fundraising.

This opportunity removes the requirement for the nonprofit to come up with an event or appeal and puts power in the hands of your supporters. Given this power, supporters can amaze and reward you. Online fundraising pages can be created for:

- Weddings
- Birthdays
- Anniversaries

CASE STUDY: LUCKY DOG

Lisa Maturo, the director of Lucky Dog Rescue in Phoenix, Arizona (formerly the Phoenix Dalmatian Station), set up 15 online fundraising pages in 2006, raising over $22,700 for her organization.

Lisa's use of online fundraising pages highlights the flexibility of the product. She has used it for:

- Ticket sales for a fundraising event (www.firstgiving.com/JinglePaws)
- Pledges for a bowl-athon fundraising event (www.firstgiving.com/bowl-arama)
- Funds needed to rescue specific dogs (www.firstgiving.com/luckydog is a great example)

Animal supporters tend to be particularly passionate about their cause; couple the power of a personalized fundraising page with a great story and cute photo of a dog, and you have got the recipe for fundraising success.

Lisa's first dog-specific page was set up to benefit Joey, a Dalmatian in need of serious medical care. Her fundraising effort was picked up by the Phoenix local press, and 134 online donations were made, totaling over $7,100. A month later, she set up a page for another Dalmatian named Ralphie (www.firstgiving.com/Ralphie) and raised the $2,100 she needed to care for him.

Lisa's subsequent pages were successful, too, even without media coverage. With 12 pages set up to support specific dogs' care, Lisa raised a total of $11,100 online, coming from an average of 15 online donors per page.

Lisa really truly embraced all that the power of an online fundraising page can do: She included a photo of the dog being supported and a detailed message about what the funds would be used for in each case. She also used the page as sort of a "blog" to give updates on the progress of the animal. The community of donors is well represented, too, with donor comments offering words of support for both the dogs and for Lisa.

Case study by Laurel Ackerman.

- Marathon runs or other athletic endeavors
- Holiday fundraising
- In memory of a loved one
- Et cetera . . .

The best way to make this option available to your supporters is to put a "Create a Fundraising Page" link behind the "How to Help" section of your site. Besides offering your supporters the ability to donate money and volunteer, you should give them the opportunity to fundraise for your organization.

CASE STUDY: PANCAN AWARENESS MONTH

The Pancreatic Cancer Action Network (PanCAN) has an extraordinarily passionate supporter base, as would be expected for an organization centered around such a serious illness.

On October 25, 2006, Angela Johnson, the director of Community Outreach and Affiliate Relations, sent an e-mail to supporters suggesting that in honor of November being Pancreatic Cancer Awareness Month, they set up an online fundraising page for PanCAN.

Over the course of the next three weeks, 62 online fundraising pages were set up, raising a total of $13,500 (as of December 18, 2006).

This is a great example of how an organization can benefit simply by letting its supporters know that there is an easy but effective way to help.

If you give your supporters this ability to act on your behalf, they will surprise you with their creativity, passion, and commitment to your cause. The next case study provides insight into how you can engage your supporters at a grassroots level.

ONLINE FUNDRAISING BEST PRACTICES SUMMARY

This summary of best practices is based on feedback, observations, and analysis from hundreds of nonprofits and tens of thousands of individual fundraisers. These tips take into account the various sorts of activities that were used to separate those who used online fundraising pages successfully from those who were less than successful.

Advice to Your Fundraisers (Best Practices)

Ultimately, the success of fundraisers is in their hands. If they are equipped with the proper tools, passion, knowledge, and creativity, you will see some extraordinary results. Here are eight tips directly from successful online fundraisers themselves.

1. **Personalize your page.** To achieve the best success, fundraisers add their own photo(s), personalized message, and fundraising target. Members of their personal network give primarily because of their relationship with this individual. The more personalized the better.
2. **E-mail your online fundraising page URL out in tiers.** Start out with a small group of close friends and family who will "set the tone" by donating and maybe digging a little deeper; pages with higher donation amounts early on tend to get higher donations throughout.
3. **Add a widget to your page to your blog, Web site, or MySpace page.** Do you have friends with blogs, Web sites, or MySpace page? Ask them to talk about you and include your URL or post your widget to their page or blog.
4. **Send updates on your progress.** People mean to donate, but sometimes they do not quite get round to it on the first request.

5. **Send a thank-you e-mail after your event or fundraising effort.** People who supported you love to hear how you did, and it gives those who have not yet contributed a final chance to do so. An average of 10 percent of total donations can come in on the day of your event or after!

6. **Add your fundraising page's URL to your e-mail signature so that every e-mail you send tells people about your fundraising effort.** One recent fundraiser reports receiving a donation from somebody she really did not know at all by doing this.

7. **Don't be shy about whom you e-mail.** You probably have a bigger network than you realize; include colleagues, college friends, and people you know through hobbies or volunteer work. The more people you ask, the more donations you will get (no surprise there).

8. **Do public relations for yourself.** If you are running a big race or doing something notable, let your local media know. Local papers love this kind of story, and it is a great way to publicize your fundraising page URL at the same time.

Advice to Nonprofits (Best Practices)

One of the great things about online fundraising pages is that your supporters do the heavy lifting. They create the pages and send them out to family, friends, and colleagues or promote them on a blog or Web site with a widget or link. This said, the nonprofit plays an important role in how effectively supporters are able to help you. Some nonprofits will raise 10 times as much as others that are similar in size, location, and nature of the organization, simply because of how they promote the capability of their supporters. It is very basic promotion, but it is one of the top reasons why some organizations do better than others with online fundraising pages. Two main tips for promoting online fundraising pages to your supporters follow.

1. **Enable your supporters to create online fundraising pages.**
   - **Events/programs.** Providers of fundraising pages can offer your fundraisers a special start page from which they can create their page. (See the "Resources" section for a list of companies that provide such tools.)
   - **Grassroots/third-party fundraising.** Almost every organization has individual supporters who are willing to take on the role of fundraiser. You will know some of these individuals in advance, and others will surprise you by stepping forward. You can suggest this powerful way to help by adding a "Create an Online Fundraising Page" link on the "Ways to Help" section of your site. This link will either point to a site where a special start page can be created by you or by your fundraising pages vendor for your event or to a Web site, such as Firstgiving or Justgiving, where individuals can raise funds for any tax-exempt organization.

2. **Tell your supporters about it!** If you provide it, they will come...as long as if you tell them about it! Use your existing communication vehicles to tell supporters about this opportunity. The common misperception is that nonprofits have to do nothing at all or something completely different from how they currently operate. Your supporters may not know that an online fundraising option exists, or how flexible it is.

   You need to let your supporters know that the tools exist in order for them to raise funds for you online. The proven best way to do this is to use your existing communication vehicles to inform them that the tools exist. Here are some common examples of what this idea looks like in practice:

- **Place links on your Web site.** If you have a section of your site for your walk-athon, be sure to place links there letting people know that they can create a fundraising page. If you have a "Ways to Help" section of your site, be sure to put links there as well.

- **Include links and information in your e-mail newsletters.** Most organizations send out a periodic e-mail newsletter to their supporters. Telling people that the ability exists to create a fundraising page and profiling a success story or two is not only compelling content, but also actionable content. The success stories can be as a brief as a few-sentence summary of the fundraiser's efforts and can include a link to their fundraising page. Others will get it and will follow.

- **Profile a success story in your print.** For those organizations that send out a physical newsletter to supporters, including a write-up of your online fundraisers' successes encourages other supporters to also fundraise online. If you run a pledge-based fundraising event, highlight online fundraising pages at your event kick-off sessions and in your event materials.

- **Kick-off sessions for team leaders or participants in "-athon" events are great opportunities for you to talk about online fundraising tools.** Also include a handout to demonstrate how online fundraising tools work, and show examples of successful online fundraising pages. You may also want to consider running a contest for top-achieving teams or individuals.

BENEFITS ROUND-UP

Here is a summary of benefits that online personal fundraising pages provide nonprofit organizations.

- Supporters will raise more money for your organization.
  - More asks. It is easier to solicit more people online.
  - Better asks. Because fundraisers do not have to ask, you eliminate the possibility that they ask for only minimal amounts.
  - More donations are a direct result of more asks being made.
  - Matching gifts become available. You identify which donors have matching gift potential.
- Get more people to step up and fundraise for you.
  - Online fundraising pages make the process of fundraising easier, which can translate into more people who are willing to commit to become fundraisers for you.
- Build your database of supporters.
  - By getting more people to fundraise for you, and with each of them reaching out to more donors, you introduce more and new supporters to your organization. Online tools will help your fundraisers nurture their donors for your organization. All of the online fundraising page providers listed in the "Resources" section will provide you with donor and fundraiser data in electronic format for easy import to your database.

Resources

A list of organizations that provide online personal fundraising pages follows. Each one offers varying degrees of sophistication, features, and ability to customize their services. As a general rule, the services that offer more features, flexibility, and ability to customize are more expensive. You will need to judge for yourself whether the additional features and customization options are worth the additional cost.

In determining what features are essential for your organization (and what bells and whistles you are looking for), keep in mind that it is ultimately the quality and personalization of the fundraising page itself that will make the difference in the amount of funds that are raised for your cause. Ultimately, if fundraisers find the process easy and are pleased with their page, they will make more asks on your behalf and you will raise more money.

Online Fundraising Page Providers

- ActiveGiving (www.active.com)
- Artez (www.artez.com)
- Convio (www.convio.com)
- Firstgiving (www.firstgiving.com)
- Justgiving (www.justgiving.com)—for U.K.-based charities
- Kintera (www.kintera.com)

Fees

Fees and fee structures for using online personal fundraising vary by vendor, but fees typically are divided into three areas:

1. **Setup/annual fees.** Most online fundraising page providers charge a setup/annual fee. These fees typically range from a few hundred to several thousand dollars.
2. **Transaction fees.** All providers charge a transaction fee for use of the service. These fees seem to range from 5 to 10 percent. The actual credit card processing fee percentage, which is paid to the banks processing the credit cards, will be in addition to the transaction fees.
3. **Support fees.** Most vendors provide some level of support to your fundraisers and their donors. Most do not charge additional fees for this, but some may charge an additional fee if a certain volume is surpassed. When selecting the right provider for your organization, these fees are something to be aware of as parts of the selection process..

ABOUT THE AUTHOR

Mark Sutton is chief executive officer of Firstgiving, Inc., a Web-based service that that enables individuals to raise money for any charity online through online personal fundraising pages or widgets. Mark founded Firstgiving in March 2003. The company now works with over 800 charity clients and tens of thousands of individual fundraisers who are raising millions of dollars online for charity. Firstgiving is dedicated to providing simple and effective personal fundraising tools to individuals and all nonprofit organizations regardless of their size or budget.

Mark has been on the ePhilanthropy Foundation's Board of Trustees since 2005 and has over 18 years of experience in electronic publishing, online services, and nonprofit fundraising. Prior to Firstgiving, Mark served for five years as marketing and business development director at FairMarket, Inc. (Nasdaq: FAIM), an online commerce company that was sold to eBay.

Mark graduated with a BA from Connecticut College and holds an MBA from Babson College. He lives in Massachusetts with his wife and their three children.

Target Audiences

CHAPTER 9

Social Networks Meet Social Change: From MySpace to Second Life

Sarah DiJulio
M+R Strategic Services

Marc Ruben
M+R Strategic Services

THE BUZZ

It is clear that something big, even revolutionary, is taking place in the new world of social networks and virtual communities. Consider these statistics:

- MySpace has over 150 million users and is the third most popular Web site in America.
- Over 300,000 people have already joined "One Million Strong for Barack," a Facebook group for Democratic presidential hopeful Barack Obama.
- $1.3 million were spent in the "virtual world" of Second Life in just a single day.
- YouTube viewers watch 100 million clips and upload 65,000 new videos to the site every 24 hours.

Even more impressive, the millions and millions of people who inhabit these virtual communities—blogging; posting notes, comments, and photos; announcing parties and events; consuming and creating music and new media—are interconnected. Average social network users have a couple hundred or more "friends" they communicate with, and it is not uncommon for the popular and industrious to have thousands. Celebrities on MySpace—say, Ashton Kutcher or the Dixie Chicks—often have upwards of a million friends.

It is the nonprofit marketer's dream: a telephone tree that is instantaneous, cost-effective, and almost infinite in size. But first you have to figure out how to harness all that potential for your cause.

It may seem simple at first blush. Just set up your organization's MySpace profile, create a Facebook account, and throw some videos up on YouTube. In no time at all, you will have thousands of new friends who can donate money to your cause and recruit their friends for you.

Unfortunately, it is not quite that easy.

While MySpace, Facebook, and Second Life offer valuable opportunities to reach out to new audiences and engage them in your issues, successfully converting a virtual friend to become a traditional donor, volunteer, or activist can be harder than it seems.

In this chapter we have attempted to cut through the hype that surrounds these virtual communities, explore real-world examples of how nonprofit groups are tapping into these networks, and outline some successful strategies for winning popularity on the Internet's top social networks.

THE REALITY

The bottom line: There is no "silver bullet" for nonprofit recruitment and fundraising in virtual communities. MySpace and Facebook are full of campaigns and nonprofit organizations that are simply languishing on the vine with little or no care and feeding, and few friends.

However, a number of organizations have invested significant resources in cultivating their online communities and have started to reap the results:

- Oxfam America launched its MySpace profile in February 2006 and has attracted over 15,000 friends so far.
- Planned Parenthood Federation of America launched a special MySpace profile to mobilize activists around the South Dakota abortion ban. Over 4,500 friends joined in just three months—adding to the thousands of supporters already on other Planned Parenthood MySpace pages.
- The American Cancer Society held a virtual walkathon in Second Life in 2006 that attracted 1,000 participants and raised $40,000.
- Through the "Dollars for Darfur" profile on Facebook, nearly 6,000 students are organizing at more than 850 high schools across the country, pledging to raise $200,000 to help stop the genocide in the Sudan.
- Oceana, one of the most popular branded nonprofit organizations on Care2 Connect, has over 57,000 members in its Care2 Connect group.

The savvy fundraiser might ask, however: Where is the money? Although the $40,000 raised by the American Cancer Society is nothing to sneeze at and the $200,000 pledged by high school students is promising, most nonprofits are not seeing their forays into online social networking instantly generate hundreds of thousands, or even tens of thousands, of dollars in new revenue.

So why should fundraisers care about social networking?

For many organizations, investing in social networks is an investment in the future. The average nonprofit direct mail donor is 55 to 60 years old. The average MySpace user is 18 to 34 years old, and a typical Facebook user is 16 to 24 years old.

Although investing in these strategies now may not produce immediate cash flow, these younger supporters *are your future donors*. And if you want to build a relationship with these prospective donors, why not go where they have already gathered?

THE LINGO

- **Profile.** When social network users create an account, they are signing up to have their own profile. This is their own personal Web page, which is viewable by others, and usually includes a description of themselves (with interests, jobs, schools or organizations, likes and dislikes, etc.), a photo gallery, a list of friends, comments from friends, events they are participating in, and so on.
- **Group.** Users can create groups based on specific interests, from custom cars, to political beliefs, to loving cereal. Groups also can be created specifically for an organization (though, beware that some social networks do not allow organizations or businesses to create individual profiles).
- **Gifting.** Facebook users can purchase little tokens of appreciation, in the form of images, to be displayed on other user's profiles. When a gift is given publicly, it appears in the recipient's "Gift Box" and on the recipient's "Wall," a bulletin board where people see who gave it and any message that came with it.
- **Network.** User profiles in Facebook are connected through networks based around a company, college, high school, or region. A user can be part of multiple networks. Being a member of a network grants someone permission to view most of the profiles on that network and join most of the groups.
- **Post (or blog).** Users can write message entries that appear on their profile for others to read and comment on. This part of their profile is called a "blog" or "journal," and the individual entries are known as "posts" or "blog entries." On Facebook, this is also referred to as a "note."
- **Bulletin.** MySpace users can write a message to all of their friends at once, which appears in the "bulletin" section on their profile along with other messages in their friends' accounts. Only the bulletin recipients can see these—they are not visible to recipients' friends or to people browsing recipients' pages.
- **Friends (or buddies).** These are other members that a user is connected to, which are listed in the "friends" section on the user's profile. These do not have to be real-life friends. Also, in the wonderful world of social networking, "to friend" is now a verb. Eat your heart out, William Safire.
- **Pageviews (or profile views).** Some of the social networks report how many times a user's profile has been viewed.
- **Widgets.** These are tools that can be added to a user's profile, such as playable videos and interactive horoscopes. Some fundraising tools even have donation thermometer widgets to put on a profile (also known as a charity badge).
- **Comments.** Users can leave comments, which are visible to other users, on their friends' profiles, blog entries, and pictures.
- **Custom layouts (or codes).** On some social networking sites (though not on Facebook), users can use CSS, JavaScript, and other Web development languages to modify the look and content of their profiles.

THE DRILL

Making social networks work for you requires more than just putting up a profile, as we have discussed. Before you start, you need to answer some key questions and develop a plan to support your virtual community over time. Many organizations

---

PLANNED PARENTHOOD ON MYSPACE

Date Launched: May, 2006

Current Size: 4,500 friends on South Dakota campaign page, 18,000 + friends on main MySpace page.

Recruitment: E-mail messages to current supporters, Web promotions, viral badges, and messages.

Cultivation: Blogs and bulletins two to three times a week, mostly postings from the SaveRoe blog; original music.

Activation: Many users have taken action on Planned Parenthood, though most prefer to participate through MySpace.

Lessons Learned: Use your existing list members to jump-start your campaign.

---

do not realize that this can be a long-term investment that may not pay off until later (sometimes much later), and they fail simply because they do not commit the time and effort required to sustain this type of initiative.

So what makes a successful social networking strategy? And how much work is really involved?

The first step is to decide up front what you are prepared to commit to the effort, for how long, and what kind of return (if any) is expected in the short term:

1. **Recruitment.** How are you going to attract people to your MySpace profile or Facebook group?
2. **Cultivation.** How will you keep in touch with your new friends? How often will you update your MySpace or Facebook profile? What kinds of things will you offer your supporters on these social networking sites?
3. **Activation.** Beyond branding and visibility, what is it that you are hoping your new social network of friends and supporters will do for your organization? Give you money? Volunteer? How do you plan on getting them to do these things?

It takes an organizational commitment of at least a few hours a week to keep your social networking pages "alive" with new content. Even if all of the content that you post is repurposed from other sources, you will need to be prepared to respond to comments and questions, foster discussion, and continually update your page if you want to keep people coming back for more.

We recommend budgeting four hours per week per social networking site, at minimum, to accept friend requests, review comments, and post content.

Once you have hammered out your vision and nailed down your resources, you should be ready to get started.

The next section provides some general guidelines to successfully launching your social networking campaign. Please bear in mind that social networking is still new, largely unexplored territory for nonprofits, and you should always be experimenting. If something you would like to try is not on the list, you should definitely go for it anyways.

THE "HOW TO START" PROCESS

1. **Pick the right social networks.** Don't just pick where to spend your time based on the size of the network. Other virtual communities may be smaller but more effective for you. (Later on in this chapter we give you some details on the different social networks that might help you decide.)

   Most organizations using social networks have a presence on more than one site, but remember that undertaking this kind of project demands considerable staff resources. It may make more sense to start off small—with one to three social networks—rather than trying to take the whole Internet by storm at once.

2. **Find an "expert" to help you.** Do you have someone around who already has experience with networks you would like to target? A young staffer? An intern? A relative? Get them involved. Their experience will be a big help.

3. **Extend your reach.** Once you select a social network, a "scattershot" approach within that network can help ensure that you get the most out of your involvement. What do we mean? On MySpace, do not just set up a single profile—create a group, as well, and attract more supporters that way. On Facebook, your organization could show up as a group and/or as an event, if that is appropriate. But always be sure you know what is allowed and what is frowned on by the site you are dealing with.

   Some social networking sites will also allow your nonprofit to become an official sponsor of a group or community within that site, for a fee. This might be worth considering if you have the budget to experiment. For instance, companies that pay a fee can become "Sponsored Groups" on Facebook. Other Facebook users who sign up for a sponsored group receive a monthly promotional e-mail, a brand logo appears on their personal profile, and they also gain access to the sponsor's message board on Facebook, where they can talk to the nearly 100,000 other users who typically join each sponsored group.[1] (To be fair, most of Facebook's sponsored groups so far have been huge companies, such as Victoria's Secret and Apple.)

4. **Prepare to lose control.** You cannot possibly vet every word of every person who wants to be your friend or join your social networking group. If you or your lawyers are not comfortable with the fact that you are going to lose some control over content, social networking probably is not right for you.

   On many social networks, friends can post "comments" on your page. Sometimes you can set it up to require your approval before a message is posted. But if you choose to vet every comment that is posted, make sure you are reviewing and accepting (or rejecting) new comments quickly—within a few hours, ideally. Your new friends will not like it if it takes two days for their comment to show up.

5. **Know who is already pretending to be you.** Are there MySpace or Facebook "groups" for your organization that you did not set up? Unofficial profiles set up by enthusiastic supporters? Blog postings?

   If you discover that someone else already has a profile in the name of your organization, be sure to reach out to that person. He or she is often a committed supporter who might be willing to promote your content if you ask.

> ## OXFAM AMERICA ON MYSPACE
>
> Date Launched: February 2006
>   Current Size: 15,000 + friends.
>   Recruitment: E-Newsletters and special messages to the Oxfam list, and a MySpace-sponsored "Rock for Darfur" page where Oxfam was a partner.
>   Cultivation: Blogs several times a week, bulletins once a week, usually reusing action alerts or press releases.
>   Activation: Over 1,000 people have joined Oxfam's e-mail list, but most still prefer hearing from Oxfam directly through MySpace.
>   Other Outcomes: The band Gnarls Barkley sent out a bulletin, unsolicited, promoting Oxfam's page; volunteers have come from areas outside of Oxfam's traditional support base (Utah, Oklahoma, Virginia).
>   Lessons Learned: Fundraising directly through MySpace is tough, but the new MySpace recruits are becoming active list members.

6. **Make a good first impression.** A lot of your list members may "friend" you early on and then not look at your page much after that, so it is best to prepared to wow them; first impressions *do* matter.

   Also, make sure to control what your organization will look like on other people's friend lists—pick a great picture and title that will get noticed on their pages.

7. **Post your edgiest, most viral content.** Social networks work best when people are passing content around. Think of your social network pages as a place to test out ideas that you think people will want to be associated with. This could be as simple as a great profile name or as involved as a YouTube video or Flash animation. Helpful hint: If it does not make you think "Cool!" then it is probably *not* viral and you need to head back to the drawing board.

   You may have better luck with a page based on a specific campaign or gimmick than with a more generic page plugging your organization. If you have a "personality" as part of your campaign—a candidate, a character, a target, an animal—you might want to set up a profile for him or her.

8. **Figure out which of your supporters are on social networks already, and ask them to be your first friends.** If you survey your members, find out which of them have MySpace profiles, Facebook accounts, or belong to other social networks. Then send them an e-mail asking them to become your friend or to join your social networking group; you can expect a response rate typical of your best action alerts.

9. **Continue communicating with your social network friends.** Regularly update your social networking pages with new content reflecting whatever issues you are working on. Use MySpace "bulletins" and Facebook "notes" on other users' profiles to get the word out on urgent issues and drive people to your page.

10. **Devote staff time to making your social networking effort a success.** You will need to assign a staff person to regularly accept friend requests, post comments

on other people's pages, and invite other people to become friends. Otherwise, your social networking efforts will bust.

There are a number of shady third-party programs that will automatically send out and accept friend requests on MySpace, post comments, and do other things you might want an intern to do. These programs amount to spamming. Remember, any of these sites can take down your profile any time they want, and it would be sad to lose all those great supporters.

11. **Activate your social network supporters.** Eventually you will want to start turning your "friends" into activists, donors, and volunteers. To that end, your social networking pages should always feature lots of opportunities to get involved. If you are an advocacy organization, regularly feature online advocacy actions that supporters can take.

Social networks can be a great source of offline support too, so be sure to regularly post event notices and other offline volunteer opportunities.

If you eventually want to raise money from your supporters, you should also include donation opportunities on your social networking pages. Even if you do not raise much in the short run, it helps to set expectations for the future.

Be specific when asking your friends to do things for your organization. Do not ask people to sign up if they are "interested" in volunteering or coming to events: Ask them to volunteer for a specific activity or attend a specific event. And do not ask for a general gift to your organization, but instead ask them to make a gift to support an urgent need.

Finally, brag to your friends! Always be sure to let people know what happened at an event or with a campaign, even if they did not participate. This will get them interested in joining future efforts.

Your social networking efforts may not pay off right away. E-mail advocacy and fundraising provide immediate gratification in terms of actions taken or dollars raised, but success in social networking is measured in terms of how many friends you make. Converting those friends to activists and/or donors will likely be a long-term process.

THE CHALLENGES

For many organizations, getting a social networking program up and running will require overcoming some institutional and organizational challenges. Your lawyers may not approve. Your communications department will want to review and approve every last comment before it goes live. You may lack the in-house expertise and know-how. You may lack the staff time to support and maintain a vibrant profile.

Unfortunately, even if you make it through all of these hurdles, you will still need to tackle some of the challenges put in place by the people who run MySpace, Facebook, and other social networking sites. At the time of this writing, there were a number of technical and logistical limitations in the way these sites are configured that will handicap your efforts.

These limitations have been put in place primarily to stop spammers and marketers from abusing these sites, but, unfortunately for you, they do not distinguish between a legitimate nonprofit cause and a spammer. Here are two examples of how the sites might limit your ability to organize your supporters and friends.

WHOM TO KEEP AN EYE ON ...

MySpace has about 80 percent of the market share among social networks; Facebook has about 10 percent. No other sites come close to the reach of these two, but more and more niche networks are popping up.

While some may not be the right place for finding new constituents online—such as the quickly growing business connection network LinkedIn—others are worth keeping an eye on.

Some up-and-coming social networks include:

- Social activism—focused Change.org
- Personal growth site Zaadz
- Google-owned Orkut, which is huge in Brazil but still tiny in the United States
- Ning, which allows communities to create their own social networks

---

1. **Limits on e-mails to group members.** On Facebook, a group is not allowed to send messages to more than 1,000 people, so there is actually a penalty if you let your group get too big. On MySpace, you can send out a bulletin that all of your supporters can see, but they do not show up on other users' pages, and they do not have the same "penetration" as e-mail.
2. **Limits on friend requests in MySpace.** MySpace has a feature where you can upload your personal address book, send your contacts a "friend request" through the MySpace system, and enable them to automatically "friend" you. You would think this would be a great way to get your current list members to be your "friends" on MySpace, right? Only if you have a tiny list. MySpace will not let you import more than 90 of these e-mail addresses at a given time.

Of course, social networking sites are constantly changing their standards, so it is possible that, with time, things will get easier (or harder) for legitimate nonprofits.

A SAMPLING OF SOCIAL NETWORKS

Here is a brief rundown on five social networking sites we think you might want to consider targeting. All statistics are current up to March of 2006.

MySpace

Keys Stats:
- 150 million worldwide registered users
- Over 100 million registered users in the United States
- Primary age demographic is 18 to 34

MySpace is the single largest social networking site on the planet. With over 100 million registered users in the United States, it has a huge audience that can allow you to reach just about any demographic you might be looking for. Because MySpace is so large, however, the site makes it exceedingly difficult to communicate with lots of supporters simultaneously (other than just waiting for them to come to your site), and there is no program in place (at the time of this writing) to support official nonprofits.

Facebook

Keys Stats
- 19 million registered users
- 80 percent of users are registered in the United States
- 64 percent of users are between the ages of 16 and 24

Once exclusive to high school and college students, Facebook has now opened its online network to the public at large and is one of the most rapidly growing social networks. Because this site was designed to network individuals based on affiliation by school, sometimes it is more difficult to create an organizational presence on Facebook than on some of the other social networks. But if you are looking for the younger generation of students and recent grads, this is the place to be.

Care2.com

Keys Stats
- 7 million registered users
- Average age is 39
- Audience is 75 percent female

Care2.com is an online social network and Web portal of civically active adults and organizations that support healthy living and social causes. It is a great place to reach a highly targeted audience of progressive activists and donors. Because Care2 is very activist-oriented, it can be easier for nonprofit organizations to promote their issues here.

Gather.com

Keys Stats
- 200,000 registered members
- 800,000 unique visitors per month
- Average age is 42
- Audience is 55 percent female
- 72 percent have a college degree

A self-titled "MySpace for Grown-ups," Gather.com reaches an older demographic than many of the other more popular social networks. Gather specifically targets an older demographic—a Starbucks-drinking, NPR-listening crowd. It offers "branded groups" which (for a fee) could allow a nonprofit to reach a targeted crowd more directly.

Friendster.com

Keys Stats

- 40 million registered members
- 77 percent of users are between ages 18 and 34
- 64 percent have a college degree

Friendster was *the* social network several years ago, but has since been overtaken by MySpace and other competitors. Friendster is still quite popular, however, especially among audiences in Southeast Asia. Because of Friendster's popularity in other countries, it might be a better choice for organizations looking to target an international audience.

THE NEW FRONTIER

There is no doubt that social networks are here to stay; whether MySpace, Facebook, or a newcomer is the next big network, hundreds of millions of people are actively using social networks, and we do not expect that to change any time soon.

The challenge for the savvy nonprofit is how to tap these immense networks to recruit new supporters and mobilize them to take action, volunteer, and give money. Unlike direct mail, telemarketing, or walk-athons, there is no proven path to follow to success in this virtual medium.

Online social networks are a bit like the Wild West: a new, largely unknown land to be explored (and settled) by the brave and innovative. As you saddle up and head off to explore this new frontier, think of it as an adventure. No doubt, there will be obstacles in your path, but if you follow these guidelines and stay creative and determined, you will reach your destination and learn a ton about advancing your cause along the way.

ABOUT THE AUTHORS

Sarah DiJulio is an executive vice president with M+R Strategic Services and oversees M+R's online advocacy and fundraising services to over two dozen major nonprofit organizations.

Marc Ruben is a senior consultant with M+R Strategic Services. He helps nonprofit groups, such as the Human Rights Campaign, Planned Parenthood Federation of America and Oxfam America, develop and implement effective strategies to raise money and mobilize supporters online.

NOTE

1. For more information, see www.mediabuyerplanner.com/2005/08/16/facebook_offers_sponsored/.

CHAPTER 10

Senior Surfer E-Gifts

Charles Schultz
Crescendo Interactive, Inc.

e Philanthropy continues to be a dynamic and developing field. Both online gifts and major gifts are now being created through Web sites, e-newsletters, e-proposals and other types of electronic methods. A new phenomenon is occurring with the advent of e-gifts, which are becoming more and more frequent as donors respond to e-media. An e-gift is a gift in which the initial contact, education, and motivation of the donor is through electronic media.

SENIOR SURFERS CATCH THE INTERNET WAVE

During the past decade, there has been steady growth in the number of Senior Surfers. Surveys on Nielsen/Netratings indicate that use of the Internet by individuals over age 65 has steadily increased from 2002 to the estimated 18 million in 2007 (see Exhibit 10.1). This is in part because of determined efforts by AARP (the American Association of Retired Persons) and other organizations to encourage seniors to acquire computers and become proficient in use of the Internet. AARP has encouraged millions of seniors to join the Senior Surfer group. All organizations with substantial senior populations have a natural reason to hope that a major part of the communication in the future can be accomplished through the Internet.

A survey posted on Marketwatch.com on January 16, 2005 indicated that 88 percent of individuals with $50,000 or more of income were on the Internet if they were age 50 to 65 (see Exhibit 10.2). For persons age 65 and above, over 65 percent are now "Senior Surfers."

While Senior Surfers over the age of 65 are clearly the last major group to join the Internet generation, once they are on the Internet, they tend to be fairly active users. Many seniors are retired and have time to explore the wealth of information available, leading them to become fairly regular Internet users.

In addition, as seniors age, they tend to be less mobile and the Internet becomes their window to the world. As a result, it is natural that an entire generation of seniors will continue to be serious Internet surfers.

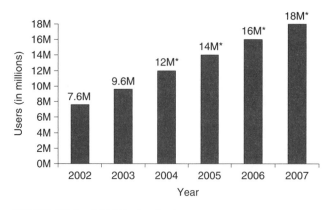

EXHIBIT 10.1   2007 Senior Surfers

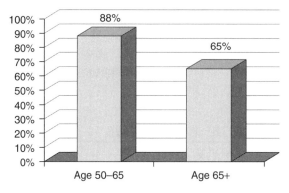

EXHIBIT 10.2   Senior Surfers $50,000 Income
Source: Marketwatch 1/16/05

WHAT DO SENIOR SURFERS EXPECT?

What are the expectations of Senior Surfers? As is true with most Internet users, within six months most Senior Surfers become familiar with and regularly visit favorite sites (see Exhibit 10.3). In addition, with regular usage, their expectations for interesting content, interactivity, and user-friendliness rise rapidly.

Internet users are exposed fairly quickly to a significant variety of sites. Seniors are similar to other Internet users in that they quickly develop Web preferences and expectations.

Surveys of Senior Surfers suggest that they are very interested in travel sites. These travels sites include Orbitz.com, Travelocity.com, Expedia.com, and a host of smaller travel sites that specialize in specific interest areas.

A second natural area for seniors is the news sites. As Senior Surfers become more dependent on the Internet for news, they are surfing CNN.com, MSNBC.com, Foxnews.com, and the other sites. A substantial number of seniors also spend regular time on finance sites. CNNFN.com, Marketwatch.com, Fidelity.com, Vanguard.com, and others are fairly popular.

Surfing Travel, News, and
Medical Sites

1. Rotating Content

2. Interactive Presentations

3. Streaming Video

EXHIBIT 10.3 Senior Expectations

Finally, seniors are regularly surfing medical sites. WebMD.com is visited frequently. However, sites maintained by the major medical nonprofits on Alzheimer's, cancer, heart, arthritis, and other medical conditions are also popular with Senior Surfers.

The second level of expectation relates to the quality of Web sites. A key aspect of Internet surfing for all users is rotating content. Since there are a million sites with rotating content, Senior Surfers may visit a static site once, but they are not likely to return.

Next, a Senior Surfer is likely to seek interactivity, which is one of the most powerful communication capabilities of the Internet. Interactivity may include calculators that explain the various benefits of a gift plan. This interactivity could be combined with an offer to speak with a representative for further personalization of a proposal or illustration.

Finally, video is now becoming widespread on the Internet. All of the major news sites offer free videos. As the Internet backbone acquires greater capacity and most Senior Surfers upgrade to broadband, the use of video will become commonplace. Video is particularly attractive for charities, since it often facilitates greater emotional connection between the message of the charity and the Senior Surfer.

SENIOR-FRIENDLY WEB SITES

Question: What capabilities decline as you become more senior?
Answer: Most everything.

In designing Web sites, it is important to understand the characteristics of seniors. Typically, vision starts to decline as people become more senior. Senior men are especially less able to discern shades of color, particularly pastel colors.

As a result, it is important to have high levels of contrast. Seniors also tend to prefer primary colors. Finally, easy navigation is a high priority. Focus groups of seniors reviewing sites have ranked easy navigation as one of their principal goals for a senior-friendly site.

WEB STYLES FOR SENIORS

Seniors desire fairly easy-to-read screens and logical layouts. Navigation bars are traditionally at the top and at the left. Placing navigation at the right or at the lower part of the screen may be acceptable, but it has a major disadvantage in that it is not the expected location.

There should be light or white background with dark text. High contrast is quite important. Graphics are excellent, but should be reasonably small and light so they load quickly. Some sites created for seniors also include the capability to increase or decrease the font size with a plus or minus button on the screen.

Integration

A key part of success with any marketing strategy is integration. Within a charitable program, typically four different areas must be combined:

1. Communications on current gifts from the development department
2. General public relations messages from the communications section
3. Major gifts of property from the major gifts sections
4. All the various planned and deferred gifts

Each of these four areas will have a different message and describe different methods for giving. However, the branding should be the same for all four. The target markets must be understood so that each market receives the message that is of greatest interest. Finally, the donor tracking system must keep track of current donors, major donors, and planned gifts donors.

Consistency: Essential for Senior Donors

A second characteristic within each of the marketing areas is consistency. For example, in the major and planned gifts area, there should be consistency within different types of communications media.

Marketing media includes print marketing, a major and planned gifts Web site, e-newsletters for donors, e-literature that may be downloaded or e-mailed to donors, audio or video communication, and individual e-proposals.

It is a special kindness to seniors when the different methods for major gifts marketing work consistently together. For example, a donor might read a story or article on a printed brochure or postcard. If an e-mail address is provided, the donor can log on and learn more directly from the Web site.

The Web site should have content similar to print media and also may provide video, downloadable e-brochures, and an e-newsletter. The "look and feel" of all of the electronic media can be very similar. In addition, the Web could offer a personalized e-proposal prepared by a staff person and e-mailed to the donor as a PDF file. Once again, the e-proposals should have colors and graphics that correspond to those on the Web site.

Consistency is a key goal. Many marketing programs struggle greatly to provide a consistent look through all print and electronic media. But all marketing researchers agree that a consistent program throughout all types of media will produce a better result. When all of the different media are familiar and easy to use, a nonprofit's outreach efforts with senior donors will be more effective.

E-MARKETING SYSTEM

A coherent and consistent e-marketing system includes five components that are designed to function together:

1. Interactive, senior-friendly Web site
2. E-mail newsletters
3. E-literature
4. Video/teleconferences
5. E-proposals

Interactive, Senior-Friendly Web Site

An important aspect of the major and planned gifts home page is a friendly hello. This defining part of the Web site should welcome the senior and encourage him or her to make use of the site's different capabilities. Take the example of a university where the gift planners use attractive photos to welcome Senior Surfers to the site. This welcome is part of the start of building an e-relationship with the senior friend.

A second aspect of the Web site is rotating content and donor stories. The rotating content on this site changes every week. It includes a combination of education news and articles that are of interest to seniors. There also should be regular stories that have strong human interest and correlate with the educational mission of the charitable organization.

Donor stories are very powerful methods for teaching relationship building. A donor story by a 1935 university graduate emphasizes his relationship to the charity. The goal of the story is to encourage other supporters to think positively about supporting the organization. In addition, the donor story facilitates or encourages understanding of a specific gift strategy. The donor expressed his delight in funding a gift annuity that has benefits for both the donors and the university.

Contact Us Page A primary object of the Web site is to encourage donors to contact the charity. There should be contact us buttons on the header navigation bar. In addition, it is very helpful to have a contact us page. If there is a large staff, which is common in colleges and university fund development departments, it may be useful to divide the "Contact Us" page geographically.

This university example shows the contact us page for a national charity with field staff in each state. By selecting one of the states, a donor is able to find both the contact information and background information on gift planners. The contact page should be friendly, open, and inviting.

Branding Branding facilitates both identification and emotional connection. The colors, look, and feel of different types of media should be consistent. Each organization will want donors to understand immediately that they now are looking at electronic or print media from that specific charity.

In addition to the logo and colors, photos are another type of branding. Many organizations have a specific mission in education, healthcare, relief services, or religious services that are clearly identified by photos. These photos and accompanying donor stories are an excellent way of building emotional attachment for donors.

Finally, branding is facilitated by cross-media links. If there is easy access from one area of media to other similarly branded media, then the donor's e-relationship with the charity is continually bolstered and reinforced.

Easy Navigation and Reading   When senior focus groups have reviewed Web sites, one of the highest priorities was easy navigation. Most navigation links are by convention placed on the left side. However, navigation can be at both the top and the lower part of the page. A return button at the lower part of the page is especially helpful, since users do not need to find the back arrow at the top left of the browser bar.

Large fonts, white space and short paragraphs complete the prescription for senior-friendly Web sites. Many seniors do not see as clearly as they once did. Since video screens do not have resolution as high as printed material, it is important to have reasonably large fonts. In addition, short paragraphs with white space between the paragraphs are much more readable.

All in all, the senior-friendly Web site can be very engaging, and it is helpful to recall that seniors will spend more time on Web sites than any other group if the sites are senior-friendly.

Interactivity Leads to E-Relationships   Interactivity is both challenging and promising. The interactivity of a Web site can be enhanced in several ways. One example is to make sure that it is personalized and carries forward the message of your charity. An interactive Web site attempts to engage the emotions of the donor. If the donor has a tie to your organization, he or she will appreciate the way that the Web site speaks through a "heartstrings connection" to the mission of that charity.

Some sites make effective use of cause-related photos to present their mission. As noted, the donor stories communicate your message.

After connecting emotionally with the organization, the donor should be offered the opportunity to explore personal illustrations. A gift involves two basic steps.

1. Decide that the organization is worthy of support.
2. Understand the best benefit from the chosen gift agreement.

A personal illustration or personalized brochure is an excellent way to achieve this result. The personal illustration could include a flash presentation with audio. A personalized brochure could then be produced as a PDF file and e-mailed with a friendly note to the donor.

E-Mail Newsletter

The e-newsletter should have the organizational logo, colors, look, and feel. When a donor sees the e-newsletter, he or she immediately understands that it is from your organization.

E-newsletters will be read only if they have great content. Content needs to be timely, engaging, fresh, and senior-specific.

It is desirable to give an opt-in frequency choice. Some donors may prefer to receive the newsletter on a weekly basis, but many will prefer twice a month or once a month. If donors have the choice of frequency, there is also a natural incentive to make the content lively and fresh so that more donors decide to receive and read the e-newsletter weekly.

There should be multiple links within the newsletter that take the donor directly to the Web site. By including many links in the newsletter, the donor will regularly be viewing content on the Web site and may easily click the "Contact Us" button to make a personal contact with the charity.

This e-newsletter is sent by a community foundation to friends in the area. It includes the colors, look, and feel of the Web site and starts with a friendly greeting from the principal gift planner. There is a special offer for a downloadable brochure, followed by a human interest article. As the Senior Surfer scrolls down, there also are current articles on national news and financial information that applies specifically to seniors.

E-Literature

E-literature is different from traditional print literature. While both e-literature and traditional print literature attempt to educate and motivate donors, e-literature is specially designed to encourage donors to move from print to electronic media.

Most organizations have developed a large mailing list over several decades. Now that more than half of donors over 65 (soon to be half of over-age-70 donors) have e-mail addresses and Internet access, it is a high priority for marketing directors of all charities to encourage these print readers to move to electronic contact.

The primary method for facilitating this movement is literature that is friendly in content and relational, but encourages the seniors to move to the Web site for further information. For example, a monthly postcard could promote articles on the Web site. If there is a senior-friendly URL or Web address that can be typed in easily by the senior, then he or she can go directly to the Web site to learn more.

The short URL should be seven or eight characters followed by .org, and there should be no front slash, back slash, underscore, or period in the URL. This short URL may require an exception to organizational policies, but that exception has been granted by many of America's largest charities in order to increase Web site accessibility.

A postcard could also offer a brochure by either electronic download or print. Charities will find that offering both types of response methods will lead to greater response generation.

Video

Video is rapidly becoming more popular on the Internet. Over half of computers in the nation have broadband Internet access. Within a fairly short period of time, fairly large numbers of seniors will have broadband. Once broadband is available, nonprofit Web sites will make frequent use of short video clips.

A primary use of the Internet is for family members to e-mail photos to grandparents. The next level of capability will be sending short video clips from cell phones. When this becomes more popular, Senior Surfers will be greatly interested in Web video.

Many sites now include a one- to two-minute friendly video hello from the gift planner or a well-known person from the charity. The friendly hello thanks the donor for his or her support, offers the services of the Web site, and communicates a "we are here to help" message. It is a chance to start building an e-relationship with the donor over the Web.

Other video could include donor testimonials or vision-casting by the chief executive officer of the charity. Since all Web videos are highly compressed, they should be short and use simple sets with minimal movement by the speakers.

E-Proposals

A desired pattern is for your donor to read printed e-literature, log on to your Web site, and request the weekly e-newsletters. After learning about the benefits of a gift plan, he or she now contacts you and expresses interest in a gift annuity, a gift and sale, a unitrust, an annuity trust, or other planned gift.

Typically, a gift planner will call the donor and discuss the gift plan benefits. In the past the gift planner would print an illustration and send it by mail.

Now there is a better option. Since the donor has an e-mail address and nearly all computers have PDF reader software, the gift planner may create a color illustration and print it to a file with PDF writer software. The gift planner may then send a friendly e-mail with the illustration as a PDF attachment.

Nearly all donors with e-mail understand how to click on the attachment and open it on screen. The donor can then view, print, or save the PDF illustration.

It is very helpful if the illustration has the same general look and feel as illustrations available on the Web site. Being kind to the senior donor means not expecting him or her to learn new ideas or methods with different colors or different graphics, but rather providing a consistent look to the illustration both on the Web site and through the e-proposal.

MAJOR E-GIFTS THROUGH PROFESSIONAL ADVISORS

While a senior-friendly Web site and e-newsletter is important, the professional advisor may also facilitate large gifts. Increasingly, major planned gifts may be initiated by a certified public accountant, attorney, trust officer, certified financial planner, life underwriter, or other professional advisor. There is great potential benefit for charities if these advisors can use electronic media to facilitate philanthropy.

A weekly e-newsletter for tax advisors needs to provide current and relevant information. Once again the e-newsletter should have the look and feel and branding of the charity. Another option is a video teleconference to facilitate education of professionals and provide a great special event.

The Web site typically will contain updated content, tax rulings, regulations, and other IRS rulings. In addition, an effective Web site includes a comprehensive tax guide and a Web site calculator.

Finally, the charity may offer to provide e-proposals on an anonymous basis to clients of the professional advisor.

E-TESTING

Half of my marketing money is wasted—I just never know which half!
                                                              —William Wrigley

Mr. Wrigley was a very successful marketer. As he correctly noted, there is no way to know in advance which marketing strategies will work best. You must implement the marketing methods and then test donor response.

There are a number of ways to engage in e-testing of your marketing system. First, over a period of years, the monthly unique visitors to the Web site should gradually track higher. Second, e-newsletter circulation is easy to track; it also should increase year after year.

When potential donors read e-newsletter articles, they will be interested in certain articles and click on to the Web site. It is possible to track both the selected e-newsletter frequency (weekly, biweekly or monthly) and the preferred topics.

Finally, charities should offer special response options on a weekly or monthly basis. These options will produce donor responses that may be tracked on a monthly basis.

The result of the e-testing will provide a better understanding of methods that are most successful. It also is likely to show that there is value in the linking characteristics of the print media, Web site, e-newsletter, e-literature, video, and e-proposals. That is, the whole will frequently be greater than the sum of the parts. An integrated marketing plan will produce the greatest total response.

E-POTENTIAL

Charities have historically built print mailing lists. Many charities have been working for several decades to build these lists.

The e-potential is the number of individuals on a print mailing list to have an e-mail address or Internet access. A simple way to calculate e-potential is to divide the organization's print list by two. Assuming that over half of the print list prospects have e-mail addresses, this e-potential is the potential number of individuals with which a charity could have an e-contact on a weekly or monthly basis.

E-CONTACTS

E-contacts are the next level of measurement. Based on the print mailing list, it is possible to determine the e-newsletter, Web site, and other monthly e-contacts. The e-contact ratio is the number of monthly e-contacts divided by the total print mailing list.

Many charities start this process with an e-contact ratio of only one percent. However, through consistent efforts to build e-mail lists and to encourage use of the Web site and receipt of e-proposals, a charity can build to 20, 30, or even 50 percent e-contacts over a period of several years.

It takes some time and effort to build e-contacts. However, gift planners should recall that most charities have spent several decades building print mailing lists. The initial indication is that building e-contacts to 20 or 30 percent on a monthly basis will dramatically increase major and planned gifts. It is quite possible for many charities to double their major and planned gift production through a consistent program to build e-contacts into the 30 to 40 percent range.

MILESTONES FOR E-SUCCESS

There are three principal milestones in measuring e-success for a major online gifts program:

1. Creation of an e-marketing system
2. Development of substantial circulation for the e-newsletter and a high contact rate for the Web site
3. Actual receipt of major or planned gifts of $1 million or more per year

A successful e-marketing system includes the Web site, e-newsletters, e-literature, video, and e-proposals. Normally implementing and coordinating a fully operational e-marketing system takes one to three years. The various electronic and literature components can be developed quite quickly. However, often it takes the charity a few years to modify and customize all of the different electronic and print components to communicate its unique message to donors.

A second milestone is e-newsletter circulation. Successful gifts come through e-contacts from the Web site. However, the e-newsletter provides weekly rotating content that facilitates use of the Web site. E-gift generation has correlated to a very substantial degree with the level of e-newsletter circulation, particularly if the e-newsletter includes links to the Web site. Since most articles in the e-newsletter are actually viewed on the Web site, the e-newsletter is the most effective means for regular transition of donors to the site.

Major E-Gifts of $1 Million Per Year

In the chart in Exhibit 10.4 an actual history of one nonprofit is shown over a period of five years. In 2002 this nonprofit implemented an integrated e-marketing system. It was able to build e-newsletter circulation fairly rapidly because the state

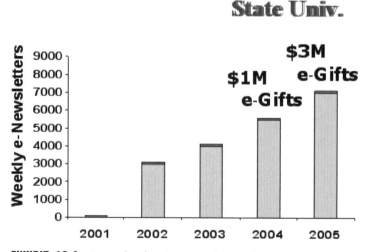

EXHIBIT 10.4   Example of an Integrated E-Marketing System

university had an extensive list of e-mail addresses. As a result of the circulation of e-newsletters, within a year donors began to contact the gift planner and create planned gifts. By 2004 donors were creating well in excess of $1 million in planned gifts per year. This amount grew to over $3 million in planned gifts in 2005.

This e-marketing system worked effectively. The Web site, e-newsletter, and e-proposals were all supportive. There was extensive cross-marketing. For example, the e-newsletter marketed the Web site and seminars. Seminars marketed the Web site and the e-newsletter. By effective use of cross-marketing, the overall result was greatly enhanced.

In 2002 the gift planner was receiving approximately 1 inquiry per week. By 2005 the gift planner was receiving over 15 contacts or inquiries per week. The net result of the e-marketing system was a dramatic increase in donor contacts. As would be expected, increased contacts led to more gifts; total planned gifts productions approximately doubled.

WHY EPHILANTHROPY SUCCEEDS: SEVEN PILLARS OF E-SUCCESS

There is a huge transition under way. The Internet and e-mail have opened up powerful new interactive ways to communicate with donors. The key for most organizations is learning how to personalize electronic publications so that they are able to produce an emotional response in donors who view the e-media. By understanding how to create this emotional response, charities will benefit greatly from e-marketing methods.

But what is the future of e-marketing to seniors? And what are specific reasons that some charities are now seeing significant Web traffic with Senior Surfers? Based on a survey of 75 charities with 100,000 to 500,000 page-views on their planned giving sites during 2006, there are seven pillars for e-success.

1. **Personalization.** An effective Web site expresses a "resonant" message. Each charity has a specific mission. It may be in healthcare, education, social service, the arts or religion. The Web site, e-newsletter, print literature, or video must act together to communicate that uniqueness. A combination of pictures and stories is an essential part of that communication effort. When your donor is on your site, he or she is motivated to assist in your mission.
2. **Senior Surfers.** Seniors are a rapidly growing and enthusiastic group of Internet users. A recent poll of seniors in the United Kingdom discovered that the individuals over the age of 65 for the first time have found a new avocation. Gardening is a longtime favorite activity among seniors in the UK. The beautiful foliage and flowers of English gardens are world famous. However, for the first time surfing the Internet has replaced gardening as the number-one activity in England. While the English Senior Surfers are spending nine hours per week on the Internet, the survey suggests that the American seniors are spending between six and seven hours on the Internet.
3. **Rotating content.** Live people prefer live sites, which provide new and fresh content on a regular basis. Within a few months of becoming a "Senior Surfer," donors discover that there are dynamic live planned giving sites and some static

sites. The overwhelming majority of donor activity occurs on live sites. These sites have regular new weekly articles, senior help columns, finance news, and Washington updates. Future sites will include attractive and changing video on the sites.

4. **Home page access.** Active sites have one- or two-click access from the home page to the gift planning section. These sites have large marketing departments that work diligently to draw thousands and even millions of prospective donors to the sites. Most of these donors will enter through a home page. It is hoped that senior donors who view a home page also can easily move to the gift planning section. Several Web sites have a visible link for "planned giving" on the home page. A number of the sites also use drop-down menus, which offer the donor the opportunity to select "donate now" or "ways to help" or a similar link. When the mouse is held on the first link, the drop-down menu provides a single-click access to the gift planning page.

5. **E-newsletter access.** Several sites have produced extended activity through links from e-newsletters for donors and professional advisors. Since the articles are on the Web site, anyone reading an article is immediately transferred to the site. E-mail address acquisition to build e-newsletter circulation is a high priority. Many of the sites have been successful because they have steadily worked to build the list. Effective use of the e-newsletter is an extremely important e-relationship-building tool. If a retired person finds articles of value, he or she will be come a regular reader. Fifty-two contacts per year over five years equals 260 separate contacts. This is the type of reinforcement in today's media-oriented world that is likely to build strong ties and strong relationships. Historically, planned gifts have resulted from similar strong relationships.

6. **E-literature.** Many charities use printed literature to lead donors to their Web site. An essential part of success is e-literature—literature that not only educates and motivates donors, but leads them directly to your site. This literature frequently encourages donors to view timely information on GiftLegacy Web sites. Charities should have a short Web address for the planned giving site that is about eight characters with no punctuation. This easy-to-type Web address also should be printed on literature.

7. **Three-year goals.** Top sites have reasonable and yet challenging circulation and gift goals for the first three years. Virtually all marketing programs require three years to move to maturity. The first step is to build circulation. After donors who represent tens of millions of dollars of potential planned gifts are regularly on the site, the next step is to encourage response by donors. Some will respond by e-mail, but many pick up the phone and call the gift planner. After researching the gift and making some tentative decisions, donors frequently would like to speak directly to the gift planner to go to the next step. The end result of the process is substantial e-gifts.

MARKETING 2010

Where are you today, and where are you headed by 2010?

Many organizations still are focused mainly on print marketing. Some organizations are 90, 95, or even 98 percent print in their marketing. The balance of their effort is electronic marketing.

Will the picture be different by 2010? Most communications directors from major charities believe that by the end of the decade, there will be a dramatic swing toward electronic media. Even seniors 65 and above will be very comfortable using electronic media in the same way they now use telephones, even cell phones.

Will e-marketing be 50 percent or more of the total marketing for your organization by 2010? Major charities are moving steadily toward that goal. Each nonprofit should estimate its target percentage of electronic media that will be electronic by 2010. Many organizations find that they expect a substantial difference between today and the end of the decade, with a dramatic increase in electronic marketing. The future is shifting toward online education that leads to motivation that leads to major e-gifts.

ABOUT THE AUTHOR

Charles Schultz is a California attorney who specializes in charitable giving and estate planning. He is president of Crescendo Interactive, Inc., and is the principal author of the Crescendo Planned Giving Software and the GiftLegacy Pro e-Marketing System. Each year he is producer and moderator for the popular Gift-Law teleconferences. In addition, he is editor for the GiftLaw.com charitable tax planning Web site and the GiftLaw Pro charitable tax service, and he also edits the weekly GiftLaw and GiftLegacy e-Newsletters. Charles writes, speaks, and publishes extensively. He teaches over 30 planned giving seminars per year and is the creator of GiftCollege.com, an Internet education program for gift planners and professional advisors. Charles is certified as an ePhilanthropy master trainer and serves on the board of the ePhilanthropy Foundation. He also is chair of the board of the Christian Foundation of the West.

CHAPTER 11

Online Marketing to Ethnic and Other Special Interest Communities

Vinay Bhagat
Convio Inc.

INTRODUCTION

All nonprofit organizations—whether ethnic or cultural groups; special interests, such as the environment, animal welfare; or disease and disorders groups—seek to connect as effectively as possible with their audiences. In April 1999 I founded Convio after volunteering at a public television pledge drive and being struck by the opportunity to leverage Internet technology to build better constituent relationships and as a result drive improvements in fundraising. Today Convio's solutions help nonprofits leverage the Internet to develop stronger relationships with all constituents to increase donor/member retention rates; to realize operational efficiencies in fundraising and communications; to manage a dynamic Web presence without requiring significant in-house technical expertise; and to manage online grassroots advocacy programs. In this chapter I address how nonprofits that target specific segments of the community can most effectively leverage the Web to reach their target audience, raise funds, and further their mission.

Using several case studies, this chapter draws on the online constituent relationship management (eCRM) framework and discusses emerging technologies and techniques, such as social networks and new forms of peer-to-peer fundraising, that nonprofits can use. Each section includes a case study from one or more nonprofit group that represents the latest thinking and best practices in each area of online marketing. The chapter concludes with case studies of two nonprofits that have expanded their online marketing programs relatively recently.

eCRM FRAMEWORK: A STRATEGY FOR BUILDING RELATIONSHIPS ONLINE

Online marketing is a cost-effective way for nonprofit organizations to reach new constituents and sustain regular contact with existing ones. Online constituent relationship management involves leveraging the Internet strategically to recruit, engage, and retain constituents. Exhibit 11.1 illustrates the concept.

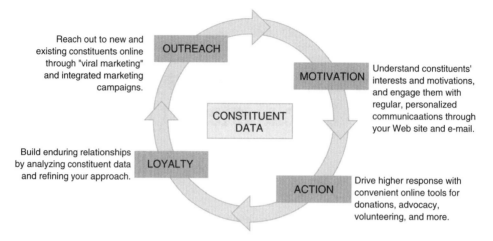

EXHIBIT 11.1   Online Constituent Relationship Management Framework

What follows are details for each step in the eCRM framework, highlighted by case studies from nonprofit groups that represent the latest thinking and best practices in each phase. The case studies draw from organizations that are trying to reach specific ethnic groups or special interest communities (e.g., the Anti-Defamation League, the Jewish National Fund, Defenders of Wildlife, and the SPCA of Texas), but the recommendations and insights are largely applicable to any nonprofit organization.

Outreach

In order to reach new constituents online, nonprofits first need to focus on driving traffic to their Web sites and then to motivate those individuals to provide their e-mail addresses. It is imperative to capture constituents' e-mail addresses and get their permission to opt them into your communications and marketing programs. To drive Web site traffic, nonprofits should provide compelling content, leverage offline media exposure, optimize their Web site for search engines, and encourage existing constituents to forward messages and site links to friends. To maximize the number of site visitors who convert to subscribers, nonprofits should present a compelling case why someone should volunteer his or her e-mail address; determine how to best promote e-mail sign-up on their site; and deploy multiple ways for people to volunteer their e-mail address beyond just signing up to receive an electronic newsletter, such as allowing them to download a special report, participate in a poll, or submit a personal story.

It also is important for nonprofits to collect e-mail addresses from existing constituents in order to communicate with them more frequently and economically, instead of using only direct mail and hard-copy newsletters. Research shows that engaging direct mail donors electronically in tandem with direct mail enhances their annual value (how much they contribute each year) and also boosts retention rates (the percentage of constituents who elect to renew their support each year). In fact, research conducted by Convio and StrategicOne, an integrated marketing analytics

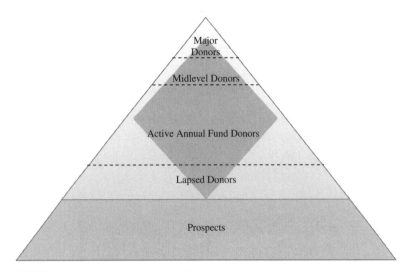

EXHIBIT 11.2 Outreach and Collection of E-Mail Addresses

firm, showed that the increase in multiyear donor retention rates could be more than 10 points.

Simple techniques to collect e-mail addresses from existing donors include asking for e-mail addresses through direct mail reply devices, phone interactions, or at events. You also can capture e-mail addresses when directing individuals to specific Web site content or by encouraging them to donate online. Using these tactics will help you collect e-mail addresses for a reasonable portion of the current constituency, especially active donors.

Another technique to quickly grow e-mail files is to conduct an e-mail append. This typically involves working with a service, such as Fresh Address, to try to identify e-mail addresses for your organization's current constituency through a review of other consumer marketing databases. Although an e-mail append can help you drive much faster growth of your e-mail file, the cost and the relative responsiveness of an appended list may make such a service less appealing. We also have found that constituents who are appended versus those who opt in themselves tend to be less responsive.

Nonprofit organizations should aim to acquire e-mail addresses for at least 50 percent of their existing donor file. This is represented in Exhibit 11.2 in the diamond-shaped area in the upper triangle. In addition, organizations should aim to build an electronic prospect list of constituents that is one to three times the size of their existing donor e-mail file, represented in the exhibit by the trapezoid below the triangle.

Motivation

Online marketing is a cost-effective way to strengthen constituent relationships. Organizations have two primary online constituent engagement vehicles at their disposal: their Web sites and the e-mails they send. In addition to site content,

CASE STUDY: ANTI-DEFAMATION LEAGUE

The Anti-Defamation League (ADL; www.adl.org), whose mission is to stop the defamation of Jewish people and secure justice and fair treatment to all citizens alike, keeps constituents apprised of the latest news and updates through a comprehensive and compelling electronic communications program. ADL has used several techniques to expand its reach and grow its e-mail file. From late 2004 to late 2005, the organization grew its e-mail file from 26,855 to 166,797 addresses.

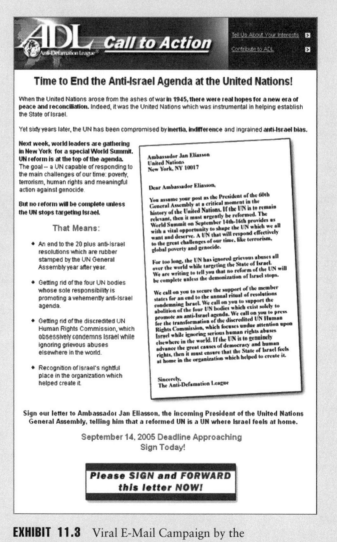

EXHIBIT 11.3   Viral E-Mail Campaign by the Anti-Defamation League

For example, ADL ran permission-based e-mail campaigns, also known as viral marketing campaigns, specifically designed to build its e-mail file-. One such e-mail sent in September 2005 advocated for reform of the United Nations' attitude toward Israel as part of a larger reform agenda. The e-mail also asked ADL constituents to sign an online petition and forward the message to others. Of the 111,560 e-mails delivered, 20.49 percent of recipients opened the e-mail, 12,238 signed the petition, and ADL added 2,308 new e-mail addresses to its file as individuals forwarded the message on to other contacts.

ADL also has used "nonorganic" file-building tactics, including e-mail appends, to grow its file. In 2005, the organization added 125,354 addresses to its file by conducting e-mail appends to its direct mail file (see Exhibit 11.3).

Web site–based engagement vehicles include surveys or polls, advocacy alerts, and constituent story submission opportunities.

It is important to maintain fresh content on your Web site that is of interest to your target audiences. If the content is not compelling and updated regularly, people will not return. More advanced tactics to increase content relevance include personalization—offering content according to specific constituent interests and their previous actions on the site—and localization—offering content according to where individuals live. (Visit the American Society for the Prevention of Cruelty to Animals® Web site at www.aspca.org and register to experience a good example of content personalization based on your profile.)

People often visit an organization's Web site because of an e-mail they receive or exposure to offline media, such as an article in a newspaper or magazine, a direct mail piece, or a television spot, for example. This is why maintaining regular and compelling electronic communications is critical. It also is important to provide more than just an organizational update in your communications. In addition to discussing topics that your group is proud of or finds interesting, you should also try to take the perspective of your constituents and think about what subjects they might find interesting and would want to read more about in a brief update, message, or article online. Just like Web content, personalizing or localizing e-mails can help improve their relevance.

The Web is a two-way medium, and it is important to motivate constituents to become more engaged by asking for their feedback and participation. Tactics for doing this include embedding surveys and polls within e-mails or asking constituents to submit their stories on your Web site.

Action

After building an e-mail file and engaging constituents, it is important to encourage individuals to take actions that support your organization. For most organizations, this means fundraising. For others, it can include advocacy actions requesting constituents to send messages to legislators.

In order to maximize the number of actions on your Web site, it is important to present compelling support opportunities. In the case of fundraising, donation appeals should be as tangible as possible and designed to strike a chord with donors, such as appeals tied to current issues in the news or appropriate to the time of year.

CASE STUDY: JEWISH NATIONAL FUND

The Jewish National Fund (JNF; www.jnf.org) is an organization that serves as caretaker of the land of Israel on behalf of its owners—Jewish people everywhere. The organization has had a strong Internet communications program for several years and has developed an e-mail list of more than 280,000 constituents.

JNF has used several techniques to maximize engagement of its online constituency. The group maintains rich, regularly updated content on its Web site that is timely to readers and also provides regional content to help maximize its appeal to people living in different parts of the country. One strategy that JNF has used on its Web site is including content submitted by donors. The organization has designed its site to be easy to use as well as to accommodate its older donor base.

In addition to its Web site, JNF also maintains regular e-mail communications. To make e-mails as relevant as possible, the group localizes its online communications by geography, publishing 26 different versions of each edition. As a result, JNF experiences strong open rates regularly in the 18 to

EXHIBIT 11.4   Home Page of the Jewish National Fund Web Site

EXHIBIT 11.5   Regionalized E-Mail Newsletter From Jewish National Fund Web Site

30 percent range, and the organization's e-mail file has consistently grown. For example, in the fourth quarter of 2004, JNF had 180,000 addresses; by the third quarter of 2006, its file had grown to more than 280,000 e-mail addresses (see Exhibits Exhibit 11.4 and Exhibit 11.5).

Visually, it is important to design your Web site so that it is clear and makes it easy for constituents to give, advocate, or perform other actions.

In addition to regular e-mail updates, it also is important to send stand-alone e-mail appeals. The appropriate frequency for appeals depends on your organization's e-mail file and appeal history. Organizations new to online fundraising should plan to send four fundraising e-mail appeals per year. Organizations that have been marketing longer and have conditioned their audience to expect a higher frequency may send as many as 12 e-mail appeals per year. In the case of advocacy groups, it is important to strike a balance between fundraising appeals and advocacy appeals. I do not recommend trying to combine fundraising and advocacy appeals in the same message, as doing so can confuse constituents in determining which action is more important.

The response rate to an e-mail appeal is measured by the percentage of people who click through multiplied by the percentage who then actually donate or advocate. To maximize the click-through rate for e-mail appeals, it is important to develop a control—a standard appeal format against which your organization can compare future appeals. It is important to then test against the control over time, varying the creative, content, subject lines, and so on. Such testing will help your organization determine whether the response rate can be improved. The e-mail subject line can have a significant impact on open rates and, therefore, response rates. In a test conducted by the Anti-Defamation League, varying the subject line for one appeal showed a 15 percent difference in open rate and an 81 percent difference in click-through rate between the best- and worst-performing variants.

For most nonprofit organizations, only about 10 percent of individuals who visit donation pages actually donate. The other 90 percent "abandon." To minimize abandonment rates and, conversely, to maximize conversion or donation rates, it is important to optimize the donation form layout, flow, creative, and messaging. Modern online donation systems like Convio provide a good amount of flexibility to fundraisers to adjust and fine-tune donation forms to help improve conversion rates. Tests that you can conduct include designing one-page versus multipage donation flows, testing the use of images, inserting additional questions into the donation flow, testing the use of premiums, and testing the use of directed giving options. One other best practice is to remove the navigation instructions, or page wrapper, as a constituent enters the donation flow, much like the checkout process at Amazon.com.

In addition to maximizing response rate, it also is important to focus on securing the highest gift possible to maximize revenue. Techniques to help do this include testing different ask arrays and asking for sustainer gifts, such as ongoing monthly contributions, or installment payments for large gifts. If a constituent is a returning donor, modern online fundraising tools also make it possible to present a gift array that is tailored specifically to that individual and reflects some multiple of his or her highest previous contribution.

Loyalty

As noted earlier, I founded Convio because I was struck by the rate at which nonprofit organizations churned their supporter base each year. Most nonprofit organizations churn 35 to 65 percent of donors each year from their direct mail programs. This is a very costly outcome, considering that a nonprofit then has to replenish its program by conducting expensive acquisition efforts. In the case of special event fundraising, it is common for 50 to 70 percent of event participants not to renew.

Online marketing can play a major role in improving retention rates and commitment levels, such as average gift size and gift frequency. There are multiple tactics at your disposal to increase constituent loyalty through online marketing.

First, it is important to provide regular donor updates to keep them informed of how your organization is using their funds and to continue to acknowledge their support. You can do this using e-mail updates tailored to donors based on which campaigns they have supported in the past. Such e-mails should not be overt asks for additional funding. By using personalization or segmentation technology, it is possible to e-mail different versions of such stewardship updates to different donors based on specific appeals or programs they have supported.

Another technique to help increase loyalty is to encourage individuals to become sustainer donors, such as becoming a monthly donor or making a larger-than-usual donation using an installment payment plan. In both cases, not only is the annual gift value much higher than usual, but it also is common to see a substantial improvement in retention rates. Sustainer contributions can be made with a credit card or by automated bank transfer. In the United Kingdom, automated bank transfers are

CASE STUDY: DEFENDERS OF WILDLIFE

Defenders of Wildlife (Defenders; www.defenders.org) is a national environmental organization dedicated to the protection of all native wild animals and plants in their natural communities. To help maximize action and response rates for both fundraising and advocacy efforts, Defenders conducts a rigorous e-mail testing program. The organization's key steps in testing and learning from its campaigns include:

1. Test design and setup.
   - Defenders sets a clear goal for what element is being tested and how to measure results.
   - It is important to test only one element at a time.
   - It is important to ensure that there is an adequate sample size for test significance.
2. Test execution.
   - The organization removes all external and confounding factors to the extent possible, such as ensuring that variants are sent at the same time and days of the week or ensuring that the sample is randomly selected.
   - Implement source codes or other tracking functionality.
3. Test measurement and analysis.
   - Defenders measures the test results, keeping in mind the significance of the test variant on improving performance on key metrics (e.g., open rate, click-through rate, conversion rate, and overall response rate).
   - Results are analyzed, conclusions drawn, and new hypotheses formed. Defenders also discusses potential additional or new tests that emerge from results.
4. Implement insights.
5. Continue to innovate and test new elements.

One fundraising test that Defenders conducted included two different campaign variants. One e-mail appeal focused on a matching gift opportunity, and the second appeal had a wolf-focused message (wolves are a key symbol used by Defenders). The organization found that the wolf-focused message resulted in a 0.17 percent response rate, or a 29 percent increase compared to the matching gift appeal.

As a result, in part of its test-and-learn approach, Defenders has achieved very strong outcomes, such as increasing its online fundraising and online advocacy actions by 50 to 100 percent over the previous year.

Defenders provides these cautions in implementing a test-and-learn approach such as the one just described:

1. Do not assume that test results are absolute. Results from one test cannot always be applied to different situations.
2. Remember to account for external and potentially confounding factors.

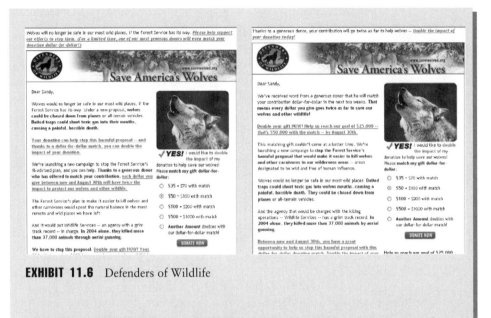

EXHIBIT 11.6   Defenders of Wildlife

3. It is possible to make data measurement and implementation errors. If you do not believe the results, do not hesitate to test it again.
4. Do not forget creative innovation. Without creative innovation, a test-and-learn approach will rapidly lead to only very small improvements and largely stagnant results (see Exhibit 11.6).

the predominant fundraising vehicle and result in annual donor retention rates greater than 95 percent. One additional strategy to drive loyalty is to encourage involvement in other programs that support the organization, such as advocacy or volunteer fundraising.

EMERGING TECHNOLOGIES AND TECHNIQUES

Leveraging Social Networks

Online social networks allow people to come together around shared interests or causes, such as making friends, dating, business networking, hobbies, interests, and political discourse. The number of visitors to online social networks has grown exponentially in recent years. In June of 2006 alone, MySpace.com had an estimated 55 million visitors. Although most social networks attract a very young demographic (the primary age group for MySpace.com is 14 to 34), there are several networks geared toward older individuals, such as Gather.com, which appeal to audiences such as Public Radio listeners.

Virtually every nonprofit organization seeks cost-effective ways to reach new supporters, and often many are interested in attracting younger constituents. Will

CASE STUDY: SPCA OF TEXAS

The Society for the Prevention of Cruelty to Animals of Texas (www.spca.org) is a regional animal welfare organization based in Dallas, Texas. The group has been engaged in online marketing for several years and has a well-established marketing program, especially for a regional organization. In particular, the SPCA of Texas has done a great job building a robust e-mail file of more than 40,000 contacts. As an organization that has a long history in direct mail fundraising, SPCA of Texas still receives a vast majority of donations from postal mail—89 percent of active donors provide donations using solely postal mail. An additional 10 percent have donated using both online and offline channels.

Research conducted by Convio and StrategicOne in conjunction with SPCA of Texas found that online marketing has a major impact on donor value and retention rates, even if donors continue to donate solely offline. In 2005, direct mail donors who were engaged online by the SPCA of Texas and continued to donate solely through postal mail gave more than three times per year. In comparison, direct mail donors who were not engaged online and to whom the organization communicated only through postal mail gave just under two times per year. The annual "value" for such donors was similarly higher. In addition, the research showed that the organization's 2005 retention

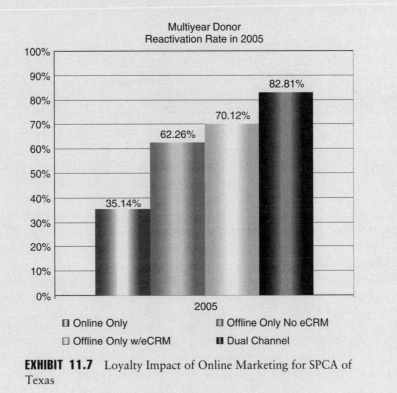

EXHIBIT 11.7 Loyalty Impact of Online Marketing for SPCA of Texas

rates for direct mail donors engaged in online marketing also were much higher. For example, multiyear direct mail—only donors engaged in online marketing renewed at an average of 70.1 percent versus 62.2 percent for those not engaged online. Multiyear donors who gave through both channels renewed at 82.8 percent (see Exhibit 11.7).

social networks represent an effective way to access and engage new supporters in the future? This section gives a brief overview of this emerging technology and techniques that have evolved in recent years, including how nonprofits use social networks like MySpace.com to reach new supporters and extend their brand.

Profiled are the efforts of two environmental conservation groups that have both been active in experimenting with online social networks—The Nature Conservancy and a return visit to Defenders of Wildlife. Long known for their progressive use of online marketing, these two nonprofit organizations have begun exploring new ways to leverage online social networks and, thus, provide valuable insight on this topic.

In summary, social networking sites have proliferated in the last few years, and certain ones like MySpace.com have begun attracting huge volumes of traffic and members. Although current results for most organizations exploring an online social networking strategy have been modest, these sites represent a new and cost-effective way for nonprofits to reach new and younger constituents. Because creating a simple social network presence and testing constituent recruitment strategies require a minimal amount of time, nonprofit organizations should consider experimenting with these sites to help better understand the potential benefits of online social networking for their organizations.

NEW FORMS OF PEER-TO-PEER FUNDRAISING

For several years, special events fundraising has been conducted online using volunteer fundraising tools from companies that provide software and services specifically to nonprofit organizations. These tools enable event participants to create personal fundraising Web pages and then market to their friends and family using e-mail messages that encourage them to donate. Moving special events fundraising online in this fashion has been a major success. Almost all major healthcare fundraising events have a strong online fundraising component today, and it is common for groups to raise more than 20 percent of funds online. Some high-involvement events, such as two-day walks, have garnered as much as 75 percent of funds online. Internet fundraising has not only brought operational efficiencies but has also driven stronger fundraising results. Online fundraisers tend to raise more money through higher average gifts and a greater number of contributions.

Early on, special events fundraisers realized that some participants wanted to support them financially but did not want to take part in the actual event. This resulted in the creation of virtual races or virtual participation options. In 2003 the Howard Dean campaign used the concept of peer-to-peer fundraising to support widespread grassroots outreach via so-called house parties, gatherings where people invited friends and strangers to convene at their homes to show their support.

CASE STUDY: THE NATURE CONSERVANCY

The Nature Conservancy maintains an informal presence on several social networking sites including Gather.com, Care2.com, and Wikipedia. The Conservancy's senior manager of digital marketing, Jonathon D. Colman, often represents the group on these social networks as an environmental enthusiast and an individual representative of the Conservancy rather than as an official voice of the organization. The Nature Conservancy believes that this approach resonates well across various audiences. Overall, the organization spends about three hours per week maintaining its presence on these social networking sites.

Since the Conservancy has begun its online social networking efforts, hundreds of individuals have joined as friends or connections on the various networks, and thousands more have visited its Web site. Depending on the network, the conversion rates from friends to donors, members, or e-newsletter subscribers is mixed. Although Jonathon makes an effort to provide links to the Conservancy's Web site when relevant, more people are interested in engaging in dialogue within the network compared to visiting The Nature Conservancy's Web site at www.nature.org.

The Conservancy's social network presence has, however, been very helpful in finding a few "superenthusiasts"—individuals who join the organization's file and become very involved. One such person, who previously was not a Conservancy member, ran a 24-hour "blogathon" to raise money for the organization. Another positive outcome was enhancements in optimizing the Conservancy's search engine placement. As more Nature Conservancy links appear on social network pages, the organization's Web site relevancy increases, which in turn helps the group's site appear higher on search result listings.

Early on, The Nature Conservancy concentrated its social network efforts on reaching new constituents. Its involvement with one network, StumbleUpon, resulted in nearly 35,000 visitors to the Conservancy's Web site by the end of 2006. The organization also experimented with promoting its Gather.com presence to current constituents on the Conservancy's home page and by way of its e-mail newsletter. This test yielded approximately 60 new members to the Conservancy's Gather.com group. Gather.com is particularly interesting to the Conservancy because of the closely aligned Public Radio demographic, enabling increased brand building and easy navigation for a key audience.

One challenge The Nature Conservancy has encountered is that most social networking services do not provide good details for page visitation or other metrics. This makes it difficult to accurately gauge the success of these initiatives outside of actions constituents take on the Conservancy's Web site.

In the last two years, peer-to-peer fundraising, also known as volunteer-led fundraising, has been applied to other areas, including tribute and memorial campaigns. Tribute giving is an important part of the philanthropic mix for healthcare organizations in particular. One major health charity indicated that more than 80 percent of its online donations were tribute or memorial gifts. One challenge with tribute and memorial gifts is that they frequently come from only one person

CASE STUDY: DEFENDERS OF WILDLIFE REVISITED

Defenders of Wildlife, mentioned earlier, ventured into the online social networking world by launching both an individual profile and a group on MySpace.com. By the end of 2006, Defenders' individual profile page at www.myspace.com/defendersofwildlife had attracted more than 2,000 "friends." At the time, the organization purposely was not fundraising on MySpace.com but, instead, focused efforts on advocacy.

To create a viral effect, Defenders offers a "site badge," or banner. This is a piece of HTML code that constituents can insert within their MySpace.com personal pages to help the organization promote their campaigns and recruit activists (see Exhibit 11.8).

The early results of Defenders' efforts are encouraging: Hundreds of advocacy actions can be directly attributed to their network of MySpace.com "friends." These numbers are very small compared with what the organization can generate through its online direct response efforts, but the organization considers the conversion rates to be promising.

Perhaps most exciting is that a number of passionate individuals have taken it upon themselves to help advance the work of Defenders by creating their own personal campaign pages. For example, the group http://groups.myspace.com/savethewolves has more than 1,000 members and links to an advocacy campaign page on Defenders' Web site.

EXHIBIT 11.8   Defenders of Wildlife MySpace.com "Site Badge"

rather than being a giving opportunity for an extended group of friends or family. A second challenge is that individuals who give tribute and memorial gifts generally are one-time donors and do not renew.

Providing donors with online tools to create tribute and memorial Web pages for their loved ones or people they are honoring is proving to be a successful

CASE STUDY: TRISOMY 18 FOUNDATION

The Trisomy 18 Foundation is a small nonprofit group focused on raising public awareness, funding research initiatives, and providing support for families dealing with the hardships of Trisomy 18, an often fatal chromosomal disorder in infants. The organization's annual operating budget is less than $500,000. The Trisomy 18 Foundation realized early on that the World Wide Web could be a very strategic tool for fundraising, reaching its primary target audience—families with children who would be born with Trisomy 18—and helping to unite these families online to support each other. Upon deploying its new eCRM system, the organization set a goal to raise $100,000 online in its first year. It exceeded this target within nine months, while simultaneously doubling the number of registered constituents during the same time period. More than 50 percent of this growth in online giving was from newly mobilized first-time donors.

One strategy that the Trisomy 18 Foundation uses is to encourage constituents to conduct their own grassroots fundraising events, such as local golf tournaments, open houses, or even school "penny drives." Such events are not run by the Trisomy 18 Foundation, but instead are organized directly by volunteers. In each case, 100 percent of event proceeds are donated directly to the organization.

The Trisomy 18 Foundation now plans to launch in April a new campaign called "Our Child's Legacy" (www.trisomy18.org/legacy). The organization plans to promote the campaign as a new support program for parents in which they can share their children's stories and begin to heal. The fundraising aspect of this campaign is appropriately downplayed, but it still should be a great path of funding for the foundation (see Exhibit 11.9).

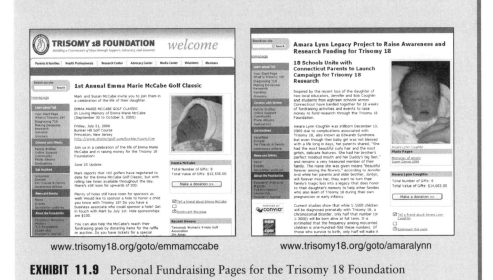

www.trisomy18.org/goto/emmamccabe   www.trisomy18.org/goto/amaralynn

EXHIBIT 11.9 Personal Fundraising Pages for the Trisomy 18 Foundation

formula. Whereas, there are many similarities to the tools and strategies involved in online special events fundraising, there also are many important differences. In particular, the tone associated with a memorial or tribute constituent interface and public Web page needs to be very different from that of a special events site. For example, the scrolling contribution thermometers, which have been an integral part of special event personal Web pages, are omitted and replaced with guest books. The messaging used within the constituent center to encourage a volunteer to raise funds also is quite different compared to special events fundraising.

When it comes to new forms of peer-to-peer fundraising, Trisomy 18 Foundation, a small disease and disorder group, has done an excellent job of building a peer community online and driving strong volunteer fundraising results.

GETTING STARTED

As stated earlier, the eCRM framework, along with the recommendations and best practices articulated by each stage, can be applied by any nonprofit organization regardless of its size, mission, or maturity of its online marketing program. Many of the case studies presented thus far have focused on organizations that have been engaged in online marketing for several years. The next two case studies, however, involve organizations that are newer to online marketing and have recently begun stepping up their online programs.

CASE STUDY: LEAGUE OF UNITED LATIN AMERICAN CITIZENS

The League of United Latin American Citizens (LULAC) is the largest and oldest Hispanic organization in the United States and is committed to advancing the economic condition, educational attainment, political influence, health, and civil rights of Hispanic Americans. As a national organization, the league operates 700 councils across the country.

LULAC considers the Internet to be its primary tool to help expand the organization's membership. In late 2006, the league had approximately 150,000 dues-paying members—almost all offline. The organization also had about 3,000 online members, or "e-members," and also operated a Listserv in Yahoo! Groups. LULAC's goal is to grow its e-mail file to 150,000, to match the size of the group's existing offline file. Over time, the organization also wants to convert its e-members to dues-paying members.

LULAC is deploying several strategies to build its e-mail file and engage its constituency. First and foremost, it has deployed an integrated eCRM system that uses a single database and encompasses all of the applications required for an organization to engage and interact with constituents online. Previously, LULAC used several systems, which resulted in data silos and made it difficult to properly engage constituents across different programs. The organization's new eCRM system includes capabilities for event management, fundraising, membership, e-mail marketing, content management, and advocacy.

One of the league's primary vehicles for constituent outreach is its 700 council network. With its integrated eCRM system, LULAC can provide each of its councils with a mini–Web site called a "club page." Each of these mini–Web sites is tied into the organization's Web site. Council administrators can update content on the "club page," post events and photos, publish a blog, and send e-mails to their local constituencies. Whenever constituents register on a club page, they also join the national LULAC file. So, as LULAC councils promote the usage of their own club pages locally, they also are supporting the national office's file-building efforts.

As an advocacy organization, LULAC also aims to grow its e-mail file through conducting online advocacy campaigns. Another strategy the organization has planned is to build its e-mail file through online event registration. The league operates a number of events around the country. Using offline promotion, the organization will encourage people to register and buy tickets online, thereby capturing e-mail addresses in the process. LULAC also aims to provide other incentives for constituents who register on its Web site, including participation in the group's online community.

One final strategy LULAC plans to pursue is promotion on partner organization Web sites and e-mail lists (see Exhibit 11.10). As an organization

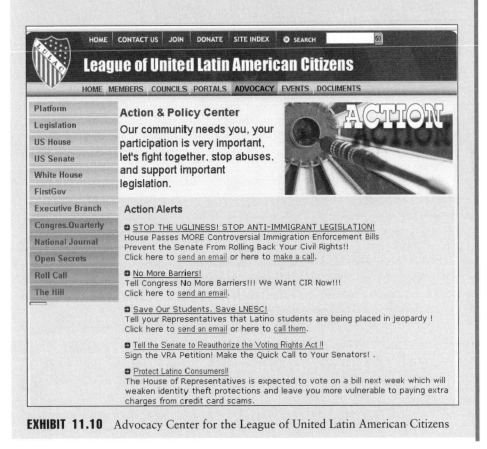

EXHIBIT 11.10 Advocacy Center for the League of United Latin American Citizens

with a defined target constituency, it is easy for LULAC to identify other organizations that reach its desired audience. By encouraging partners to present LULAC's issues on their Web sites and in e-mail communications, the organization can increase traffic to its Web site and help drive additional registrations and ongoing support.

CASE STUDY: UNITED NEGRO COLLEGE FUND

The United Negro College Fund (UNCF; uncf.org) is the nation's oldest and most successful minority higher education assistance organization. Its annual campaign raises approximately $100 million each year from corporate, foundation, and independent donors. Unrestricted donations are especially important to UNCF, because it is from these funds that the organization provides operating support to the 39 historically black colleges and universities (HBCUs) that belong to UNCF and from which the charitable organization draws its own operating budget.

In recent years, corporations and foundations—UNCF's traditional sources of unrestricted funds—have increasingly targeted and restricted donations to carry out their own mandates. This has led the organization to look increasingly to individual donors for unrestricted contributions, hoping both to widen its base of individual donors and to persuade present donors to increase the size of their contributions. With these objectives in mind, UNCF has increased its focus on the potential offered by the Web.

UNCF already has an active Web presence. Many thousands of students and their parents visit uncf.org to apply for financial aid from the 325 scholarship programs that UNCF offers or to find out more about its member colleges.

UNCF's primary focus in expanding its Web-based activities is toward increasing its unrestricted support by identifying and cultivating individual donors. The organization would especially like to use the Web's generally younger, upscale audience to engage a new generation of donors. To these ends, UNCF will explore several strategies:

- Create a dedicated "Give" subsite, which will highlight a variety of donation campaigns, each directed at a different constituency and which will feature a redesigned user-friendly donation page.

- Create microsites for special-appeal campaigns, such as UNCF's annual nationally broadcast entertainment special, *An Evening of Stars*, and the "Wave of Hope" campaign, which is based on the leadership of former presidents Bill Clinton and George H. W. Bush for efforts to assist Katrina-devastated HBCUs along the Gulf Coast.

- Build traffic to the site with special Web-based content, such as unbroadcast "extras" from performers who appear on *An Evening of Stars*.

- Use online communications to increase the reach, impact, and yield of UNCF's direct mail campaign.

The United Negro College Fund also is interested in exploring a number of other approaches to using the Web to carry out its mission. The lower cost of online communication would make it feasible to provide stewardship of current and prospective donors by sharing information outside the context of specific requests for contributions. The organization could build on its service to scholarship applicants by extending its communication with them through and after graduation to provide a "landing place" for students, alumni, and like-minded members of the public. By helping these constituents stay abreast of issues in minority higher education and of the needs of HBCUs, such an online space can provide alumni the opportunity to support UNCF's activities in this area.

The organization could modify its scholarship application functionality to retain applicants' e-mail addresses and expand the UNCF e-mailing lists. And UNCF could use its Web site and Internet to build a wider constituency among corporate diversity officers, key corporate contacts both for seeking out job-seeking UNCF alumni and developing UNCF workplace-based fundraising campaigns.

CONCLUDING COMMENTS

Online marketing can be a very powerful tool for groups targeting specific segments of the community—whether ethnic or cultural groups or segments that represent special interests. In this chapter I have presented a comprehensive set of recommendations to follow and case studies of organizations that have been engaged in online marketing for varied lengths of time.

If your organization is new to online marketing, do not be intimidated. Begin the journey today toward establishing a successful online marketing program. Adopt the eCRM framework presented in this chapter to help identify priorities and key tactics. Starting out, you do not have to follow all of the recommendations and strategies used by the nonprofits that are presented here, but they are illustrative of the direction in which your organization should be heading.

Nonprofit online marketing is growing and evolving at a rapid rate. According to the *Chronicle of Philanthropy*, groups not involved in tsunami or Hurricane Katrina fundraising grew online funds by more than 50 percent from 2004 to 2005. In our own client base at Convio, we saw similar annual growth trends from 2005 to 2006. Not only is this growth exciting, but so is the innovation. Whether experimenting with social networks or trying new peer-to-peer fundraising techniques, many organizations and the vendors that serve them are trying to evolve successful models, learn from the commercial sector, and leverage new assets, such as social networks. Not all of these experiments will bear immediate results. For example, most experimentation to date with social networks has provided good insights but few significant results. Some innovations, however, like the new forms of peer-to-peer fundraising, including tributes and memorial campaigns, are showing promising early results, as illustrated by the Trisomy 18 Foundation case study.

Last, this chapter and, indeed, this book focus primarily on fundraising. It is, however, important to note that with all organizations cited, online marketing plays just as important, if not a more important, role in effecting the mission of each organization.

Constituents who support your organization financially also want to, and are able to, support your mission in other ways, such as spreading the word, volunteering, advocating, and the like. In some cases, as with the United Negro College Fund, the same constituents who can provide financial support may also have been beneficiaries or your organization's services at different points in their lives. As such, it is important to always consider the strategic mission, priorities, and fundraising goals of your organization as you define your online strategy.

ABOUT THE AUTHOR

Vinay Bhagat is the founder, chairman, and chief strategy officer of Convio Inc.. Vinay founded Convio, Inc. in April 1999 after volunteering at a public television pledge drive and being struck by the opportunity to leverage Internet technology to drive better fundraising results. Today, as chief strategy officer, Vinay oversees business and corporate development, strategy, and consulting services and works with many of Convio's largest current and prospective clients.

A frequent speaker at conferences, Vinay has addressed events hosted by the Association of Fundraising Professionals, Direct Marketing Association Nonprofit Federation, Council for the Advancement and Support of Education, Independent Sector, Integrated Media Association, Politics Online, Public Broadcasting System and National Voluntary Healthcare Association. Vinay also is a widely published author, with chapters in *The Nonprofit Handbook: Fund Raising Third Edition 2002 Supplement* and *Nonprofit Internet Strategies: Best Practices for Marketing, Communications, and Fundraising Success*; his articles appear regularly in *DM News, Journal of the Direct Marketing Association Nonprofit Federation* and on OnPhilanthropy.com. Vinay serves on the board of the ePhilanthropy Foundation and the Education Committee of the Direct Marketing Association Nonprofit Federation.

Integration Strategies

CHAPTER 12

Integrating Online and Offline Activities to Build Stronger Relationships

Mark Connors
Amergent, Inc.

Relationships of trust depend on our willingness to look not only to our own interests, but also the interests of others.
—Peter Farquharson, Executive Director, Habitat for Humanity Northern Ireland

INTRODUCTION

The quotation by Peter Farquharson clearly articulates what is needed for a successful relationship: Both parties' "interests" must be considered, and both parties must "benefit" in order for a relationship to be successful. This is true both in personal relationships and in the relationships nonprofit organizations have with their various constituencies. And, like personal relationships, building strong, lasting ties between a nonprofit organization and donors takes time, effort, and creativity.

Whether your focus is direct mail fundraising, major and planned gift cultivation, online giving, advocacy, or any other type of nonprofit activity, it likely involves relationship building—or, as the title of this book suggests, *People to People Fundraising*. Even "institutional giving"—giving to an organization by foundations or companies—is primarily driven by individuals within the nonprofit organization building relationships with individuals within the donating institution. So, no matter what type of activity you are involved in on behalf of your organization, it is critical to view each contact as an opportunity to build a stronger relationship between those you are communicating with and your organization.

As many of this book's chapters illustrate, advances in online technology are enhancing existing interactions and creating new opportunities for people to form and build relationships, both with like-minded people and with the organizations they support. And the exciting part of this for nonprofit organizations is that although online giving has increased dramatically over the last few years, even the most aggressive estimates for the amount of money being raised online indicate that it is still *only one to three percent of the total amount of money being given by individuals*. This fact proves that online fundraising is in its infancy, meaning that there is still time—and huge potential—for nonprofits to become more effective and efficient in online fundraising. It is also important to note that raising money online is not the only factor to consider. It is also important to consider the impact that online relationship-building activities are having on offline giving. We discuss this topic later in the chapter.

Despite early claims by many companies involved in online fundraising that traditional methods of fundraising would quickly be replaced by online giving and e-marketing, most experts agree that the real success stories will come from organizations that embrace a holistic approach to building relationships. This requires the development of comprehensive strategies to leverage and integrate both online and offline activities across the entire organization.

This chapter explores what is needed to develop integrated online/offline—or "multichannel"—strategies that will ensure stronger relationships with your donors and other constituencies.

BECOMING "DONOR-CENTRIC": UNDERSTANDING YOUR SUPPORTERS AND *THEIR* VIEW OF *YOUR* ORGANIZATION

Here is an interesting and eye-opening experiment to perform before reading further:

Step 1. Select five to ten people from within your organization. Be sure to mix it up a bit by choosing one or two each from different departments or with different job titles and/or responsibilities. For example, include an administrative person, a program staff person, a fundraiser, a manager or executive-level person, and so on.

Step 2. Ask each to do: "Describe, in your own words, how you would explain what our organization does to a friend or family member unfamiliar with our work. Give the top two most important aspects of our work in your view, then rank them #1 and #2." *(Get written answers if possible.)*

Step 3. Write down what each person ranks as his or her "Top Two." Count how many different answers you have.

Step 4. Repeat Steps 1 through 3 with a small sample of nonstaff people who have a connection with your organization. Again choose a cross section of people: donors, volunteers, advocates, board members, and so on. You can vary the instructions slightly to ask: "Tell me how you would describe to a friend or family member your reason for getting involved with our organization and the top two most important things that you feel our organization does or should be doing."

It is likely that you now have a list of several—and perhaps many—different answers. There is a good chance some of them do not reflect what your leadership feels is the mission of the organization. *Don't fret; you are not alone.*

Many of the organizations that perform this experiment find that people, both within and outside of their organization, have very different views of the same organization. And while this may concern the folks who crafted your organization's very succinct and crystal clear mission statement, it really should be seen as an opportunity.

If all of the answers on your list are similar, take a look at the narrative of what these people are telling their friends and family. Are there any major differences in the way they are describing your organization? Again, there may be some more subtle differences in what people think is most important about your organization, and perhaps there is an opportunity to widen your focus or alter your message to attract more people to your cause.

A Real-Life Example

While this "experiment" is fairly unscientific and only involves a small number of people, the same types of results are often found by organizations that invest in focus groups and broad-based surveys of their constituents. For example, Amergent (the direct marketing agency that the author of this chapter works for) performed a project for a large international fraternal organization that had decided to begin a national fundraising program targeting its members. Until then all fundraising for the organization was done locally through the organization's "chapters."

In order to craft the most powerful fundraising appeal, the organization and the agency wanted to understand the membership better and really get to the bottom of what the members thought were the most important initiatives of the organization. To do this it was decided that the organization would ask the members directly.

The first step was to overlay the organization's membership data with demographic and wealth information provided by Target America (www.tgtam.com). Amergent then identified segments of the file to be invited to take the survey. The segmentation algorithm was fairly complex and involved making sure that there was equal representation of members geographically as well as by age, length of membership, wealth, and other factors.

To perform the survey, Amergent sent out direct mail invitations that directed members to an online survey site. (This is an example of using traditional direct mail to drive online results.) Amergent used a powerful online survey solution from Communitas Online (www.communitasonline.com) that allowed us to ask a series of open-ended questions to which respondents could answer in their own words with as much text as they liked. The open-ended questions were interspersed with multiple-choice and ranking-type questions to make up a complete survey. The answers from the survey were then fed into Communitas's powerful CALCAT™ software, which identifies and organizes recurring thoughts, frustrations, needs, or ideas, so that meaningful analyses can be produced from open-ended questions.

The results were eye-opening for the organization. Not only did the results show that the membership had different ideas than the organizational leadership of what was most important, but it also revealed that there were two major segments within the membership that felt very different about the importance of various organizational issues. In this organization's case the results also showed that these segments were pretty clearly delineated by age. From this analysis Amergent recommended that the organization craft two very different messages for its initial appeal in order to maximize results.

Despite the very clear data showing that there were two distinct groups who needed to hear different messages from the organization, the organization's leaders

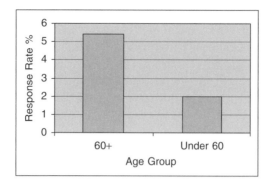

EXHIBIT 12.1   Appeal Response Rates by Age

decided to stick to a single message for the inaugural appeal. The organization chose to develop an appeal around the themes that the older member segment indicated were most important. The response rates to the appeal are shown in Exhibit 12.1.

The older members told the organization what they wanted to hear from the organization. The organization responded with an appeal that spoke directly to those issues and reaped a 5.4 percent response rate from this segment. The younger members, while still responding at a respectable two percent rate, were not as inspired by the message and therefore responded in much lower numbers. Armed with these results, the organization is now planning future messaging that will take into account the differences among their member segments.

What this all goes to show is that even organizations with very narrowly defined mission statements (like a fraternal membership organization) typically have groups of constituents involved with the organization for very different reasons. Understanding why these different groups are involved with your organization and what they want or need from it is critical to building long-term relationships. Only by understanding these different segments can your organization become more "donor-centric"—building long-lasting relationships by focusing on meeting the "interests" and needs of your various constituent groups while at the same remaining true to the mission of your organization.

So now you probably want to know how an organization goes about becoming donor-centric. Here are a few steps to get you started.

TAKE A LOOK IN THE MIRROR

Think of this as taking the "e-Harmony Personality Profile Quiz" for nonprofits.

The first step to becoming a more donor-centric organization is to have the leadership of your organization take a long hard look at your organization and ask some tough questions. This includes looking at:

- Organizational structure
- Current communications (branding, messaging, segmentation, media/channels, etc.)
- Systems, processes, and data flow

Taking the time to look in the mirror before starting an online fundraising program will help your organization avoid many pitfalls. It will also help you develop a strategic approach to online efforts that complements your offline initiatives, aligns with the organizational mission, and avoids creating an undue burden on your staff.

Some of the questions to ask include:

- Are there organizational barriers to understanding the full relationship we have with our donors/members?
- Are the technology solutions we use sharing data in an efficient and effective manner?
- Do we have a complete picture of our constituents and their activities with our organization?
- Are we allowing donors/members to truly interact with us—and their fellow supporters—via multiple channels?

BREAKING DOWN ORGANIZATIONAL SILOS

For many nonprofit organizations, one of the most significant barriers to successful donor-centric communication is created by the very structure of the organization itself. This can be true for any size nonprofit but is particularly true in midsize and larger organizations. As nonprofits grow, they often become organized into departments that are focused on particular functions: Development, Marketing & Communication, Volunteers, Advocacy, Web and Online Activity, Program Delivery, and so on. And within these departments there may be further divisions. For example, Development is often further divided into separate groups that handle Direct Mail, Online Giving, Major Gifts, Planned Gifts, In-Kind gifts, and the like.

Policies, procedures, and data management systems that are put in place by the various departments often cause a silo effect, where individual departments or groups can become both isolated in their thinking and disinterested in what other departments are saying to or doing with the same donors, volunteers, and other groups. In many cases, the silo effect is not evident to those within each department as they continue to meet their goals and provide the appropriate service to their constituent group, whether internal or external. However, when viewed from the outside—the donor/constituent view—it often is clear that the organization is not be meeting the interests of its constituents in the most effective and efficient manner possible. In other words, the organization is creating relationships that are lopsided: giving each department what it needs, but not necessarily meeting the needs of donors and other constituents. This is a recipe for a short-term relationship.

This is not to say that an organization needs to completely change its structure. But it could point out the need to rethink how the departments within the organization interact with each other. While the various groups within the organization need to be focused primarily on their particular aspect of the relationship with a donor, they also need to be cognizant of how the other groups within the organization are interacting with that same donor.

Here is an example, based loosely on a real-life situation faced by a large national nonprofit organization, of how the silo effect can impact an organization's relationship with a donor.

XYZ ORGANIZATION: A LARGE NATIONAL CHARITY

Mary Smith has been donating clothing and household items to XYZ organization for 10 years. At one point she even donated a used automobile. In addition, Mary has been volunteering in her spare time at the local office of the charity over the past two years. After 10 years of donating "in-kind" gifts to the organization and two years of volunteering, Mary received a particularly moving direct mail piece from the organization and decided to make a cash donation. To her surprise, she received a letter of acknowledgment thanking her for becoming a "new donor" to XYZ and explaining all the additional ways she could become involved with the organization.

While she was pleased to receive the acknowledgment, she was a bit upset that the organization had referred to her as a "new donor." After all, she had receipts for her in-kind gifts dating back 10 years, and she was on a first-name basis with the local volunteer coordinator. Mary picked up the phone and called the organization to find out why she had been referred to as a new donor. During her conversation with the very pleasant customer service representative, she was told, much to her surprise, that while they were sure Mary was a very loyal longstanding donor of "in-kind" gifts and an active volunteer, they had no record of that in their system. She was told that "those types of gifts" are tracked by a different group and that volunteer information was managed locally by each chapter. After the call Mary had a nagging feeling that the organization did not really appreciate all she had done for it over the years.

From donors' perspective, they have a relationship with your organization, not with a particular department within your organization (volunteer, direct mail, online). They expect everyone representing your organization to understand and appreciate the full depth and breadth of their relationship.

The term coined to describe this in the commercial sector is "CRM," or customer relationship management. Countless books, systems, and training courses have been created around the concept. Yet many people are still confused about the true meaning of CRM. What it really boils down to is having a comprehensive understanding of the relationship a customer has with the organization or, in the case of nonprofits, becoming "donor-centric."

There are many examples to illustrate the importance of being donor-centric and the negative impact that the silo effect can have on the relationship between your organization and your constituents. Here are just a couple of additional examples. Do you think any of these types of things could be happening at your organization? You might be surprised!

One of the most challenging issues is that many organizations maintain segmented databases to manage their "in-kind" gift donors, direct mail donors, volunteers, and other constituent groups separately. And many organizations still "protect" certain segments of constituents—such as volunteers, advocates, and event

ABC ORGANIZATION: A LOCAL PERFORMING ARTS ORGANIZATION

George, a five-year season ticket holder and patron-level donor, had grown very fond of ABC and had begun to consider "doing more" for the organization. After visiting the organization's Web site to look into his options, he decided to talk with his financial advisor about making a large gift of stock.

While on the Web site, George was pleased to notice a new option to sign up for the organization's e-newsletter. He signed up and then used the tools provided to e-mail several of his close friends to suggest that they also sign up for the e-newsletter to learn more about the organization he had been telling them about. In addition, he also took advantage of an opportunity to register for a guided tour during a rehearsal.

After a week passed without receiving an e-newsletter, George called the organization to see when he could expect to receive the next edition. He was dismayed to learn that the organization did not yet have an e-newsletter and that it was simply "building an e-mail file" so it could send out e-mail newsletters and other communications "in the future."

Two days later, George attended the guided tour. At the end of the tour, he was asked to consider becoming a season ticket holder. His guide was a bit embarrassed when George pointed out that he had been a season ticket holder and patron of the organization for five years. George began to wonder if the organization really had its act together and began to rethink his plan of making the large stock gift.

participants—from getting solicitations because they feel that would be asking too much of these loyal people who give their time.

However, it has been proven that these people respond quite willingly and generously to solicitations without cutting back on their other activities. The key is to have a complete view of each individual's activity and to constantly thank them for all that they do for the organization. In fact, quite a bit of evidence supports a direct correlation between the number of different touch points that you have with donors and their "long-term value"—the total amount they will end up donating to your organization over time.

A second challenge being felt by many charities is the pressure to rush to hop on the online bandwagon. Fueled by news accounts of the wonderful successes nonprofits are having online and the aggressive marketing of online and e-marketing tools, many organizations have been quick to jump without first creating an effective strategic plan. As the examples given show, it is easy to start asking people to visit your Web site to leave an e-mail address. But without an effective plan for how you will use e-mail addresses and how your online activities will integrate with your offline activities, you may be creating more problems than solutions.

People interacting in the online world have a much different set of expectations than when they are offline; primarily they expect a much more immediate response to

EFG MISSIONS: A RELIGIOUS CHARITY

Mrs. Jameson, a widow on a fixed income, had been a very faithful donor to EFG Ministries for more than 20 years. She really enjoyed receiving the monthly magazine from the organization detailing the works of the missionaries around the world. She read every issue from cover to cover. While her gifts were always small—$5 (cash) every other month—she did what she could.

At one point, Mrs. Jameson called the organization to let them know she was leaving them in her will. She spoke with a Major Gift officer who noted this fact in the bequest database—a database kept separate from the main direct marketing database. About a week later, Mrs. Jameson received a personalized thank-you letter from the executive director of the organization, which made her feel very good about her decision.

Not long after, however, her health condition changed and she required more expensive medical care. Sadly, she could no longer afford to donate regularly to EFG.

Later that year, the direct marketing department of EFG began looking at costs and decided to cut back on the distribution of the magazine only to donors who donated at least $25 per year. For everyone else, EFG would begin publishing articles from the magazine in an e-newsletter format. An e-mail was sent to donors informing them of this decision, and an insert was included in several of the direct mail pieces encouraging people to go to the website and sign up for the e-mail version of the newsletter/magazine.

Mrs. Jameson read the insert and understood the organization's need to control costs, but because she did not use a computer she was disheartened to think that she would no longer receive the monthly magazine she enjoyed so much. Not one to raise a fuss, she did not bother to call the organization. In two months' time, the magazine stopped coming.

A few months later, she noticed a direct mail piece from a different mission organization in her mail and realized that this organization was offering a *free* printed magazine. She promptly put a few dollar bills in the business reply envelope and mailed it off.

their online activities. An organization must have a plan to meet these expectations or risk alienating people who might otherwise become very involved with the organization. Even worse, you could turn off an existing and generous donor.

DOES YOUR ORGANIZATION HAVE A PLAN?

Based on what you have read so far, is your organization prepared to truly integrate online tools into your cultivation plans? And, more important, do you feel that your organization is really prepared to respond to constituent needs in this new medium effectively? If yes, congratulations! If not, it is definitely time to prepare to take the leap into the online world—if it is done properly, the benefits to your organization can be enormous. What follows are some basic steps to take in developing a truly integrated strategy for your organization.

MINING YOUR DATABASE

While it is imperative that organizations begin to utilize online tools as part of their marketing mix, it is important that this be done in a well-planned manner. A major key to developing a solid strategic plan and spending your budget effectively is to first understand your existing donor base and the groups (segments) that make up that base.

The key to identifying the segments within your donor or member base is to have enough of and the right type of data, which can then be transformed into information. Most organizations collect and store plenty of "data" about their constituents; however, the data must be turned into actionable "information" in order to perform truly strategic fundraising. This is where the use of technology comes in handy.

Most nonprofit organizations today have some type of database system in place to keep track of their donors, and most of these systems do a good job of tracking who has donated what (Gift Type and Amount), when they have donated (Gift Date), and why they have donated (Source/Appeal Code), along with how they wish the gift to be used (Fund/Restriction). From this information, an organization can begin to build some very basic "segments" by searching for and grouping people by these various data points. For example, all people who have donated for a particular restricted fund might be considered a segment. Or all donors who have donated to the same appeal in each of the last five years might be considered a segment.

Where many organizations fall short is in keeping a complete history of each and every "outbound" communication and "inbound" interaction or touch point with each and every constituent in a manner that can later be turned into information. After all, in building a relationship with someone, it is just as important to know as much about their dislikes as it is to know about their likes. Translating this to the nonprofit world, it is just as important to know what a particular donor/constituent *does not* respond to (telemarketing, appeals for general funds, volunteer requests) as it is to know what he or she *does* respond to (direct mail, appeals about children, event invitations). Organizations that keep track of each and every outbound contact, whether it elicited a response or not, have a lot more data that can be turned into information. In the direct marketing business, turning data into actionable information is called "data mining"—digging for those nuggets of informational gold that help us better understand constituent behavior.

Many people have the misconception that data mining has to be a very complex process involving statisticians, intricate data modeling, and sophisticated analysis. The fact is that data mining can take many forms and can vary in the depth (complexity) necessary to unearth the gold (information). Basic data mining often can reveal very useful information that can be applied to significantly help a program.

The first step to successful data mining is making the most of the data you already have. This sounds simple enough. But in many organizations, data are fragmented across multiple systems and have been recorded in an inconsistent fashion throughout the years, making even the most basic analysis difficult. And without good data, it is almost impossible to develop a good understanding of what is driving donor behavior. In order to properly mine a database, often it is necessary first to perform a bit of reorganization, cleaning, and consolidation. Here are a few things to consider doing first.

MAKE THE MOST OF THE DATA YOU ALREADY HAVE

Identify Where Constituent Data Are Kept

While most organizations believe they have a single donor database, a little digging and asking questions often proves that there are a number of additional shadow databases being maintained by various departments and/or individuals within the organization. Often these additional databases contain more accurate and more detailed information on specific segments and/or activity than the primary donor database. It is important to consolidate these data in order to have a complete picture of your donors.

Count the Codes in Your System

Over the years databases can get quite cluttered and dirty, especially if there have been multiple changes in organizational management and/or high staff turnover in the data management area. Each group typically brings new ideas that they then translate into new coding structures in the database. Over time the database ends up containing lots of codes that may have never been used or used only once or twice. Sometimes several existing codes stand for the same thing. This can significantly affect your ability to understand the segments in your database. Taking the time to clean up and consolidate your database can lead to increased efficiency and better segmentation.

Look at Donor Records with Activity History and "Do Not Solicit" Flags

You may be surprised at what you find if you run some queries that look for donors who had at one time been very involved with your organization but are now flagged as "do not solicit." When performing file analysis for clients, we often uncover groups of donors who were excellent donors but at some point were flagged as "do not mail" or "no solicitation." And in attempting to understand what caused these donors to be flagged this way, we sometimes uncover startling information.

One of the most common reasons for good donors to be flagged "do not mail" is because they have been identified for a potential major gift ask. The trick is that, in many cases, if they do not respond to the major gift ask, the "do not solicit" flag is never removed. This prevents them from once again being solicited for the projects they supported so readily in the past. In other cases, the system is automatically flagging donors this way based on outdated business logic, but they are not being handed off to a major gift officer. Often these types of issues can be overlooked, as usually only a small number of donors are being flagged at any one time. Over the years, however, this segment can grow to be significant. And since they were regular donors in the past, this group is often a ripe opportunity for recapture.

Another common problem that is often identified is the improper handling of donor complaints and feedback. Many times donors or constituents contact an organization in reaction to receiving too many solicitations or to voice their displeasure with a particular message or issue. In some cases, they may have written on a response device "Don't mail me this again." All too often, this type of response is handled by simply flagging the donors as "do not solicit," when it should really be treated as an opportunity to have a dialogue with donors and to learn how the organization can better meet their needs. Often donors may be happy to continue to receive communication from your organization; they may just want you to mail them less, not include them on mailings about a particular issue, or contact them only via a certain channel (no phone calls, e-mail only, etc).

These types of issues point out the importance of having good procedures in place for handling donor complaints and how to flag donors appropriately. They also point out the importance of documenting any business rules and automatic coding procedures that are set up in your system, helping future staff members understand what is happening in the database.

It is a good idea to perform this type of data review, reorganization, and cleanup on a regular basis—at a minimum annually. Just like housecleaning and maintenance, performing database cleanup on a regular basis can help avoid much larger and more costly problems down the road.

COLLECT THE RIGHT TYPE AND AMOUNT OF DATA IN THE ONLINE WORLD

As you move toward integrating online and offline activities, it is more important than ever to plan in advance for the capture and management of data. With today's technology, including new online tools, it is crucial that you balance the amount of data you collect with what you will actually use. With the automated nature of some of the online tools, there can be a tendency to collect too much data, which then gets in the way of discerning the real information. Many online tools include databases of their own. Take the time to determine which pieces of data from these systems need to be added to your primary donor database and which can be left in the online tool databases.

For instance, many tools can track each and every mouse click as a person navigates your web site. While this might be useful information for looking at traffic patterns, abandon points, and the general flow of visitors to your site, keeping this amount of granular information in your primary donor database is not likely to be useful for segmentation purposes. Rather, tracking the number of times a person visits a Web page or area on your site focused on certain activity (advocacy, volunteering, particular program information) or clicks on links in your e-newsletters focused on similar themes or programs will be far more useful in identifying potential segments of like-minded constituents.

In addition to choosing what types of data to capture, you must also consider how frequently you want to synchronize your online and offline data. Some systems can be set up to support real-time data synchronization. But for many nonprofit organizations, a nightly or even weekly synchronization is sufficient. Again, the key is to balance your needs against the cost and the technology capabilities.

LOOK AT YOUR EXISTING DATA THROUGH A DIFFERENT LENS

A wise college professor once told a class full of undergraduates that one of the most important things to do in life was to "constantly alter your perspective, especially when dealing with things that you are very comfortable with or feel you are knowledgeable about." Often, when viewed through a different lens, those familiar things reveal an entirely new dimension or set of characteristics that previously went unnoticed.

In applying this lesson to marketing and fundraising, it is always important to constantly question what we believe causes certain results and donor behavior. An example of this can be found in the way many nonprofits develop segmentation strategies based on RFM (recency, frequency, monetary) of the various appeals to which a donor has historically responded. While this is a fairly sound strategy, it may not tell the whole story or give you the biggest bang for your buck.

A number of ways to apply a different perspective to looking at response history have shown some significant results. One is to consider seasonality—the time of year that the person is giving. For a religious organization, an initial view of what donors are responding to may tell us that they like to give once a year to appeals with a Christmas theme. If we look at the data differently, with seasonality in mind, we may learn that a certain donor likes to give in the fall and winter, not just to Christmas appeals. This could be significant because it could present new opportunities to get such donors to give when they are more likely to be in the giving spirit. Other donors may turn out to be springtime donors when we had originally thought they were Easter appeal donors. Even if donors are giving at several different times of the year, it can be important to understand if there is a particular season during which they seem more inclined to give. This might allow the organization to cut back on contacting certain people at certain times of the year, saving money, which can then be used to send additional solicitations to these people when they are more likely to give.

Another thing to consider, especially as you begin to solicit via multiple channels (e-mail, direct mail, online, etc.), is whether it is the channel that affects response or some other factor, such as theme. For example, some donors may appear to only donate online; others may seem to give only to direct mail. However, looking at things from a different perspective may reveal that certain donors respond, or do not respond, to any message having to do with certain themes, regardless of channel. In these cases, you have to consider the types of messages being sent via the different channels in order to fully understand the cause and effect.

These are just a few examples of how looking at your data through a different lens can reveal additional information and opportunities. There are many more. And while some of this information can be uncovered by running queries on your database, often the real gems are revealed only through a more detailed analysis that goes deeper and considers multiple data elements and their impacts.

If an organization does not have the reporting and analysis tools to perform this type of analysis in house, a number of companies offer services to help discern this information. Often this type of analysis is well worth the cost as it uncovers opportunities both to save money on unproductive segments and to raise more money by targeting more responsive segments at the right time with the right message.

Two companies that offer in-depth data analysis:
        Amergent: www.amergent.com
        Strategic One: www.strategicone.com

EXHIBIT 12.2 Integrated Offline Strategy

Once you have a good understanding of your current data file segments, you have the key building blocks to begin developing an integrated online offline strategy (see Exhibit 12.2).

MULTICHANNEL MARKETING: OPPORTUNITIES AND CHALLENGES

Most organizations have begun to market in multiple channels, but far fewer are actually doing effective multichannel marketing. While the new online tools are creating incredible opportunities for nonprofit organizations to interact with various constituencies more effectively and efficiently, these tools also create new challenges. One of the key challenges faced by organizations using both online and offline techniques and media is how to truly understand what is motivating constituents to take action.

The old model—donor receives mail piece, donor sends check—is changing. It is now likely to look more like this: Donor receives mail piece, donor visits Web site, donor signs up for e-newsletter, donor receives e-mail from organization, donor donates online or sends check back with reply device from original mail piece. This new world of online/offline is raising lots of questions and "issues" for organizations including:

- How does the organization track the appropriate "source" of these gifts?
- What department gets credit for raising that gift?
- What is really causing the person to take action?
- How should we spend our marketing dollars going forward?
- What is the best method of communication or mix of media for different types of constituents?

While these problems can be frustrating, they are good ones to have and good questions to be asking. The fact is, as stated earlier in this chapter, the use of online fundraising tools is still in its infancy, and in most cases organizations are still learning to walk when utilizing these new tools to enhance their marketing programs. While there are some definite dos and don'ts emerging, there is still plenty of uncharted territory to be explored and testing to be done. What works for one organization may not work for another. What works for one segment of your donor file may not work for others. This is why the old marketing rule of "Test, Test, Test—and Then Test Again" still holds true. Each organization has to learn what works for its constituent base and the various segments within that base.

A brief sampling of some ways that multichannel marketing is being used with success in the nonprofit sector follows.

USING MAIL TO DRIVE ONLINE ACTIVITY

The first big challenge to an organization's online success is getting people to visit the organization's Web site and/or provide an e-mail address so that ongoing online communication can take place. In the early rush to get online and reap Internet gold, most organizations focused on building Web sites. And only after spending lots of money to build these sites and having disappointing results with online fundraising did they realize that the Field of Dreams approach to online success—build it and they will come—simply does not work. There were not (and are not) vast numbers of people randomly searching the Web for new organizations to support.

Most fundraisers now know that in order to have online success, they must be constantly driving traffic to their Web sites. And while one of the easiest ways to do this is through regular e-mail communication, the challenge is getting people to provide their e-mail address and to give you permission to interact with them via e-mail in the first place. This is why it is so important for organizations to take every opportunity to use their direct mail pieces to drive not only offline results (donations), but also online activity.

Rule #1 in integrated online/offline marketing is that every piece of printed material that an organization produces should have the organization's Web site (URL) printed on it. And, when appropriate, every direct mail piece should give the recipient a compelling reason to visit the organization's Web site and begin or continue an online relationship. In addition, printed response devices should ask for and provide a space for respondents to include their e-mail addresses.

While this may sound like a pretty basic concept, it is surprising how many organizations are still not doing a good job of using their direct mail to drive online results. In most cases this is due to some form of the organizational silo issue discussed earlier. Often one group "owns" the Web site while a different one is responsible for direct mail fundraising. The direct mail group does not want to lose credit for gifts by sending donors to the Web site. The web group does not want to share credit for online gifts, even if the donors are driven to the site by a direct mail package. This territorial mind-set often gets in the way of doing what is best for the constituent and the organization as a whole.

USING E-MAIL AND ONLINE TOOLS TO BOLSTER DIRECT MAIL RESULTS

As mentioned earlier, for most organizations, direct mail fundraising is still the primary source of revenue and will likely continue to be for a number of years. Therefore, one of the best opportunities available to nonprofit organizations is figuring out ways in which to use e-mail and online activity to drive greater direct mail results.

Here are just a few examples of what is working for organizations today.

E-Mail Announcement, Alert, Spotlight

One use of e-mail to bolster direct mail results that is working quite well is the use of e-mail to alert constituents to an upcoming direct mail piece. An e-mail or series of e-mails is sent in advance of a direct mail campaign telling recipients to "watch for" the direct mail piece in the coming days. Often these e-mails utilize images and artwork from the upcoming appeal, a brief explanation of the importance of the mail piece, and a call to action asking the donor to go online to give today.

Many organizations have used this "spotlight" approach with particularly important campaigns, advocacy petitions, and other mailings for many years in the offline world by sending a postcard in advance of the primary mail package. Now an e-mail can serve the same purpose at far less expense.

E-Mail "Sandwich"

The term "e-mail sandwich" has become popular for describing the practice of sending an e-mail (or e-mails) both before and after a direct mail piece. Often the up-front e-mail serves as an alert or spotlight to the mailing, and the follow-up e-mail(s) reinforce the message of the mail piece and offer the recipient an additional opportunity to respond. E-mail sandwiches have proven very effective in raising response rates to direct mail campaigns and in some cases allow organizations to stretch their direct marketing budget by replacing a follow-up direct mail piece with a follow-up e-mail at a lower cost.

Many membership organizations are moving to adjust their membership renewal series by adding e-mails to the cycle or replacing mailed renewal notices—both at the front and back end—of the series with e-mails. If the organization can get people to click on an e-mail and renew online at the front end, it saves time, money, and reduces mail volume for the direct mail renewal pieces. Back-end e-mails reduce the costs associated with chasing those people less likely to renew as they get farther out past their renewal date.

E-Mail "Supplements" to Special Interest Segments

Because e-mail is an inexpensive form of communication, it provides the ability to segment and target your message to smaller audience groups within your database. This can allow you to communicate in a much more specific way with groups that may have been too small to communicate with via mail. In addition, e-mail can be used to send more detailed "supplemental" information to these smaller groups when a direct mail piece with a more general message is sent out. The supplemental e-mail can reference the more general direct mail piece, which may have included a request for a donation, and then highlight in more detail how a donation would help in an area that is of specific interest to that donor. For instance, a cancer center's direct mail piece may discuss the need for funding for cancer research while supplemental e-mails to different groups of donors might focus on the work of a particular researcher working on a type of cancer that is of direct interest to the donor.

USING PRINT AND GENERAL ADVERTISING TO INCREASE BOTH OFFLINE AND ONLINE RESPONSE

As with direct mail pieces, all forms of print and general advertising should contain the organization's URL. This is true for everything from billboards and magazine ads to subway posters and radio spots. Wherever you post your message, you should provide an opportunity for those seeing it to learn more about your organization. And the technology available today affords nonprofits an added advantage—the use of microsites and landing pages to help identify what form of general advertising is driving traffic to the organization's sites. Furthermore, microsites allow an organization to continue the branding and messaging from a print or general advertisement, increasing the likelihood that the person visiting the site will stay engaged and take action. For the most part, print and general advertising are still primarily focused on generating awareness rather than driving specific action, but through the use of microsites and other online innovations, organizations are having more success in measuring the impact of these forms of media and, in some cases, driving specific action.

USING ONLINE TOOLS TO SPUR INTEREST IN AND SUPPLEMENT OFFLINE ACTIVITY

Many online tools have been developed to aid nonprofit organizations with their offline activities. Combining an online component with an offline activity has proven very successful for many organizations. Some examples of this include:

1. **Using online ticket sales and registration to aid in preparing for special events.** Online advance registration can significantly reduce the chaos that often occurs at the beginning of events. A variety of options for online ticket sales and registration tools handle all aspects of the process.
2. **Adding an online auction component to an offline auction.** Even the smallest organization can now turn its annual golf outing auction into an international event. Several online auction tools allow organizations to easily an online component to their auction event, increasing the number of bidders and money raised.
3. **Providing online tools to help offline event participants raise more money for pledge-type events.** Many of the organizations that have hosted "-athon"–type events, in which event participants raise money on behalf of the organization, have seen huge increases in the amount of money raised and the satisfaction of the event participants through the use of solutions like Convio's TeamRaiser or Kintera's Kinterathon.
4. **Hosting an online event or activity in conjunction with offline activities to increase participation.** Organizations continue to come up with innovative— and successful—ways to use online technology to build on offline activities. A number of organizations have hosted online "events" that coincide with or are built around existing offline events. These online events allow a much larger audience to "participate," including people who may not be able to join the actual event. Other solutions include taking something that works well offline and building an online counterpart. For example, The Salvation Army has taken its traditional Red Kettle Holiday Fundraising activity and built an entire "Online Red Kettle" system that utilizes technology from Artez Interactive to allow people to "host" their own Virtual Red Kettle and collect donations from family and friends.

So now you have the building blocks and some ideas of what is necessary to implement an integrated online/offline strategy. But what about the creative side of the equation: How do you go about developing a concept for an integrated campaign? What follows is just one example of how an organization might consider developing the creative side of an integrated campaign.

EXAMPLE OF ONLINE/OFFLINE INTEGRATION IN A CAMPAIGN EXECUTION

This example depicts a creative concept for a truly integrated, online/offline, multichannel campaign.[1] This particular example is focused on a hunger relief organization, XYZ Food Bank, but a similar campaign could be built around almost any message.

Campaign Theme: The problem of—and solution to—hunger in Anytown USA is closer than you think.

Timing: Leading up to National Hunger Awareness Day (June)

Primary Objective: E-mail collection

To build a database of e-mail addresses—both from current constituents and new constituents—through an integrated campaign consisting of some, or all, of these media: direct mail, radio, billboard, print, guerrilla marketing, online.

Secondary Objective: Awareness

- To combat the misperception that *XYZ Food Bank* is "just another food pantry" by showing the scope of your work in a very visual, interactive way
- To show participants how hungry people really are their neighbors, that the problem of hunger—and the solution to hunger—truly is "closer than you think"

Tertiary Objective: Fundraising

Participants will be given links to XYZ Food Bank's "Donation" page.

Approach: Create a multichannel campaign that builds curiosity around a microsite (www.XYZMicrosite.org).

Participants driven to the microsite will be asked to enter their e-mail address and zip code. If this information is provided, they will be taken to a second page that includes both a Google Map and Google Earth portal framing XYZ Food Bank's service area.

Both portals will contain an individual "thumbtack" corresponding to each of XYZ Food Bank's many member agencies. Each thumbtack will contain information relating to services provided, the number of people helped, and, when possible, photographs and a link to each agency's Web site. Every agency thumbtack will contain a link to XYZ Food Bank's home page or perhaps to the donation page.

By seeing the huge number of agencies served by XYZ Food Bank in this visual, interactive format, the scope of your work will be immediately recognizable. And, more likely than not, participants will see that there is an agency supported by XYZ Food Bank close to their home—perhaps "closer than they think."

Creative Execution

Visual: white space with collage of three to five silhouetted people

Copy Option 1:

Headline: It has many faces. It has many names. And it's closer than you think.

Subhead: Learn more at www.XYZmicrosite.org.

Copy Option 2:

Headline: Do you know where they are?

Subhead: Find out at www.XYZmicrosite.org

Logo: To build curiosity, no XYZ Food Bank logo or branding will be used.

Potential Channels

To maximize the awareness and success of a multichannel campaign, the approved creative execution should be pulled through across as many of the channels below. When possible, and when budget necessitates, corporate partnerships can be leveraged to obtain donated or discounted services and/or space (this applies primarily to outdoor, print, radio and Direct TV marketing efforts).

- **Direct Mail.** Send a campaign postcard to acquisition lists (perhaps renewal as well), and include inserts in appropriate renewal mailings.
- **Guerrilla Marketing.** Place business cards with campaign creative at strategic locations throughout XYZ Food Bank's footprint (restaurants, grocery stores, convenient stores, universities, community centers, etc.).
- **Outdoor.** Billboards, subway posters, bus siding, taxi-wrappers can all be used to increase campaign visibility.
- **Print.** Place print ads in regional publications and/or inserts in supermarket circulars.
- **Radio Sample 30-second spot:**
  Father: Within a week, both our companies downsized. One week we're celebrating a new house and the birth of our son. Then, just like that, we're unemployed.
  Grandmother: I'm 83 years old. I need my pills. That's what happens when you get old. But after paying for my medication, I don't have much money left.
  Single Mother: Times are tough, but I will *never* send my baby to bed hungry. If that means I have to skip lunch and dinner, I'll do it. I've done it. And I'll do it again.
  Announcer: We pass them on the streets. We sit next to them on the subway. They are our neighbors. And they don't know where their next meal will come from.
  Hunger in our community is closer than you think. But so is the solution. Learn more at www.XYZmicrosite.org.

- **Online.** People driven to the campaign microsite will be greeted with a Flash presentation. Initially, only the black, silhouetted figures from the campaign creative will be shown. One by one, the silhouettes will fill in with real faces of real hungry people, along with a brief quote—perhaps the same as, or similar to, the quotes from the radio spot—explaining each person's situation.

Once all the faces are revealed, this copy will appear:

> *Hunger. It's closer than you think.*
> *But so is the solution.*

Readers will then be prompted to provide their e-mail addresses and zip codes before clicking through to the aforementioned Google portals.

- **E-mail.** While the primary objective of this campaign is to build an e-mail list for the organization, if the organization has a limited number of e-mail addresses and permission to communicate with this group, a subcampaign focused on driving donations or other action (petition signing, advocacy action, etc.) could utilize similar creative to drive traffic to a different microsite—or a different landing page within the microsite—asking the person to take action.

This campaign execution is just one example of how integrating both online and offline efforts can be leveraged for better overall results.

SUMMARY

As the use of online technology continues to spread through the nonprofit world, new and innovative ideas continue to come to light, many of which are highlighted in this book. As discussed in this chapter, the key to succeeding in utilizing these new technologies and techniques is careful strategic planning, implementation of the appropriate technology to help support the plan, and targeting the right audiences at the right time with a compelling message. In the end, by using multiple channels in a cohesive, well-planned manner, and by providing multiple opportunities for people to get involved, your organization will build stronger relationships and realize greater results.

ABOUT THE AUTHOR

Mark Connors is vice president at Amergent, Inc., in Peabody, Massachusetts. Amergent is a full-service provider of database management solutions and integrated direct marketing services for the nonprofit sector. Mark has spent his entire career working with companies that help support nonprofit organizations through the application of technology solutions. He also serves as a board member for the ePhilanthropy Foundation.

NOTE

1. This integrated campaign concept was provided by Colin Booth, creative director for Amergent, a leading nonprofit direct marketing agency.

CHAPTER 13

How the Telephone and the Internet Are Beautiful Partners for People to People Fundraising

Mike Johnston
Hewitt and Johnston Consultants

The tool shapes the task.
—Ursula Franklin, Engineer and Social Technology Thinker

We have all heard the murmurs, but are they true? Will conventional fundraising tools like mail and the telephone become less powerful with the growth of e-philanthropy?

How will the shift in the tools of communication shape our task of fundraising? As fundraisers, we are charged with the responsibility to invest in new tools of raising money to support our causes. New tools and methods like the Internet imply risk, but when connected in a cautious, tested way, the combination can increase the value of both the Internet and the telephone in fundraising. The case studies in this chapter show that when managed creatively and carefully, the telephone, combined with the Internet, becomes a powerful integrated approach in fundraising.

On their own, online tools have their strengths and weaknesses. At their best, they can serve as a 24/7 reception desk for your organization. During emergencies they can reach many potential supporters and give them the opportunity to help pitch in with emergency efforts. The downside of online fundraising tools is that they can be alienating and distancing. There is a preponderance of evidence to prove that the Internet is a wonderful medium for getting new donors through the door (in an emergency, e.g.), but it has been extremely difficult to renew those first-time (one-time) Internet donors by using the Internet to get them to give again. The phone is the key to renewing their support.

Most fundraisers are coming to the conclusion that while your online database can create large prospective lists (of both prospective warm supporters and real supporters), the Internet has to be coupled with more personal tools to connect with donors. If the tool shapes the task, then we must employ the right tool according to the task we need to accomplish. Just as you would not use a screwdriver to hammer in a nail, we must use both the phone and the Web for the tasks they can best accomplish. The phone, another mass marketing medium, has different abilities to connect to people on a more personal level. According to Scott Keys of Keys Direct Marketing & Communications Inc., a full-service direct marketing agency providing strategy, planning, and deployment of integrated campaigns based in Ottawa, Canada, "The phone allows for follow-up and person-to-person reassurance, the phone personalizes the communication, it allows donors to ask questions in a personal way versus the typical FAQs (frequently asked questions) online. The phone can also serve as an educational tool." Keys has described the marriage in this way: "Online to phone integration is an excellent one-two punch." By combining the two mediums, fundraisers have the potential to marry the impersonal with the personal to create a greater sense of identification between the donor and your organization.

HORMONAL ADVANTAGE OF THE TELEPHONE OVER THE INTERNET IN FUNDRAISING

Why is the phone personal? How can this tool shape a more personalized interaction that the Internet often cannot? It is probably worthwhile to give a quick cheerleading exposition on telephone fundraising at this point. Human beings are biological beings. They produce hormones that create feelings of trust when there are harmonious interactions. When someone opens a letter or opens an e-mail, there are fewer hormones produced to create the feeling of trust and the emotional connection that often spurs a gift. Of course, face-to-face interaction is the most powerful form of fundraising due to the very fact that seeing a person in front of you kicks your biological fundraising hormones into gear.

Pregnant mothers-to-be produce higher levels of hormones that produce the feeling of well-being and trust and safety. However, all individuals produce these hormones when meeting someone face to face. The telephone is simply the second level of hormone-producing methods. The human voice produces levels of trust and safety that encourage prospects to make a gift. By using the phone (after the more passive and less hormone-producing e-mail or Web), we are tapping into the biological side of fundraising.

The biological efficacy of the telephone in fundraising connects back to the original quote that "the tool shapes the task." A more impersonal, distant medium like the Internet is going to produce a less-connected donor to renew. A more personal tool like the phone is going to shape the task—the task in this case of renewing someone's emotional commitment to an organization though an additional financial commitment.

Beyond biology, this chapter addresses four key areas where the phone can be used to support online initiatives and build your e-mail database for the future:

1. Integrating the phone with online pledge events to cultivate high-end registrants/fundraisers
2. Using the phone to acquire or renew memberships from Web-based lists
3. Using the phone to motivate online activists to become donors
4. Using the telephone to motivate single-gift Web donors to become monthly donors

We explore these four potential areas of integration and, in addition, provide tips and examples in each section and at the end of the chapter for maximizing this integration strategy.

INTEGRATING THE PHONE WITH ONLINE PLEDGE EVENTS

More and more, organizations are turning to online tools to support their events. Online tools can allow supporters to register for all manner of events, from hosting a fundraising event in their own home or office, to becoming personal fundraisers, soliciting pledges by sending out e-mails to friends, family, and colleagues and directing them to a personal Web page. While offering online registration tools to supporters has helped many organizations raise more money, more efficiently, this form of interaction between the organization and its supporters can be somewhat impersonal. That is why integrating the phone with such online tools can successfully bridge the gap between the impersonal and personal. We look at relationship management and building relationships with enthusiastic supporters by integrating these two mediums.

The unique fundraising paradigm of online event fundraising creates two very important categories of donors in any online event: Those individuals who are the *star performers* and those who make an online event page but never get their fundraising off the ground; we will call them the *shy bottom feeders*.

Star Performers

As Exhibit 13.1 shows, the majority of the money raised in social network fundraising online is often concentrated in the top five percent of participants. The value of the top fundraisers is even more exaggerated online than offline. Offline, traditional

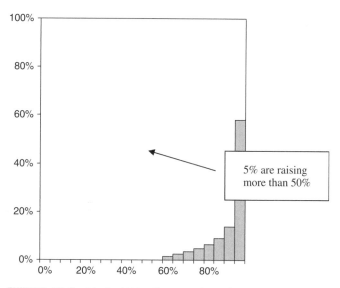

EXHIBIT 13.1 Typical Distribution of Fundraisers for a Pledge-Based Event Online

fundraising relies on the idea that the Pareto's principle (80/20) will be at play. This means that the top 20 percent of donors will raise 80 percent of the total dollars raised. Online, that ratio is even more extreme.

If this top five percent is so important online, how do we stimulate these *star performers* to do even more? The answer lies in the biological reference earlier: the hormone-producing human voice as sent down the telephone line! The telephone can be used to thank and further motivate those top registrants to do even more, and then the telephone can be used to motivate those at the bottom to get raising money. Imagine the potential impact of calling the top performers to thank them personally and urge them to do more.

The top five percent of participants who register online tend to raise more than 50 percent of total dollars raised by all registrants.

Shy Bottom Feeders

On the opposite extreme of the top five percent are the folks who make a social network fundraising page (going to the effort of setting it up) but who do not ask for anyone to give to their page. For whatever reason, these individuals do not e-mail their friends, family, and colleagues to give.

Now imagine if they received a phone call to praise them for making an online page, but urged them just to e-mail a few family and friends to get a donation. Even more, the caller tells them that it is easy and they will feel good getting those first gifts online.

Inspiring the Top and Bottom in Social Network Fundraising with the Phone

A children's aid organization offered their supporters the chance to register for a fundraising walk and solicit donations using a newly licensed online tool. Donors had the opportunity to create a personal Web page and upload their own images and text. From this Web page they sent out e-mail solicitations to their list of personal contacts, raising money from their own social network in an easy and convenient manner. After the event (which raised more money using the online module then the organization had in previous years), the aid organization and the technology provider created a matrix segmenting online fundraisers by amount of money raised.

The organization designated a follow-up caller based on how much money the registrant raised. This method of cultivation served both to thank the registrants for their fundraising efforts and to build a stronger personal relationship for future endeavors. The top registrants/fundraisers received calls from the organization's president; other levels of donors received call from either regional managers or volunteers. The volunteer callers were given scripts to use when calling online fundraisers.

During the thank-you call, high-end fundraisers were also asked to participate in a survey, asking them why they got motivated to raise money on behalf of the children's aid organization and why they decided to do it online. This allowed the organization to better understand their supporters and to deliver messages more effectively in the future.

Now let us look at this children's organization and calculate what the calling might do to improve results. Exhibit 13.2 shows how much more money might be made with the use of the telephone.

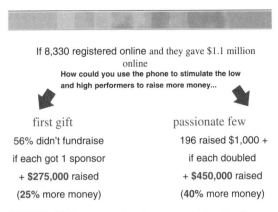

EXHIBIT 13.2 How the Phone Might Be Used

With a selected use of the phone to stimulate the top and bottom social network fundraisers, the children's aid organization could raise an additional $725,000. Those additional dollars would come from a result of getting the 56 percent of personal page donors who had not received one donation on their personal page to get one donation. That improvement would raise an additional $275,000. In addition, stimulating the top performers to raise 40 percent more per individual would bring in an additional $450,000. This gross revenue improvement would have to be matched against the costs of calling the low- and high-end performers to calculate the final net revenue.

If your organization is running online social network fundraising campaigns now, we urge you to think of these bottom and top performers and make a plan to use the phone to stimulate these two important categories to improve your overall fundraising results.

Tips from Experts for Using the Phone

- Segment your online fundraisers.
- Use the telephone to call and thank the top-performing online registrants.
- Use the phone to survey online fundraisers to determine not only their motivation for the cause but also for fundraising online.
- Use the telephone to call those who have registered but have not raised any money yet.
- Who makes the call is more important than what they say. The success of your phone call depends on the style of the person making the call. Put away the script! Intonation and inflection and a friendly manner count for a lot.

USING THE PHONE TO ACQUIRE OR RENEW MEMBERSHIPS FROM WEB-BASED LISTS

Phoning for membership renewal is nothing new for organizations like political parties and arts organizations. What is new and interesting though is that following up with one-time online Web donors or ticket purchasers and asking them to become members at a low price can acquire many new supporters to your cause. This method has worked out differently in the cases of political and arts organizations, but nonetheless, combining these two mediums had far more power than each one on its own.

A grassroots political party in Canada had an urgent need to increase membership before an upcoming election. The need was great, and the price was low with memberships for $10. The party ran an internal e-mail campaign for membership renewal and acquisition before the upcoming election. That is, it constructed an e-mail to its current e-mail database; some were former donors, others were members whose memberships were due for renewal and still others were simply individuals who were warm to the organization but had not yet made a gift.

The party sent out an e-mail internally and followed up with a phone call. The call had 45 to 69 percent response rate, a 15 percent improvement in the pledge rate over past campaign, which used only the phone. The party has learned that Internet donors for political campaigns were very receptive to the phone to make additional gifts.

Arts organizations are in the unique and challenging position to acquire new members or donors via the phone yet sourced from their Web sites. Unique, because they may have access to vast prospects who may have come knocking on their Web door through the purchase of a ticket for an event or exhibit. The organizations may be in a challenging position, as privacy of the ticket purchaser must be respected at all times and adherence to local privacy laws may limit the number of people who actually can be contacted.

A national arts center in the United States can teach us a few lessons about using the phone to recruit new members who may have become part of your database by purchasing a ticket online or by subscribing to one of your e-newsletters. Single-ticket buyers for this organization are contacted four times per year to become members. These are people who bought tickets to an event or exhibit in person or online. That is how they become included in the Web names on the database. The segment of Web names (including people who did not necessarily purchase tickets online but may have asked for more information) converted at a 10 percent higher rate than the other names.

Why do you think the renewal rate was higher? We all know that there are so many variables at play. For example, it can depend on the performance that they bought tickets to. Was it good? Did it get good reviews? How soon after performance did you call? The telefundraising firm in this example found that if the performance had great reports, the response rate was higher. From this we can garner a notable lesson. Lisa Drane, from the U.S.-based telephone fundraising firm Direct Marketing Advantage, lends some of her expertise to this discussion by saying "Phone-web integration is about conversation; it is a dialogue from many complimentary or competing mediums. The call should never be a sales pitch. External factors and all other aspects of the whole experience effect response rate."

USING THE PHONE TO MOTIVATE ONLINE ACTIVISTS TO BECOME DONORS

The Internet is proving to be a powerful tool in building warm lists very quickly. Its task is to spread information rapidly and allows gateways for people to take action impulsively. It also allows people to stand up for their beliefs easily, quickly, and, one could argue, relatively anonymously. The pass-along or viral marketing strength of the Internet is building massive lists of people who sign an online petition or take some click-of-a-mouse action on a particular issue. A number of charities are now successfully converting these online activists to donors by incorporating the phone into their communications. There are two examples to draw on in this section, the Brady Campaign and Amnesty USA. We examine what happened when warm leads were called. What was their response? What worked and what did not? What was the pledge fulfillment rate? Would the organizations do it again? What was the cost of calling? By exploring these questions, we determine how the phone can be used to convert Web activists to donors.

Brady Campaign

The Brady Campaign, a U.S.-based organization, has been successful in the last few years in its online campaigns. In the fall of 2003, it launched a microsite (www.nrablacklist.com) that urged citizens to put their names and e-mail addresses on an online list. The National Rifle Association had created a "black list" of individuals who had been active in opposing its policies and positions. The Brady Campaign cleverly took that list and urged like-minded individuals who opposed the NRA to put themselves on that list—and join well-known Americans like Jack Nicholson who were on the original NRA-created list (see Exhibit 13.3).

EXHIBIT 13.3 NRA Blacklist.com Home Page

EXHIBIT 13.4 StoptheNRA.com Petition Page

The microsite was popular and helped grow the Brady Campaign's overall e-mail list from 38,000 to 101,257 in just under three months.

Throughout 2004, the online petition signers were given further actions, such as signing urgent federal legislative petitions. In addition, these initial NRA black list online activists got a chance to participate in a new online campaign: www.stoptheNRA.com (see Exhibit 13.4).

Throughout 2003 and 2004, most e-mails asked these online activists to make a donation, and the results were significant. Overall, the Brady Campaign had great success in raising money in 2004 from online activists and donors. For example, online donors generated approximately $60,000 in 2002, $167,000 in 2003, and $339,000 in 2004. The most successful approach to get these online activists to give was to send e-mails asking them to give to TV and print ads that would be run with their money (see Exhibit 13.5).

As the next table shows, the results of the e-mail solicitation were a promising component of the Brady Campaign's online fundraising program.

E-mail Sent Date	21 Oct 03	27 Feb 04	3 Jun 04	15 Jul 04
Number of E-mails	48,000	123,700	135,600	141,000
Response %	0.37	0.37	0.19	0.27
Donors	177	461	251	382
Avg. gift $	$46	$39	$40	$24
$ Raised	$8,142	$17,979	$10,040	$9,168

EXHIBIT 13.5 StoptheNRA.com Supporter Letter

While the Brady Campaign had success in generating income online, it wanted to add to the success by integrating online activists into mail and phone contacts so that they had the opportunity to respond in other ways. The campaign was pleased with the income raised via the Internet but wanted to boost overall performance. So it went to the phones for those who had not responded online. The big fundraising breakthrough came about when the telephone was used with these online activists. The Brady Campaign decided to call a test segment of these online activists, many of whom came on board in 2003 with the NRA black list campaign and had received e-mails to both give money and to take action throughout the rest of 2003 and 2004. In the spring of 2005, approximately 20,000 individuals who had taken action online in March 2005 were called. These e-mail activists had a phone match linked to their e-mail addresses so that 20,000 individual addresses were matched correctly and then called. The results were a significant improvement over the e-mail results seen earlier in this section:

- Online activist pledge rate: 21 percent
- Online activist average pledge: $27.38

The earlier e-mails had tiny percentage responses while the telephone had a 21 percent percentage pledge response. That darned biological impact of the voice!

EXHIBIT 13.6   700women.org Violence Against Women Campaign

Amnesty International USA

In June 2006 Amnesty International USA called people who had participated in one of its online campaigns (700women.org) around reauthorization of the Violence Against Women Act (see Exhibit 13.6). Amnesty International joined with the National Organization for Women and Break the Cycle to deliver a petition with 100,000 signatures to key lawmakers as they negotiated the final version of the bill. More than 90,000 of these signatures came from the petition hosted on the 700women.org site. Due to the tireless efforts of these organizations, Congress subsequently reauthorized the Violence Against Women Act (VAWA), to help combat domestic violence and stalking in the United States.

Some who participated in the campaign by signing the online petition were activists who were not donors; others were current donors who were taking an online action in addition to making their gift. The campaign took place over the summer of 2005, concluding with passage of the legislation in the fall.

A year later, in June 2006, Amnesty International USA polled people who had participated in the campaign as activists but had not yet supported them financially. It worked pretty well, with net profit on acquisition despite the expensive acquisition technique of calling (see Exhibit 13.7).

As the exhibit shows, 23.60 percent of those contacted pledged their financial support through a gift, and of them, 67.35 percent fulfilled their pledge. Amnesty International USA shared with us the basics about the activity it had from both those activists who newly joined via the phone and those who were already donors. There

Names on List	7,149
Number of Phonable Names	3,671
Number Contacted	1,246
Contact Percentage	33.94%
Number Pledged	294
Pledge Percentage	23.60%
Average Pledge	$28.91
Gross Pledged	$8,501.00
Number of Returns	198
Fulfilled Response Percentage	67.35%
Gross Income	$5,920.00
Average Gift	$29.90
Total Cost	$5,777.05
Net Income	$142.95

EXHIBIT 13.7   Amnesty International Activist Campaign Results

were 198 responses to the June telemarketing and of those, 72 (36 percent) were join gifts (new donors); the rest came from existing donors. The 72 new joins to the June telemarketing gave gifts totaling $1,935.00. Of those new joins, 14 percent (i.e., 15) have made subsequent gifts. For those who were already donors when they signed the petition, after the June telemarketing, 121 donors made 126 gifts for $3,985.00. And of those 121 donors, 35 percent have made subsequent gifts.

This is a small test, and though the numbers are not extremely high, a net return on an acquisition and such a solid pledge percentage imply its success. There are three major lessons to take from this example:

1. Web activists can be inspired to become donors. We must test the phone as the medium to reach out to them.
2. Organizations have to incorporate the capturing of phone numbers in their online campaigns, donation forms, and so on.
3. Timing is everything. We have to test the time we reach out to Web activists. Segment Web donors and activists, and respond to them via phone both two months after their action online and three months after, to see if one segment performs better than another.

USING THE TELEPHONE TO MOTIVATE SINGLE-GIFT WEB DONORS TO BECOME MONTHLY DONORS

When we ask ourselves about how the phone can be used to motivate single-gift Web donors to commit on a monthly basis, timing is everything. Crises are the best times to both acquire and convert new Web donors. This section explores how you can use the Web-phone combination in both times of crisis and times of calm.

Motivating in Emergency Situations

AN OPPORTUNITY AWAITS OXFAM CANADA

Many North American charities found tens, if not hundreds, of thousands of new Web donors after the Asian tsunami and Hurricane Katrina. The intense media attention of these natural disasters drove many individuals to go to the Web sites of relief and development agencies and donate online. The various development and aid organizations asked themselves: "With so many new, single-gift online donors, what should we do with them?" Do they send a follow-up e-mail that asks for a second gift? Do they send an e-mail to convert them to monthly committed giving?

For Oxfam Canada, the solution to maximizing the value of their new online donors was to test different combinations of media. After the tsunami, Oxfam had acquired thousands of new donors who had made single gifts by going to the Web or by picking up the phone. Oxfam was mentioned by media outlets as one of the choice charities to donate to, and people had chosen one of two media to make that "flash" philanthropy gift.

Oxfam broke its testing into three distinct groups. The first group consisted of donors who had made a gift during the tsunami relief effort through the Web. This subset of Web donors received an e-mail follow-up solicitation approximately four months after their initial gift. The second group consisted of donors who had made a gift during the tsunami relief effort by picking up the phone. These donors received a phone call approximately four months after their initial gift. Finally, another set of Web donors to tsunami relief received a phone call four months after their initial gift. Which group converted best to monthly committed giving? Would it be those donors who initially gave through the Web and got an e-mail, or the donors who received calls but had initially made their call by phone or online? Often fundraising is counterintuitive, and the results of this study tend to reinforce that fact. The winning combination of media was using the phone to call Web donors.

In April 2005, HJC New Media and SIRIS Solutions Group were contracted by Oxfam Canada to contact approximately 7,000 Canadians who responded to the tsunami disaster with gifts of financial support. This unprecedented show of support overwhelmed many of the agencies that work in this geographic region.

Once the disaster settled both on the ground and in the media, the question was whether these newly acquired supporters would extend their trust to Oxfam by renewing their support and joining other responsive Canadians in helping international development organizations build and develop emergency response funds.

Based on past emergency campaigns, HJC and SIRIS knew that time was of the essence and the donor conversion program needed to start as close to the event as possible. At the time when the second communication was being planned, four months of relief effort had passed and attention to the disaster was minimal.

Oxfam decided that only first-time tsunami response donors (those whose first gift ever to Oxfam was made in the wake of this disaster) would be contacted, and a different campaign would be used to approach current donors who gave to the effort. Initially the idea was to raise funds for the tsunami relief effort, but Oxfam decided to launch a new emergency response program instead. Thus, the tsunami response donors' second gift would go toward this program. As this was the first time Oxfam was launching the program, the consultants did not have any historical data on which to forecast revenue.

The goal of this campaign was twofold: to contact and convert single-gift donors to monthly supporters and to test various methods of conversion. With respect to the first goal, and recognizing that many of these individuals had limited knowledge of the development work that Oxfam does, the campaign strategy became a multistep, multicontact process to inform, cultivate, and develop these donors. The second goal aimed to test communication channels and their ability to convert single-gift tsunami donors to regular monthly donors (or recurring single-gift donors). The Web and the phone were pitted against one another. In addition, multiple messages and integrated medium tests were conducted to find the most effective combination of converting donors.

Who Were the Donors and Why Did They Give? In the immediate response to the disaster, we can presume that these donors had access to cash, were moved by the media, and that response increased due to a federal matching gift ($80 million) and an extended timeline for tax credits (e.g., 14 percent of donors gave on January 11, 2005, the last date on which a gift made could be claimed on the previous year's tax returns). Based on typical online demographics, we know that online donors, for most organizations, are younger than the average direct mail donor. Through associate feedback and by monitoring calls, SIRIS found that the online and phone donors sounded younger, seemed busy, and were informed. By the larger than average gift size from this group than Oxfam's typical donor, we presumed that their ability to give was either greater or that they were not stretching all their fundraising dollars across many different charities.

Process that Occurred before the Phone Call In order to understand why the phone as a conversion tool worked so well, it is important to have a background on the communications that took place in between the initial donation and the eventual conversion call. Next we highlight the process that took place.

Donors who gave to the tsunami relief effort:

- Received a tax receipt (e-donor immediately after making the donation)
- Mail/phone donors: 4 to 8 weeks
- A thank-you postcard, which was mailed *only* to the phone/mail donors in February, noting how much money had been raised
- An e-thank-you letter was e-mailed to the Web donors with the same message

Before any calls were made, donors were contacted with a pre-call letter (phone donors) or a pre-call e-mail (Web donors) to prepare them for upcoming contact and to recognize their gift. The donors needed a pre-letter/e-mail that would:

EXHIBIT 13.8   Pre-call E-Mail to 6,000 Web Donors

- Reconnect them to their gift and how it was used
- Create a need for ongoing immediate access to funding
- Personalize Oxfam and the work that it does
- Prepare them for the phone call ask by not putting an ask in the letter
- Speak about long-term ongoing projects
- Mention that there would be follow-up about the emergency response fund

(We originally wanted to include a newspaper article with the letter, but it was felt that the article that was chosen had some "unconfirmed information" and was not used.)

Since this chapter concerns itself with Web-to-phone conversions, we briefly describe the pre-call e-mail sent to donors.

- The pre-call Web donor letter was personalized and used HTML programming (graphics were embedded in e-mail) (see Exhibit 13.8).
- The letters and e-mails were sent, and then the donor received the follow-up call.

The Call: Scripting Is Crucial   SIRIS tested two scripts on the various donors. Script A had a slightly higher conversion rate to single gifts, and script B had a slightly higher conversion rate to monthly gifts.

Script A
- Restated Oxfam's immediate response in East Asia
- Overviewed the needs when disaster strikes, for example:

- Importance of preparedness and planning, along with immediate funding for disaster relief
- Oxfam's emergency response fund
- Monthly giving

Script B

- Spoke about the tsunami and the disaster and how unprepared East Asia was due to a lack of sensors, etc.
- Highlighted what preparation was needed to help the developing countries with disaster plans
- Oxfam's emergency response fund
- Monthly giving

Exhibit 13.9 presents the results of the phone call to the various streams of donors.

Phone Results The use of the telephone as the primary contact point to these phone and Web donors proved the most effective. Web donors converted at the highest level, followed by phone donors.

It is important to note the overall difference in response rates depending on the combination of media or tools. The online donor group who received a subsequent e-mail solicitation converted to monthly giving at 0.2 percent. Web-to-phone donors converted at 8.85 percent. What an enormous difference!

The lesson learned is that the next time you have an outpouring of online gifts, call the donors and ask them to make a monthly committed gift. Do not just send a subsequent e-mail to convert them. How many organizations stick to one medium for their donors? Clearly, from these results, it could be to their significant detriment. In this case, the testing of different media revealed one combination (the Web and phone) that was significantly more effective than other combinations. If the tool shapes the task, then we can infer that, as fundraisers, we need to have a strategic vision of what our task is (acquisition, action, conversion) and then choose the tool that can best accomplish both our immediate and our long-term goals.

Another crucial lesson for postemergency one-time gift conversions comes from Oxfam and other post–Hurricane Katrina initiatives. The lesson learned is that timing is everything. One organization called its Web donors (donors who went online and made a single gift during and right after Hurricane Katrina) a month after the hurricane, asking these Web donors to become monthly donors. The organization had amazing results. When it called other Web donors a month later (a couple months after their initial donation), the conversion rate was cut in half. When it called online donors in December, the rate was cut in half again.

In disasters or emergencies, timing is everything. While your organization may be apprehensive about getting on the phone too soon and appear to be capitalizing on the disaster, the best time to call is sooner rather than later. Emotions are high during and right after the disaster is in the media. People's hearts are open to your message. Contact them, engage them. Some marketing firms call this the "honeymoon phase." Individuals felt strongly enough about helping that they went online and gave a gift. Successful emergency fundraising campaigns got them on the phone while they feel the weight of the event.

Tag	Segment	Type	Calls	Pledged Revenue	Cost Per $	Pledges	Single Conversion	Monthly Conversion	Total Conversion
A Total	0.00-99.99	Phone	969	6,850.00	$0.83	109	4.54%	6.71%	11.25%
B Total	100-499.99	Phone	1,207	13,069.00	$0.53	118	3.40%	6.38%	9.78%
C Total	500+	Phone	89	1,749.00	$0.32	7	5.62%	2.25%	7.87%
D Total	0.00-99.99	Phone	106	810.00	$0.74	16	3.77%	11.32%	15.09%
E Total	100-499.99	Phone	625	8,160.00	$0.43	60	3.20%	6.40%	9.60%
F Total	500+	Phone	45	300.00	$0.93	2	4.44%	0.00%	4.44%
G Total	0.00-99.99	Web2Phone	1,397	15,234.36	$0.53	162	3.36%	8.23%	11.60%
H Total	100-499.99	Web2Phone	2,263	30,711.88	$0.42	259	1.99%	9.46%	11.44%
I Total	500+	Web2Phone	126	2,580.00	$0.29	12	4.76%	4.76%	9.52%
Total			6,827	79,464.24	$0.50	745	3.13%	7.78%	10.91%
A		Phone - Script "A"	2,265	21,668.00	$0.61	234	3.97%	6.36%	10.33%
B		Phone - Script "B"	776	9,270.00	$0.48	78	3.35%	6.70%	10.05%
C		Web2Phone	3,786	48,526.24	$0.45	433	2.59%	8.85%	11.44%

EXHIBIT 13.9 Phone Results of Disaster Relief Donors Who Gave by Phone and by the Web

Tips and Notes from the Experts　Kathleen Bradshaw, a telefundraising veteran from SIRIS Solutions Group, offers this advice after conducting a second successful wave of calling Oxfam's Web donors a year after the tsunami:

- Two things to note with the web-to-phone calling:
  1. Obtaining credit card information is crucial to ensuring fulfillment, and we found that credit card conversion was substantially higher with the Web donor group: at least 50 percent higher than when we phone typical direct mail donors.
  2. The average single gift was also much higher than typical direct mail donors.
- The address and phone number verification could be a challenge as we rely on donors' entries when they made their donation. In the Oxfam case, the tele-fundraising firm had to do phone and address appends as the entries were not always accurate.
- Call length to convert these Web-based relief donors to monthly giving was also much less then our telefundraising firm was used to.

We attribute this to the younger age group who do not spend as much time on the phone and are much quicker to make their decisions.

Motivating in Nonemergency Campaigns

The successful conversion of Web donors by phone is not limited to emergency campaigns only. We now take a look at converting single-gift Web donors, who gave to nonemergency campaigns, to monthly giving. The first example comes from a local humane society and compares the conversion of Web donors to other donor segments. The second example comes from a gift-giving campaign from CHF, a Canadian international development agency.

A local humane society ran a monthly conversion telephone campaign in October of 2006. Web donors converted to monthly donors at a four percent higher rate than the average, which included such other streams as mail donors, event donors, and Direct TV donors. Exhibit 13.10 shows how Web donors converted to monthly giving when compared with other segments of donors.

For the purpose of comparison, we have extracted only some of the donor types. Therefore, the numbers in annual and total revenue will not add up. Here we omit such donor streams as direct dialogue and special events.

The second example of converting single-gift online donors to monthly committed donors comes from CHF-Partners, formerly known as the Canadian Hunger Foundation (see Exhibit 13.11). In November and December 2005, it launched an alternative giving campaign online. Following in the tradition of Heifer International and World Vision, CHF-Partners. It asked individuals to buy someone a donkey to help a family in Ethiopia instead of getting a gift for someone on their gift list, a gift they probably did not really need.

The campaign was a success. Overall, it found 632 donors giving an average gift of $67.74 (85.6 percent of whom were new to the database).

CHF spent $20,000 to raise $39,383. For an acquisition campaign, that was a very good, reflecting a 2 to 1 return on investment (ROI).

CHF wanted to improve its ROI by calling these one-time gift donors as part of its spring 2006 renewal phone campaign and convert them to monthly giving.

	Completed Calls	Total Pledges	Total Response (%)	#	Summary Monthly Conversion Rate(%)	Avg.	Annual Rev.	#	Summary OTG Conversion Rate(%)	Avg.	Total Rev.
Projections					6.00%	$14.00			10.00%	$ 35.00	
Campaign Total	27,762	4,344	15.65%	1,985	7.15%	$14.00	$337,204.00	2,359	8.50%	$ 33.37	$78,719.00
Donor Type											
Event	2,421	412	17.02%	261	10.78%	$16.00	$ 50,712.00	151	6.24%	$ 30.03	$ 4,534.00
Mail	128	29	22.66%	19	14.84%	$19.00	$ 4,272.00	10	7.81%	$ 31.00	$ 310.00
Other	3,450	502	14.55%	187	5.42%	$14.00	$ 30,524.00	315	9.13%	$ 41.48	$13,066.00
Telemarketing	294	78	26.53%	33	11.22%	$13.00	$ 5,016.00	45	15.31%	$ 43.22	$ 1,945.00
TV	2,906	543	18.69%	317	10.91%	$16.00	$ 61,456.00	226	7.78%	$ 34.62	$ 7,824.00
Web	1,000	155	15.50%	108	10.80%	$14.00	$ 18,156.00	47	4.70%	$446.23	$ 2,173.00

EXHIBIT 13.10 Web Donors Converted to Monthly Giving

Starting March 31, 2006, CHF called 5,210 individuals, of whom 592 were online donkey donors from the November–December 2005 donkey campaign. The phone campaign resulted in a total of 635 recommitted donors, 19 of whom were monthly commitments. Of those 19 donors, 12 were from the year-end alternative-giving Web group. That meant the online alternative gift donors responded at a 2 percent rate while the non–online donors responded at a 0.13 percent rate. That is a difference of almost 1,000 percent. In this case, the online single-gift donors seemed more responsive to converting to monthly giving than the direct mail and telephone single-gift donors.

EXPERT TIPS FOR USING THE PHONE AND ONLINE TOOLS TOGETHER

Using the Phone to Collect E-Mail Addresses

Whether you are calling Web donors or donors from any of your other donor segments, capturing e-mail or confirming e-mail addresses (since they change often) should be included in every call. Building your e-mail database is an investment in the future. Even if your organization is too small to be able to afford an outsourced calling campaign, you can ask any donors you have phone chats with for their e-mail address.

Tips
- If you do not have enough e-mail addresses, you can use the phone to get them.
- Have your telemarketing company or volunteer callers explain how e-communi-cations and e-receipting saves the organization time and money. Incorporating something like this into the script would help to boost e-mail: "E-mail saves money, paper and helps us keep you updated about how your gift has made a difference."
- Let donors know they can choose how they would like to be communicated to. E-mail communication offers donors the opportunity to say how they want to be communicated to (when, how often, and by which means), thereby allowing them to have control over they types of communications they receive.
- Remember that phoning centers should be donor-centric. Asking for e-mail should be too.
- Offer your callers a small bonus. If you do have an outbound or inbound calling program set up, make sure that the callers are capturing e-mail addresses. Even if you have to offer the call takers a bonus ($0.50) per address captured, gathering these data will increase your communications scope.
- Offer donors a reason or incentive to give their address: "We'd like to send you our monthly online newsletter. Could we get you e-mail address in order to do this?"
- Younger and more progressive demographics tend to be more flexible about giving their e-mail address. Susan Paine of the Share Group has told us that "calling for the LGBT organization yielded 35 percent of people giving their e-mail addresses."

A gift of a donkey, made in your name, will bring new hope to a family in Ethiopia.

Season's Greetings

Why a donkey? To read the story about Zahra and how a donkey transformed her life, click here.

CHF
partners in rural development

EXHIBIT 13.11   E-Card Donors Could Send to Those for Whom They Gave Gift

Using the Phone for Nonsoliciting Purposes

Fundraisers can consider keeping their eye off the prize and on the process. Too often, due to our limited budgets, we do not put money into nonsoliciting phone campaigns. This is shortsighted. The phone is a great way to build relationships and can be used successfully to:

- Thank Web donors
- Prime people for upcoming campaigns
- Survey Web donors

Tips for the Weary

The biggest impediment is the organization itself, which is often "silo-ed," slow to respond, and gives up phone numbers of online donors. A key recommendation is to take down silos between online departments and direct fundraising.

CONCLUSION

The tools that we use in fundraising shape the scope of what we are able to achieve. More impersonal tools allow us to communicate with a wide audience, inviting huge numbers of potential supporters to take action and join us in our cause. But we need the more personal media as well to reach out them after they have expressed an interest. It is like dating—or online dating to be more exact. There are only so many e-mails you can send before it is time to pick up the phone and ask for a date in person.

The phone and the Internet are beautiful fundraising partners. Whether it is using the phone to stimulate online social network fundraisers or to approach potential or past members, to convert online activists to donors, or to convert online single-gift donors to monthly committed giving, the combination needs to be used by more organizations.

The examples in this chapter show that improved results in this online/phone synergy are wide ranging.

Truly, the tool shapes the task. The Internet is a powerful broad-based collector that allows massive numbers of individuals to give quickly and easily. It is that mile-wide and inch-deep tool that shapes its own task: to find donors and to make first contact so easy.

But its shape does not allow it to accomplish another crucial task: to deepen the donor/organization relationship. In the examples provided, another tool has that task, a tool that uses the human voice to build deeper relationships: the phone. We urge you to use both tools in combination to reach your goal—to build a larger donor file and to then deepen the loyalty and profitability of the file thereafter.

ABOUT THE AUTHOR

Michael Johnston is the president and founder of Hewitt and Johnston Consultants, cofounder of the Washington, DC, based Legacy Giving Group, and new media partner with the Netherlands-based fundraising company Delphi. He has been a fundraiser for over 18 years, and has worked with hundreds of nonprofit organizations in Canada, the United States, Europe, Latin America, and Asia Pacific. Mike is an expert in direct response fundraising innovation, especially in the use of new technologies like the Internet. He is the author of *The Fund Raiser's Guide to the Internet, The Nonprofit Guide to the Internet*, and the editor of two books: *Internet Strategies: Best Practices for Marketing*, and *Direct Response Fund Raising: Mastering New Trends for Results*. Mike was a founding board member of the Washington-based ePhilanthropy Foundation and was the first chair of its Education Committee. In addition, he was the founding foundation chair for the first global charity online lottery, www.globelot.com.

CHAPTER 14

The Web of Integration: Fully Integrated Fundraising Campaigns

Ryann Miller
Hewitt and Johnston Consultants

Patricia MacArthur
Hewitt and Johnston Consultants

A ccording to the dictionary, "integration" is "an act or instance of combining into an integral whole."

As simple as this may sound, properly executing a fully integrated fundraising plan is not an effortless process. The act of integrating fundraising is like that of weaving an intricate spider's web. The more weaving and interlocking, the more complicated the web—but the stronger and more resilient it is. Like spiders, we want to weave intricate webs in which each strand stands on its own but is also part of an interconnected, greater support strategy.

This chapter explores the many pieces of a fully integrated fundraising campaign. More specifically, we explore how ePhilanthropy can and should be used as the next step toward a unified fundraising program. Today many nonprofits are looking at adopting some ePhilanthropy practices and techniques but are overlooking the critical next step to building a holistic program. This leaves many charities wondering why their fundraising programs are not as successful as they could be. Piecemeal ePhilanthropy and thinking divisionally—the shortsighted enemies of nonprofits—are the things we are warning against.

The concept underlying this chapter is *strategy*: the need for a clearly laid out strategy for a successful integrated fundraising campaign. We also explore the three levels of integration that all organizations should know and incorporate into all levels of fundraising and "friend-raising" campaigns that will increase Web site traffic, build brand awareness, strength donor relations, and increase revenue potential. Additionally, we examine how both traditional mediums, such as direct mail and the phone, and nontraditional methods, including e-appeals, e-newsletters, the Web site, social network fundraising, videos, and online marketing, can be collaborators when building a fully integrated fundraising campaign strategy.

ePhilanthropy stands apart from traditional fundraising practices because of its defining characteristic: *It is new*. While not exactly rocket science itself, this simple and shallow fact has large and complex implications. As the new kid in school, ePhilanthropy has an obligation both to work with traditional and offline mediums *and* to incorporate innovative yet complementary online fundraising techniques.

To start thinking about integration, we share with you the story of the organization Save the Greasy Spoon. It failed, and its proponents could not figure out why. This hypothetical case study is followed by the cardinal rules of integrated fundraising. At the end of this chapter, we provide a worksheet that applies many of the best practice principles we discuss. Through the review process, the worksheet will help create a fundraising plan and schedule that incorporates many of the best practice elements of a fully integrated fundraising plan.

Save the Greasy Spoon was excited about their new eat-athon to promote its campaign, Grease Is Good. Adherents did not approach the campaign with an integrated strategy, but instead added parts and pieces as they saw fit. They thought they had their integrated marketing strategy all worked out by virtue of the fact that they *had* online marketing. They planned, they cast their marketing nets wide, and they marketed the campaign, confident in their equation: multiple marketing streams = success.

Save the Greasy Spoon decided to market the eat-athon for the campaign "Grease Is Good" via three streams: in a direct mail package with an insert about the campaign, creating a Web page that could be found in the "Events" section of its Web site, and putting banners online. Staff members had considered a broadcast voice message, other online advertising, and print ads, but decided against them because of cost. They knew that e-mail was a good idea but because their support base were activists, and Save the Greasy Spoon had just sent out two e-mails to their house e-mail list urging them to tell their elected officials to end the media's unfair war against grease, they felt their e-mail list was fatigued and might not be interested. Concerned that this new ask would turn supporters away, instead they sent an e-mail to their e-mail warm list, which were people that had signed up the year before for Save the Greasy Spoon's yearly Greasy Spoon Watch: a list of restaurants around the country that had closed and any new ones that had opened (though this tended to be an "endangered species" list).

The Development team brought in the Communications and Marketing team of Save the Greasy Spoon for this campaign, but all were too busy beyond a few meetings to delegate tasks for any real combined group buy-in or ownership. Though they each had their responsibilities, these two groups rarely interacted beyond what was necessary. Surveying their marketing avenues, which were direct mail, Web page, online banners, and a warm list e-mail, the group decided that their bases were covered. "Grease Is Good" would be a smash hit.

The first cardinal rule of integrated campaigns for any nonprofit is to start at home. Before integration of mediums, you must have integration of departments. Integration of fundraising and marketing mediums means that the Development department and the Communications and Marketing departments must work together as a team. While one group may be spearheading the project, the first key to success is the organization coming together as a whole so that all integrated mediums support each other. In this case, Development brought in Communications and Marketing but did not ask them for their input. Communications and Marketing saw "Grease Is Good" as a fundraiser, did what they were asked to do, and assumed no ownership beyond that. This situation, though perhaps common, is not inevitable. It is less a matter of politics than a matter of knowledge of sharing for success. Communications and Marketing had no ownership and felt no allegiances. They were not invited in and did not come to see this campaign as dependent on their marketing expertise.

"Grease Is Good" was a fundraising failure and did not break even. Those who got the direct mail piece needed reminding before the actual day and did not know where to turn, as there was no unique URL driving people to a microsite or even a unique spot on the Web site home page. The insert was used because it was inexpensive. It was also ineffective: People were more focused on the letter than the insert. Some people went online, but gave up because they saw no evidence of the "Grease Is Good" campaign on the home page. Others did find it under the "Events" section and judged the campaign not to matter that much to the organization because it seemed so hidden away. The reason there was no major Web site home page presence was because those responsible for the Web site, Communications and Marketing, were not keen to alter the home page. They felt it would be distracting and potentially confusing to users. In truth, they had not been given enough input and subsequently did not have buy-in in the campaign and the importance of home page presence.

The online banners were not on properly targeted Web sites, with no concentration on foodies and/or grease lovers. One banner appeared on an online newspaper, and another on answers Web site (the kind where one types in a question and receives popular answers) because the organization did not know enough about online marketing and group targeting and thought all Web sites were more or less equal. Moreover, staff members did not do any research into their own database to see what Web sites might target some of their main groups. Save the Greasy Spoon did not use keyword marketing, so prospects looking for an event, such as an eat-athon, did not find it on any search engines. E-mailing the warm list instead of their supporter list was perhaps the most obvious of the errors. A warm list, in this case a list of 4,000 names, should have been *in addition to*, not *instead of*, the house e-mail list of committed donors and supporters, which itself consisted of 1,500 names. Small lists usually mean committed supporters, but not in this case. They should have e-mailed everyone they could have, at least twice. They had decided that their house list was fatigued, but did they have any evidence of this? No one told them that different standards applied when the message you were communicating was related to something completely different, with a different ask, and would produce a different result.

Save the Greasy Spoon fell for the first trap of integration: "Any integration is good integration." This is not true when an organization does not have a strategy. Visualizing their marketing vehicles, Save the Greasy Spoon saw only dead ends, not a web of interlocking links and connections. They did not plan properly, then did not set out their goals; they did not know their audience or do data research to find their audience; and they did not have any public relations plan. There was no web of integration because there was no foundation and no strategy.

HOW TO AVOID ERRORS AND PLAN THOUGHTFULLY

What did the organization do wrong? What will this chapter tell you so that you can steer clear of their mistakes and lead your campaign toward integration success?

Let us start with the fundamentals.

- Integration is a strategy itself, and must be treated as such. It is not a catchphrase. It is not a passing fad.
- Integrated fundraising is more complicated than it looks, because everything must be integrated to work together as one unified fundraising program.
- Integrated fundraising is still new, and therefore it: requires new ways of thinking about fundraising; depends on new testing; and should be followed by an integrated donor cultivation model.

Fundamentals in place, next we lay out the cardinal rules of integrated fundraising:

Take that Inside, Kids!: Internal Integration before Anything Else

When people ask me what we do or what Hewitt and Johnston Consultants (HJC) does, we tell them that we take traditional fundraising, traditional marketing, and online marketing and marry them. Okay, so it is a three-way marriage, which is not legal even in Canada ... but the point sticks, right? We marry the old and the new. But at least we are honest from the start: We really *are* doing it for the money ... that is, greater fundraising revenues. Integrated campaigns in this era of fundraising also require a coming together of internal groups or departments. More and more, we are seeing that integrated campaigns require a significant coming together of Development, Campaigns, and Communications teams.

Whether traditional development or online marketing/development "owns" the campaign, the internal campaign process should be a collaborative experience. This is easy to accomplish if there is an initial strategy session before campaign kick-off. Decisions should not be made prior to this meeting, only ideas and thoughts presented. As mentioned, integration of fundraising and marketing mediums means that Development, Communications, and Marketing departments must work together as a team. At the strategy session, ideas should be presented and discussed, decisions made, and a campaign plan developed in order to ensure that all aspects of the campaign work together to carry the same message across all mediums. A well-designed campaign supported by all internal departments will ensure that all mediums support each other and the message is coherent. There is also a greater wealth of knowledge when teams overlap and a smaller risk of overlooking something. The better the internal integration, the better the campaign integration.

Weave Them Together Like a Persian Carpet with Your Plan

As mentioned earlier, the analogy of the web is the best way to describe how an integrated fundraising plan should work using both traditional and online fundraising mediums. Each strand of the web is connected from the center core as it spreads out, weaving and linking with other strands creating a network of interlocking links. For the organization, the core of this web is the Web site. The Web site has become the main source of information for the general public, donors, and supporters; it is the organization's portal to the world. It is also used as a collection device to survey donors, offer pertinent information, present questions and answers, provide contact information, track Web site visitors (including which pages of the site are most commonly visited, for how long, and with what repetition), and is a superb branding and marketing device. The Web site is the most common driving device used by most organizations, and understating the value of your organization's Web site (for fundraising or anything else) is akin to stating in Alexander Bell's time that the telephone will not change how people communicate. When people ask for more information about your organization, they go to your Web site. When they want your address or phone number, they check out your Web site. Most marketing tools, online and offline, are driven to the Web site.

As the web expands, the weaving and linking that represent all of your mediums begin to clearly work together, cohesively, as one. If some of the strands or links break or a hole develops, the web may stay together, but the hole creates a void or weakness that could spread further. This is the same if one of the campaign pieces breaks down in an integrated campaign. For example, you may have a well-designed campaign, but if the marketing devices fail, your campaign most likely will fail also.

How do you show the weaving and linking that is the hallmark of integration? Well, for starters, your online marketing should be branded the same as your offline marketing. The "look and feel"—what images you use; the placement of images and text; the slogan, catchphrase, or question; the font; the colors: These are your campaign brand. Have your online channels refer to each other, so in your first, second, and third e-appeals, the Web site is presented as the destination. But do not stop there: Use a unique URL that will stick in people's minds and galvanize your campaign. If possible, make your URL the same as your slogan. You can have this URL automatically transfer to your campaign landing page or right to your modified, rebranded donation form. If your campaign has humor or targets youth, ensure that your video on YouTube emphasizes your Web site. Whoever your market, your print material should drive people online to learn more or give. The online banner should be on a targeted Web site and link directly to the landing page of the campaign or right to the donation page. Your public service announcement should give the option of giving by phone or online, while your Web site gives the phone number of a real, live person who can take your donation over the phone or mail out material. And every time you use the slogan, design your message with the same look and feel. Brand your unique or modified donation form to match everything else, so that people are comfortable when they arrive there. What you want is brand consistency across all your marketing channels, to use more marketing channels and to overlap them, and to keep the message and destination simple and the same. Creating a unified plan between your online and offline mediums and weaving them together like a web will help build an integrated fundraising plan.

Outline Your Goals and Do Not Forget Them

When developing an integrated fundraising campaign, always outline your goals at the start. If you do not outline goals at the start of the project, it is harder to evaluate results at the conclusion of the campaign. Review your campaign elements and establish the benchmarks you want to evaluate at the conclusion of the campaign, for example: the budget, marketing strategy, public relations strategy, brand awareness, Web site traffic, organization's goals, employee performance, overall campaign goals, and results. Use these benchmarks to review your campaign plan and examine each piece individually. Each campaign component should be coordinated with a goal to assist in the overall assessment. To assess the final results, highlight the goals outlined, any important points, and feedback gathered. Goal setting provides a set of benchmarks and expectations to review your project as a whole and make improvements for future endeavors.

Know Thy Audience

No matter what kind of campaign your organization is developing, you have to know your audience. Whom are you speaking to? Why should they listen? To market a campaign successfully and strengthen the brand, you have to know and understand the demographics you are targeting. For example, are you targeting a donor file, a lapsed donor file, or a campaign to the general public? If it is the public, what age group, what socioeconomic sector, what interest group? When you know to whom you are speaking, your organization should establish the appropriate tone, language, and images. It can then begin to gauge potential results. Testing different mediums and elements gives results that can assist in fine-tuning an existing campaign.

Timing Is Everything

Integrated fundraising strategies require timing, especially if an organization wants to run a cohesive campaign connecting all of its offline and online initiatives together. There are many factors to consider when accessing the timing of integrated fundraising plan. Taking this one step further than establishing campaign timelines, assess these five factors and how timing will affect each:

1. The fundraising environment
2. Your fundraising campaign
3. The marketplace
4. Your internal resources
5. Your external stakeholders

Look at you fundraising environment. Is the timing right to launch your campaign? Will your donors and supporters be responsive to your campaign?

Is the fundraising campaign strategically planned and ready to execute on a specific timeline to ensure all of the offline and online mediums are working together cohesively?

Is it the right time to launch your campaign in the marketplace? Are there any other campaigns that might be competing for the same dollars as your organization, and if there is, is your marketplace saturated? Are there any mainstream media stories that will drive traffic to your Web site, or mean higher open rates and click-through rates on e-appeals? One animal rights organization waited until a very public animal rights event happened to broadcast its e-newsletter and saw dramatic increases in its open rate (over 25 percent) and click-through rate (over 35 percent) compared to what it usually saw.

Has each member of your campaign team had sufficient time to implement the campaign strategy properly? Is your organization ready to dedicate the resources needed to execute the campaign properly? Have timelines been developed for your employees, including their responsibilities and desired outcomes?

The last area to evaluate is your external stakeholder. Should any other factors be considered before launching your campaign? This assessment will assist in the evaluation of your overall integrated campaign strategy and if timing will have any impact on your results.

Have You Met My Wonderful Sister, Data? She's Great but No One Calls Her

Data is the shy middle sister who rarely dates and never gets recognition but is always there, always sharing valuable information that helps you get what you want, and asking only for any new useful information in return so that next time you ask, she will be able to help you more. Data is vital to the success of fundraising campaigns. Your database contains important information about your donors that is key to developing a fully integrated fundraising campaign. What mediums might work best? Check your database to see if it correlates to the figures. Depending on e-mail to get the message out? Want to try using the phone along with direct mail? Wondering what Web sites might yield the best return on investment? Check your database.

All the information you already have, as well as the information you gather about your donors, presents a clearer picture of their interests, personal milestones, which medium they prefer to receive correspondence via, giving patterns, and the level of support they can provide to your organization. Any correspondence between you and your donors/supporters online or offline should be recorded in your database. As time goes on, and your organization becomes comfortable building a more integrated fundraising plan, the next and critical reason for maintaining data integrity will be noting personal preferences and life milestones as they become known to the charity through the donor. This will give the organization an ability to communicate with donors on a personal level, *throughout the entire course of their lives*. Imagine what this might mean for legacy giving. Using your database to its full capacity is one of the best resources an organization can invest in: a reference tool and an essential resource in relationship building.

Trends Are Trends So Test

Just as in the for-profit sector, trends emerge in fundraising, and it might be hard to determine if they will be more like Billy Rae Cyrus or more like the Rolling Stones. Billy Rae was a flash in the pan—one song and then we never heard from him again, while the Stones have a longevity that is the envy of every band. But the Stones have not cruised through each decade, without a care or plan. They had a comeback that was just as much a marketing and clever promotion strategy as it was classic rock and roll. The Stones are still equal parts strategy and music. And their success is incredible. Integrated fundraising is also about the strategy in perfect harmony with the actual campaign. As the way nonprofits should approach any campaign in our era for maximized success, integrated fundraising is clearly no trend.

But other trends will emerge, and many will seem like great ideas to develop for your own organization. Some of the trends that emerge will be fantastic to test at your organization. The key word is *test*. Trends do show an inclination toward the topic at hand, but without testing the concept with your donor base, the new concept could be set up to fail. One primary way to learn what your supporters think of a campaign is to poll them online—via e-mail—as soon as you can. Ask them five questions that will help to steer the direction of next year's campaign. Do not be afraid to ask, but do not try their patience either. Make sure everything works (test!), make sure it takes under four minutes to complete, make sure you thank them for their time, and make sure you apply their information.

Know your fundraising environment and what concepts might be worth testing or not testing in your organization. Always test new ideas to see if your donor base is warm to the concept. Unfortunately, not all trends work for every organization. Test it before running with it!

PR Plan

For integrated fundraising campaigns, especially with a large marketing element, having a well-designed marketing and communications plan is the key to your success. Whether in-house or outsourced, public relations (PR) specialists are invaluable resources to your organization. They are specialists in planning, networking, and connecting with the right individuals who can give your campaign the type of media exposure necessary to make it a huge success.

Why does PR matter? Well, simply, you want people to know about your campaign. Public relations is not generally a prerequisite to working at a nonprofit, and we might want to admit that we could use help in getting the word out. A campaign geared toward retirees might want to use radio and television, while a campaign geared towards youth may want to incorporate an online video or a social networking tool. These different channels require different tools. Online videos can be inexpensive and innovative, and end up being viewed by 10 times the people in your database . . . if your video is appealing. This medium, as with e-appeals and e-cards, is concerned with viralocity[1] and plain old word of mouth. You do not require a PR plan for online video itself, though you might want to consult with someone 20 years old or younger for some expert advice. The same goes for social networking.

But radio and TV, which tend to cost more, will see a much greater return if a PR strategy also is invested in. For example, say you developed a public service announcement: Who will you send it to? Chances are you do not have many deep connections that you can leverage, but the PR specialist will. When? How will you pitch it? You do not want to miss station deadlines or fall on deaf ears, and you do not want to see your announcement aired at 4:30 A.M. on one station, just twice. The PR specialist will recommend stations, channels, producers, when to call (or the specialist will call), what to say, and how to pitch your announcement. The specialist can help you get a story "planted" in a newspaper, get an interview on the radio or on TV, or get a media personality to take up your cause. Sometimes these access channels are the most successful. The PR specialist will—or you should—create a PR plan that has who, why, and when to contact.

For example, you want a PR plan that is in line with your target group and you want to time it properly, so radio/TV spots are aired after your Web site has a modified (we call it "hijacked") home page, and in the two-week period in which you are sending out three e-appeals. Modifying your online donation forms? Do this *before* the spots air. Putting a video on YouTube? Fine, but put it on your Web site as well, and add a button on the home page that links to the video. From the video landing page, have a prominent link to your modified donation form. Whoever is doing all of this (and more!) will likely *not* have the time to create a list and call all the media sources you want to know about your campaign. Enter the PR plan (and someone to execute it). If you cannot hire a professional, integrate PR into the overall strategy, read books, and have someone assume responsibility for getting the word out. Remember, free publicity is the best kind.

And Finally: Strategy, Strategy, Strategy

Every organization needs a strategy to develop a fully integrated fundraising campaign. We will see strategy in detail coming up with our case study, but before we get there, we want to review the key points. A successful campaign is built on a solid internal foundation: Plan your integration and outline your goals; know your audience; time everything systematically; use data to its best advantage; mine your audience; test to separate the trend from the valuable; and do not forget PR—your integrated campaign needs to be seen and heard. Strategies should ideally be started a year or nine months before you want to launch your campaign. A plan should be developed and begun to be implemented six months before your campaign launches. One of the worst and unfortunate mistakes is to leave things to the last minute. Start early and you will thank yourself.

It may sound like juggling when you think about all the pieces involved, but when everything is in place, and you see how people lead from one channel through the stream toward your destination, you will recognize see the simplicity within the complication. Or vice versa. And you will see how juggling those pieces are all parts of the web that is your integrated strategy. Furthermore, you will see, when it is all over, how mediums strengthen each other and propel each other toward greater campaign success. Whether it is greater fundraising dollars or a higher level of participation and dedication from supporters, or both, integration assures you a stronger and more successful campaign.

CASE STUDY: CHF

We have looked at the cardinal rules of fundraising and what it means to have a truly integrated fundraising campaign, so the last key to the puzzle is strategy. How do you take all the information discussed in this chapter and apply it to an organization? Now we look at an example of a charity that created and developed an integrated fundraising campaign for its 2005 holiday campaign along with the results.

CHF, a Canadian international development agency, created and developed an integrated holiday acquisition campaign for its 2005 holiday campaign that strove to integrate all media. Instead of having a campaign, an e-newsletter, a Web site, currently all existing independently, CHF decided to join together the disparate pieces into one cohesive plan and carry the same clear and concise message across all mediums. Using banners, e-appeals, its e-newsletter, radio spots, search engine optimization, print media, and e-cards, CHF launched an integrated fundraising campaign that stuck to its message, exposed its campaign to new audiences, and maintained its visual consistency. All aspects of the campaign including the banner, the Web site, the e-appeal, the e-card, the donation form, and the thank-you pages carried the same familiar look and the same message across all mediums.

To look more closely at some of the marketing pieces developed for this integrated campaign, we discuss each piece and how it worked.

- Integrated giving form (see Exhibit 14.1)

  The integrated giving form incorporated many best practice elements. The logo is at the top and visible as soon as you land on the page. It gives the page credibility and increases brand awareness to a new market. The banner at the top of the donation form is consistent with the banner used in the other marketing pieces. The customized donation form also talks about the campaign and how easy it is to make a difference. The other nice element is showing donations at work with a photo. All of these elements give new donors a sense of security; they know where their dollar is going, and it is a fun and hip way to give a gift during the holidays.

- Integrated acquisition campaign banners (see Exhibit 14.2)

- Viral element: e-card (see Exhibit 14.3)

EXHIBIT 14.1 Integrated Giving Form

EXHIBIT 14.2 Integrated Acquisition Campaign Banners

EXHIBIT 14.3 Viral Element: E-Card

The banners above this image are numbers one and two of a three-part rotating banner. The same banner was used in other marketing pieces to keep the message consistent across all mediums and to strengthen brand awareness. The rotating banner has a catchphrase, colors, and images that catch the eyes of potential supporters. The viral e-card also carries the same imagery used throughout the campaign. Keeping the brand consistent creates a link between the mediums, increasing awareness and recognition of CHF and its work. The viral e-card was sent to the gift recipient. At the bottom of the viral card is a link for the recipient to go back to the donation form and make an additional gift.

- Google and Yahoo! keywords to drive traffic to CHF's Web site during the holidays (see Exhibit 14.4)

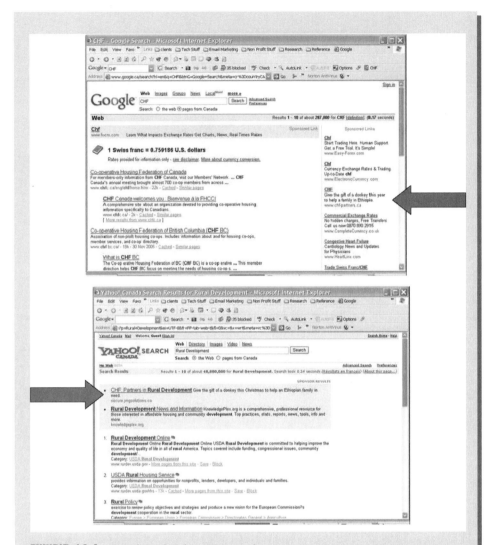

EXHIBIT 14.4   Google and Yahoo! Keywords

- Buttons and banners on company Web sites (see Exhibit 14.5)

  The CHF banner was placed on well-known Web sites to drive traffic to the CHF holiday campaign. The banner was linked directly to the CHF holiday landing page, which made it easy for people to make donations or find out more information about the campaign. Placing the banners on well-known sites also gave CHF exposure to new markets that it might not have reached otherwise.

- E-mail list rental (see Exhibit 14.6)

  The always reliable direct mail letter can be put to work as well.

EXHIBIT 14.5 Buttons and Banners on Company Web Sites

EXHIBIT 14.6 E-Mail List Rental

Dear Friend,

I know you lead a busy life so I'll make this very brief.

Most likely, your holiday season will be a time of plenty. But for some many people around the world—this holiday will be a struggle to survive. With **your help today**, we can make their lives better by giving them a donkey.

You heard me correctly—a donkey! Let me explain.

Zahra is a hard working mother who lives in the Bati district of Ethiopia—an area of the country that, for decades, has struggled with recurring drought and famine.

Once a week, to make ends meet, she walks to market with a couple of her hand-made pieces to sell. Unfortunately...

The names that received the e-mail were from a third-party rental list. Those on the list had agreed to be mailed to and had an interest in international development agencies. Other innovative marketing concepts were developed, including the distribution of branded bookmarks to all of the city's public libraries and elsewhere. The bookmarks put CHF's name out in the public sphere via the fresh and appealing holiday campaign.

The pieces of the integrated campaign that were tested for the first campaign included: keyword marketing, banners on the home page and well-known Web sites, two e-mail rental lists, e-mail to house donors, a direct mail insert to all current donors, a print advertisement in a national newspaper, a media release, two on-air radio interviews, a television interview, one radio advertisement, peer-to-peer e-mails, promotion through the internal program, and promotional bookmarks placed in public libraries and around the city. All of these pieces, online and offline, carried the same clear message and images about the integrated campaign. The most successful Web site drivers were the two radio interviews and the local television news interview. The other two major drivers were the keywords and one of the e-mail rental lists.

Overall, the integrated campaign raised $39,765 for a first-time, online acquisition campaign and exposed CHF's once-unknown brand to the public in a dynamic and multifaceted way. CHF was able to acquire 597 donors, and 82 percent of whom were new. Return on investment was 2 to 1 since CHF invested $20,000 into this campaign.

Thanks to CHF for their generosity in letting us use their campaign as a case study. For more information about CHF, please visit www.chf-partners.ca.

INTEGRATION AS AN ORGANIZATIONAL PHILOSOPHY

We have discussed integrated fundraising for campaigns, its cardinal rules, and shared a case study, but we all know that an organization is more than just the sum of its campaigns. This is the point in the chapter where we want to take a step back and ask you to look at your organization more holistically. When we remove the word "campaign," we are left with just integrated fundraising. This term, when separated from "campaign" or "event," takes on a broader meaning. What do we mean?

Integrated fundraising actually applies to three broad areas:

1. Online and offline integration (campaigns/events etc. . . .)
2. Life cycle integration (Your organization can be a part of every major event in your supporters' life cycles.)
3. Donor relationship integration (Your donors have more and many ways to get in touch with you, and you have more and better information about connecting with your donors.)

Let us explore these ideas further.

Online and Offline Integration

This first definition of integrated fundraising is the obvious one—the one discussed for most of the chapter. This is the concept that when you bring together all of your fundraising and marketing mediums and make them interrelated, you will have a stronger campaign and raise more funds.

Life Cycle Integration

This definition of integrated fundraising leans more on the word "integrated" and less on the word "fundraising." We re talking about what every organization dreams about: from birth on up, through the teen years with the start of philanthropy through volunteering, to young adulthood, where some start making personal decision on whom they wish to support, maybe some event volunteering or even attending an event as a participant. Adulthood leads to more financial support to fewer, more specific charities of choice. At this point, many will offer their expertise in their occupational field as a board member, committee member, or volunteer. Retirees who have been committed donors may become major gift donors and offer more support as volunteers. This is also the point where people who have been affected directly by your cause, either as donors or through direct experience, will consider leaving a larger donation to your organization. As lifetime supporters, these people have decades of memories of you and them: There is a real relationship and a strong foundation that both of you have come to count on. The final piece of the life cycle integration is the lasting gift of a bequest. This is a full life cycle support. This is not just a donor; this is a *lifetime supporter*.

Exhibit 14.7 explores this concept of life cycle integration more closely. At each stage of a person's life, in the lifestyle integration model, the charity is presented with an opportunity to connect with the donor on a unique level. During each stage of life, your organization can connect with the donor/supporter on a different level.

The term "donor" does not do justice to a person's lifetime of giving (time, effort, social networking, and money) to one specific cause. But keep in mind that these vital people *want* life cycle integration: It is mutually beneficial. These are the people who want interesting in-lieu programs that represent their commitment to your cause (alternative gift catalog in lieu of wedding presents or a work-vacation to an international program). They want new and interesting ways to contribute to

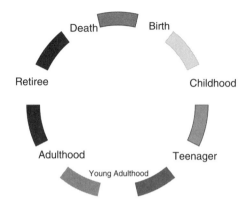

EXHIBIT 14.7   Life Cycle Integration
Model

your organization and engage others on your behalf that convey the passion they feel for your cause. These are the people who have a great lifetime value as donors. As an organization, why would you not try to fit into their life cycle to maximize their support for your cause?

Each stage of a person's life presents an opportunity to integrate your charity into their lifestyle. Let's start with birth, the celebration of a beginning of a new life. This marks a major milestone in a person's life including the start of a very new one. As technology becomes more advanced, many people look for more innovative and creative ways to mark the birth of a new child. Many charities have a tribute donation form with an e-card that can be sent to the new parents announcing an in-lieu of a gift; a donation has been made in honor of the birth of your child. This is a great start. But let us think on a larger scale. What else can your organization do to engage that new, wonderful life as part of your community of supporters?

Here are some ideas for the birth of a child.

- An alternative gift catalog or registry presents many options to someone who wants to give a unique gift.
- Enroll the baby in a monthly giving club as the newest member of your community with a special birthday wishes on the first birthday.
- Offer special e-newsletters commemorating milestones of the year including major gifts, special donations, and other milestone events, such as a birth.
- Offer a tribute section where Web pages can be created to commemorate the birth of the baby. Include a section for special pictures or messages to be posted and viewed and donations can be made to your organization instead of a baby shower.
- Design an online social networking event to raise money for your organization in honor of the birth.

The options are endless when you look at your traditional fundraising mediums combined with your online fundraising mediums. The best way to access your options is to review your online and offline fundraising tools and determine how each can be expanded and linked with each other to create innovative options for your donors and supporters.

The next piece of life cycle integration is to ensure that all of the other areas where these true supporters connect with your organization, including volunteers, board or committee members, as they also may become spokespeople for your organization. Taking this one step further than just monetary support, make sure these loyal supporters have all the necessary tools to continue to be loyal, lifetime supporters and advocates for your cause. It is even more important to nurture these relationships and develop the rapport between your supporter and your organization.

The benefit of life cycle integration is that when you are a part of people's lives from birth to death and in between, they have a very close connection and very positive brand awareness of your cause. They are natural (and often subconscious) salespeople for your organization. They have the effortless and unaffected enthusiasm that can be magnetizing and mean great things for you!

Donor Relationship Integration

As donors and supporters become more educated about your cause, they want to choose their means of communication with you. These days many of us are banking online and purchasing tickets to events online, and would prefer to control our communications with organizations to the best of our abilities. Many of your supporter might be thinking "Don't call me; I'll call you" or "Don't send me seven direct mail letters; send me two e-mail appeals instead." If your organization has a plan to integrate your donor relationships, then this is not a problem. What donor relationship integration really means is that your donors have more and many ways to get in touch with you, and you have more and better information about your donors. It is a win-win situation.

We know you want to control the relationship. You fear that if you let go, they will leave. Our response? What is that saying? If you love your donor, set them free? We are not actually suggesting setting anyone free, but we are suggesting loosening the grip a little. In one online survey conducted by HJC in 2006 for a client, we asked: "How do you prefer to be contacted?" Of the over 1,200 respondents to the survey, over 79 percent replied "over the Internet." Another online survey HJC conducted for a client that same year had a similar response: Over 66 percent of the 650 respondents gave the answer "over the Internet." The second option from both surveys was by mail. So, online donors want to choose the means of communication.

Now for the good news: We are not suggesting that you let donors *do* the communicating. You and your organization should still be communicating with your donors actively. But you should give them a choice between mail and phone, mail and e-mail, e-mail and phone, or just e-mail, and then respect their responses. They will respect you for asking and empowering them.

You now have your optional segments and should record each of these segments in your database for future campaigns. Use of these options should also increase your response rates and improve your communication with each donor in the long run.

We have now looked at all the pieces in developing an integrated fundraising plan. The next question is: How do you take this information and make a successful plan for your organization? A strategy worksheet has been developed to assist in development phase of a fully integrated fundraising campaign. This worksheet examines the components of an integrated campaign and breaks down all the pieces necessary to successful execute you campaign. Each organization may use some or all of the mediums discussed in this chapter. Use this worksheet as a guideline to develop your integrated campaign and decide which elements you need for your campaign to be a success.

Please see Appendix 14.A for the integrated fundraising plan and strategy worksheet.

Appendix 14.B is a sample timeline that has been developed for a holiday campaign season. It looks at all of the fundraising mediums discussed in the chapter and places them on a timeline showing how each element of your campaign needs to be integrated and executed. Every integrated campaign should follow a similar format to establish the length of time needed to fully implement each medium and how each piece will interact with the other elements of the campaign. Both the integrated fundraising plan and strategy and the integrated timeline will become essential tools for developing your fully integrated fundraising campaign. They combine all the pieces and illustrate how each element interacts to make your fundraising campaign a success.

CONCLUSION

Properly executing a fully integrated fundraising campaign takes planning, knowledge sharing, and a solid strategy that links all online and offline mediums with the same cohesive message. ePhilanthropy can work with traditional mediums to maximize exposure for your organization, and reach the new donor who is moving entirely to the online environment. ePhilanthropy can enhance the relationship of longtime direct mail donors with the organization by offering them more means of communication. Integrated fundraising is a strategy that ties together all the pieces of campaigns. Integration is a web pulling together strands that, standing alone, do not work to their full potential; woven together, they are stronger and more tangible. Any existing campaign can start by adding a piece of integration here and a concept there.

Integration is all-inclusive; it is not just interested in online tactics and mediums. It wants to take a warm e-mail address, get the person's phone number, call, and turn them into a direct mail donor and social networking fundraiser. It is truly integrated in that it is not linear; it works at all levels and at varying degrees of depth and breadth. Integrated fundraising is the philosophy that will take your campaign and turn it into technicolor. You can go at any pace and use any medium. Just remember to test what you do, and remember what *else* you want to do next year. Building on initial success is how we learned about integrated fundraising and gained confidence in the strategy.

Integration and working toward a holistic campaign are the keys to the Net-savvy, information-rich, communication- and technology-saturated culture in which your campaign and your brand must strive to stand out among the others. We must admit that we are always in direct competition for dollars—no matter that we call them "donor dollars" while business calls them "consumer dollars." We must rise to the challenge and win over the hearts and wallets of potential lifetime supporters, and the way to do that is through integrated fundraising. This savvy, rich, and saturated marketplace is waiting for you to catch up and show them through your next campaign that your organization is just as slick, just as Web 2.0, just as compelling and attention-grabbing and successful as any for-profit marketing campaign out there. Go show them.

ABOUT THE AUTHORS

Patricia MacArthur, Hewett and Johnston Consultants, managed accounts for a range of different clients including FoodShare Toronto, the United Nations World Food Programme, Easter Seals Society, Ontario, Alzheimer Society, Toronto, The White Ribbon Campaign, and Interval House. Her account management responsibilities included creative, marketing, deployment, analysis, reporting, and integrated ePhilanthropy audits. In addition, she completed the postgraduate certificate in Fundraising and Volunteer Management at the Humber Institute of Technology and Applied Learning under the direction of Ken Wyman.

Ryann Miller, Hewett and Johnston Consultants, left academics for a life in fundraising and has not looked back—in part she is too busy running online and offline capacity building for clients and facilitating an online course on ePhilanthropy for fundraising professionals around the globe. Ryann serves a diverse client base: from Amnesty International Canada, to CARE Canada, CNIB, March of Dimes, and others. Her responsibilities entail account management, which includes creative, online and offline marketing and deployment, analysis, and reporting, and integrated ePhilanthropy audits. Ryann is especially interested in Web 2.0 and social networking and how nonprofits may take full advantage of these fun Web toys.

NOTE

1. Viralocity is a new word that is tied to viral communications and conveys the validity of its use.

14A

Integrated Fundraising Strategic Plan Sample Worksheet - Holiday Fundraising Campaign									
Medium - Online / Offline	Objectives	Campaign Responsibilities	Budget	Target Audience	Length of Project	Desired Action(s)	Results	Outcomes/ Results	Future Recommendations
Technology									
E-Commerce Tool									
E-mail management tool									
Web Site									
Traditional Mediums - Offline Integration									
Direct Mail Campaign									
Direct mail package									
Campaign Insert and URL									
Special Event Participants									
Online Tool link for home page									
Online Promotion									
Email blast									
Broad cast Voice Message									
Memorial/Tribute									
Link or button online campaign form									
Monthly Giving									
One time special ask									
Link or button to online campaign form									
Planned Giving / Major Gifts									
One time special ask									
Link or button to online campaign form									
Corporate									
Unique online giving form									
Link or button from corporate website to campaign form									
Banner on corporate website									
Special corporate campaign ask									
Employee fundraising campaign									
Telegiving Campaign									
Campaign with online integration									
Third Party Event Fundraising									
Link or button to online campaign form									
Campaign package for third party event fundraising									
e-Philanthropy - Online Integration									
Online Marketing									
Keyword Marketing									
Social Networking Campaign									
Link or button to online campaign form									
Campaign package for social network fundraising campaign									
e-newsletter									
Campaign feature and donation options									
Create offline version for mailing and marketing									
Link to online campaign form									

Integrated Fundraising Strategy - 2007 Holiday Campaign Timeline

Sample Timeline

	September				October					November				December					January			
Holiday Schedule	3	10	17	24	1	8	15	22	29	5	12	19	26	3	10	17	24	31	7	14	21	28
Technology																						
E-Commerce Tool	Make sure all aspects are ready for October																					
E-mail management	Make sure all aspects are ready for October																					
Direct Mail Campaign																						
Direct mail package	Start creative for package	Review and refine package			Production of Holiday package					Drop Holiday package												
Campaign insert and URL		Create reminder insert			Production of Holiday insert								Drop reminder insert									
Marketing Plan																						
Social Networking Campaign																						
e-appeals	Launch an e-appeal				Review results, Update lists		Develop creative			Finalize and review	First e-mail blast			Second blast	Reminder				Collect results		Follow-up thank you email	
e-newsletter / capture	Launch fall e-newsletter	Email capture on homepage				Develop Creative	Finalize Creative				Launch holiday e-newsletter										Update lists for winter e-newsletter	
Homepage button						Create Button			Revisions	Place and test buttons	Launch buttons with campaign link										Update button for new campaign	
Banner (s)			Develop holiday banner			Seek sponsors and sites			Buy Banner ads		Test banner on host sites				Holiday campaign banner(s) live							Evaluate results
Gift Catalogue			Develop gift catalogue			Review concept				Finalize Creative and concept	Test	Launch holiday gift catalogue				Send thank you's						Evaluate results
keyword marketing				Start researching keywords				Finalize		Set-up contract		Launch holiday keywords				Send reminder		Analysis results			Evaluate results	
e-cards			Develop concepts			Develop e-cards		Finalize Creative and concept		Test		Launch e-cards			Any revisions					Analysis results		
Marketing Plan - Offline elements																						
Newsletter	Launch fall newsletter					Develop Creative		Finalize Creative			Mail holiday newsletter								Analysis results			
Annual campaigns - see below																						
Television			Contact PR to set-up interviews			Follow-up for interviews			Establish contacts and scripts						Finalize interview times	Interviews				Analysis results		
Radio			Contact PR to set-up interviews			Follow-up for interviews			Establish contacts and scripts						Finalize interview times	Interviews				Analysis results		
Celebrity	Create strategy for celebrity				Celebrity approval obtained				Celebrity incorporated into campaign			Launch Holiday campaign with celebrity							Analysis results		Update for new campaign	
Corporate Campaign																						
Unique online giving form		Establish corporate campaign support				Develop corporate giving form			Test on site	Launch corporate form									Evaluate results			
Link or button from corporate website to campaign form							Create Button		Revisions	Place and test buttons	Launch buttons with campaign link									Analysis results		
Banner on corporate website		Establish corporate campaign support				Develop Creative	Finalize Creative		Test		Launch on corporate sites								Analysis results			
Special corporate campaign ask / Employee campaign		Establish corporate campaign support			Develop campaign package					Present to corporation	Revise	Launch corporate campaign										Analysis results
Special Event Participants																						
Online Tool link for homepage							Create Special Button			Place and test buttons	Launch buttons with campaign link								Evaluate results		Update	
Email blast							Create Special Button	Collect participant email addresses		Customize e-appeal	Finalize and review			Send e-appeal	Reminder				Evaluate results	Analysis results		
Broadcast Voice Message - BVM							Create Special Button	Collect participant phone file			Review message and objective	Finalize message		Send BVM	Reminder	Reminder BVM						
Annual Campaigns																						
Direct mail - see above																						
Monthly giving				Create e-appeal			Create Special Button		Revisions	Place and test buttons	Launch button, revise e-appeal			Send special e-appeal						Analysis results		
Planned Giving / Major Gifts				Create special appeal			Create Special Button		Revisions	Revise appeal				Send special appeal						Send special thank you	Evaluate results	
Telegiving		Review telegiving campaign concept																				
Third Party Event Fundraising		Create Third Party page		Develop online concept and tool			Develop online campaign		Revisions	Launch button	Launch third party online campaign							Evaluate results			Update	
Memorial / Tribute				Create appeal			Create Special Button		Revisions	Place and test buttons	Launch button, revise appeal			Send special appeal						Send special thank you	Evaluate results	

CHAPTER 15

Your Organization in the Donor's Pocket

Marcelo Iñarra Iraegui
International Consultant

A golden lamp was shining in the night.... Three of us stood before it, feeling lucky. (It is the oft-repeated story of the lamp and the genie who grants wishes.... Anyway, let us go on and see what happens.)

There we were, three experts on different aspects of fundraising: getting large donations, seeking funds from donor foundations, and, in my case, involving as many people as possible in donating and participating in a cause: a task that I am obsessed with.

We worked up the courage and rubbed the lamp. Sure enough, the genie popped out at once. And just like in stories, he granted us three wishes. The first one to make a wish was my colleague who works with big donors—maybe because he is experienced in making requests face to face. He asked for the list of the world's richest people who were willing to donate their fortune to advance the cause he is working on. His wish was granted; the list appeared in his hands.

Next was the turn of the expert on writing the best proposal for foundations. "I want the gift of knowing beforehand what project my donor foundations are seeking, for a whole year." I know my friend was very successful in the next 12 months.

After the invention of online media such as the Web and e-mail, all of us who work on direct and interactive marketing have had a hard time imagining a medium that can raise the bar. But there was a genie before me and I was not going to waste my chance, so I asked him for a medium that was (a) portable, so I could reach my potential donors at any time; (b) personal, so each message would reach only one person; (c) instantaneous and interactive, so my message would be delivered a few seconds after being sent and get a swift reply from the donor; (d) massive, so the widest possible audience could access it; and (e) easy to use. Last, it had to be a medium through which we could collect donations.

As if by magic, the genie produced a cell phone. At that moment, my mobile phone rang, waking me from my dream. (I think I have seen too many children's movies over the last few years. Thank you, Aladdin et al., for the inspiration.)

Mobile phone communication is revolutionizing the world. There are 2 billion (2,000,000,000) mobile phone users on the planet—that is, one-third of the world's population—and the number is growing at an amazing rate. The fascination for being connected all the time is an unstoppable mania.

After the boom in the massive sale of telephones with voice message systems, cell phone companies have expanded their business toward new horizons by using data transmission technology.

The most widely used data transmission service is text messages, or SMS (Short Messaging Service). Users have become whizzes at writing messages of up to 160 characters, and they have even developed a new language. When, in December 1992, the first text message was sent from a personal computer to a mobile phone on the Vodafone network in the United Kingdom, no one could ever imagine the far reaches of this form of communication that used the tiny key pad of the telephone. *In 2006 year 2 quintillion text messages were sent worldwide.*

Text messages were followed by the customization of cell phones, by means of MMS technology (Multimedia Messaging System). Phones can be personalized with the ringtones and screensavers of your choice. Ringtones, logos, wallpapers, and the like are now part of our lives.

But the big revolution is yet to come. The convergence of almost any medium on the cell phone is becoming a reality. Mobile Internet, games, music, and television are commonplace in Asia, with South Korea and Japan leading the trend. For instance, in early 2005, an on-demand mobile TV service was launched in South Korea. In the subways of Japan, it is more common to see youngsters reading a newspaper or magazine on their cell phone than on paper.

The rest of the world is slowly incorporating these new technologies into their mobile platforms. The business sector jumped into this new technology, using the most basic SMS and MMS services for promotions, contests, multimedia games, and other uses.

WHAT HAPPENED WITH THE THIRD-SECTOR SOCIAL ORGANIZATIONS WORLDWIDE?

Ten years ago, in August 1996, I secured my first donation through the Web. Without knowing it, I was becoming a pioneer in the use of new media.

Today I sense that organizations feel the same kind of "panic" at mobile technology that I felt at the time when it came to using the Web or e-mail to seek funds or engage affinity groups that supported a certain cause.

This is not exclusive to Argentina, which is where I work. Not by any means. It is the same throughout the world. But at the same time, innovative ways of using mobile phones are cropping up. And they show others the way. The year 2005 was a turning point in this respect. Two events stood out that year: the tsunami catastrophe in Asia and the Live 8 concerts.

The urgent need for help for the tsunami victims led organizations to make ready for action, overlooking the risks in order to experience new technologies. So, they started using mobile phones to channel the aid.

In the United Kingdom, Fresh, O2, Orange, T-Mobile, Tesco Mobile, Virgin Mobile, and Vodafone joined together to provide a single, no-fee text number to accept donations, which reached €1 million in a few days. Television network Antena Tres in Spain used a similar system that got 5 million text messages, with donations reaching €4.5 million in just two days. The funds went to the Red Cross. UNICEF raised €350,000 only in Germany through 130,000 text messages. In the Netherlands, a pool of companies and organizations raised €1.7 million through a premium SMS service. The same kind of service was used in Italy, and an amazing €14 million was raised. Similar strategies were applied in Greece, France, Austria, and the Czech Republic.

But the record mobilization through text messages so far has been accomplished by the media-broadcast "Live 8" concert: More than 25 million text messages were sent in support of the concert's campaign from over 100 countries around the world.

The same model of implementing new media when catastrophes occurred was used with online media over the last decade. But one question kept coming up: What happens when there is no catastrophe? In our daily work, how can we persuade our audiences to donate using mobile phones?

The case of Greenpeace Argentina is very interesting. Greenpeace Argentina was the world's pioneer in the online fundraising model. Based on the lessons learned over 10 years of experience, it started to devise a way to use cell phones in its campaigns. In 2004 it started a plan to work on the platform of a "mobile activism" program to achieve goals in its environmental campaigns. Six months after its launch, Greenpeace has 11,500 mobile activists in Argentina. Several new initiatives aimed at developing funds were launched thereafter.

In order to reach the top of a mountain, one has to take the first step, and this is what was done at Greenpeace. The organization built its "fan base" by sending relevant, inventive proposals. The appeals for financial support will be the next step. "Mobile fundraising" is just beginning. And it is going to grow faster than expected. Our causes need funds and participation, and the opportunity is in the palm of our hands.

The next goal for Greenpeace is to secure financial commitment through mobile telephony; like any new technique, it must break a few barriers before gaining wide acceptance. Fundraising based on registered "mobile activists" would be a simple task today if telephone companies, known as carriers or integrative entities, provided not only a data transmission service (SMS, MMS, or the Internet) but also affordable, ethically defensible payment systems for donations. At present, few countries in the world have reached such a satisfactory infrastructure. Yet if we follow the rules that govern the market, we know that in the next few years this fundraising alternative will be highly viable for social organizations.

This obstacle does not hamper the experimental, enterprising spirit of the fundraising team at Greenpeace Argentina. At this time, the office is planning several tests of attractive proposals to offer its donors. The tests are targeted at those people who are already "mobile activists" and those with automatic debit for making their monthly donations. The organization's offerings include subscriptions to a newsletter about environmental alerts. If donors are interested in receiving the newsletter about the situation in the forests or the oceans in real time, all they have to do is send Greenpeace an SMS to sign up, and the cost will be added to their monthly automatic donation charge.

For several years now, we have noticed that the characteristics that define relationships among people—and especially between the new generations and organizations—are changing at great speed, almost in real time. Immediacy rules our lives, and the Internet and cellular telephony are the media that make this possible. In this context, it becomes more attractive to innovate in "instant campaigning" in order to achieve instant communication.

This is the case of MSN Messenger, which attracts over 465 million single visitors every month around the world, with localized versions available globally in 42 markets and 21 languages. This is just one example of an instant message system. We could mention others, such as Skype, Yahoo! and AOL.

With a still short life, e-mail has gotten slow for the needs of many users. Now, amid this fever for immediacy, how do we combine this "instant campaigning" formula with Greenpeace, mobile phones, and fundraising?

Let us imagine an everyday work situation at Greenpeace: A forest company plans to clear away 1,500 hectares of virgin subtropical forest. The organization has a network of monthly automatic donors who are, in turn, mobile activists, and there is an urgent need for donations and involvement. The donors receive a warning call via SMS or MMS asking for a "special appeal" or a request for an upgrade of their monthly donation in real time in order to help stop the deforestation. The donors reply, also through an SMS, indicating simply if they agree to an extra donation for the next six months. Bingo! Greenpeace will have extra funds for its work in defending those 1,500 hectares of forest.

But there is no reason to be so orthodox with the new media; why not envision using those lists of mobile activists also to conduct proactive telephone fundraising and call those people to invite them to become donors? What is important is to add techniques, to combine them and integrate them rather than replace certain techniques with others.

Chances are that in the next fundraising efforts, these plans made by Greenpeace will have actual results and will be the subject of new chapters.

ONE MORE WISH TO ASK THE GENIE

I tried to concentrate so that I would dream of the genie of the lamp once more, but he missed the appointment. I wanted to ask him to let me take a sneak peek at the future of social organizations and the new media. Without my Aladdin, I will have to manage on my own and analyze the future scenario.

It is nothing new that the communication media have an influence on and redefine relationships among human beings and that social organizations cannot be oblivious to these changes. The novelty is the speed of these changes: The settings where we perform are getting more and more dynamic and fast. We can already sense a new generational change mapped out by the new media, while new subjectivities are defined, influenced by technological change not only in the supporters' communities but also within organizations.

Regarding changes, the tendency with the most evolutionary force is the convergence of media. For instance, already mobile phones are starting to be called smart phones or pocket PC phones, incorporating all the functionalities of a computer into one small device.

In this sense, the question is: Faced with this evolution of new media and social relationships, how will fundraising and public mobilization evolve? Let us do a pretend exercise based on three rhetorical questions:

1. Will we be able to conduct face-to-face fundraising via mobile phones?
2. Will we succeed in promoting our organization using a TV spot commercial that will pop up on our cell phone when we get near a state or city where our organization is conducting an outreach program? Will we be able to ask people to attend in person or to make a donation or sign a petition?
3. Will we be able to broadcast from our own TV channel to cell phones showing how our organization works during a flood or another catastrophe and thus involve our supporters?

I believe that this and much more will be possible. Starting today, there is already a lot to do. "Mobile fundraising" is just beginning, and it is going to grow faster than we think. Our causes need funds and participation, and the opportunity is in the palm of our hands.

ABOUT THE AUTHOR

Marcelo Iñiarra Iraegui has 20 years of experience in innovative work in the nonprofit sector. He was one of the pioneers in online fundraising and campaigning worldwide.

Today, mobile mobilization and fundraising is one of his new obsessions. Defined by his colleagues as an "exotic guru," he lectures in United States, Europe, Asia, and Latin America. He was one of the six highlight speakers at the International Fundraising Conference organized by The Resource Alliance in the Netherlands in October 2006.

He works as an international consultant through his own creative agency providing marketing strategies powered by innovation for the social sector. He is also devoted to his environmental task in the fundraising team at Greenpeace International.